FENG SHUI FOR INTERIORS

Feng Shui For Interiors

Chief Editor : Jennifer Too
Managing Editor : Honey Lim
Design Editor : Andrew Yep
Published by KONSEP LAGENDA SDN BHD (223 855)
Kuala Lumpur 59100 Malaysia

Notice of Rights

Notice of Liability

ISBN 978-967-329-068-0
First published in Malaysia, August 2002
This revised edition January 2011

CONTENTS

CHAPTER ONE
PROTECTIVE INTERIOR FENG SHUI

CHAPTER TWO
ENHANCING ROOMS & CORNERS

CHAPTER THREE
PERSONALISING YOUR FENG SHUI INTERIORS

Real gold (24k) embedded in a crystal bull for success in investments.

CHAPTER FOUR
USING EAST/WEST FENG SHUI

CHAPTER FIVE
FLYING STAR FENG SHUI

CHAPTER SIX
THE DESIGN FACTOR

CHAPTER SEVEN
REVITALIZING ENERGY

CHAPTER EIGHT
SPIRITUAL FENG SHUI

Powerful Golden Amulet Medallions for protect and enhance of personal chi energy.

1

PROTECTIVE INTERIOR FENG SHUI

The best way to practice feng shui is to start by adopting a protective strategy. You must apply feng shui ways to protect your home and office from being harmed by **killing chi**, which creates bad feng shui. Do this before doing anything else. Protective feng shui can be as easy as placing key symbols in correct corners of the home. These are effective because of the special energy they generate, and today I design many traditional feng shui cures that are suitable for modern contemporary homes.

Protective symbols can be placed flanking doors into rooms and living areas. When there is a fireplace in the living room, it is excellent to place a small dragon image nearby to simulate the presence of the fire dragon. This creates powerful protection against burglary and bad people.

1 Protective feng shui

When practising feng shui, it is imperative you adopt a defensive strategy. You protect yourself from bad feng shui before trying to enhance for good feng shui.

Feng shui prescribes many methods that range from the simple placement of guardian images to the more complex application of symbolic cures used in conjunction with formula feng shui. **There are different types of killing chi and these require different kinds of protection.** Bad chi can be due to hostile structures, or they can result from intangible forces, which you cannot see. Bad feng shui can be caused by imbalances in the yin/yang chi of the space. When yin chi dominates, it can sometimes bring disaster and even death. There are different manifestations of bad chi. Feng shui opens your eyes to bad chi and teaches you to recognize when it is necessary to implement remedies to dispel bad luck and overcome energy that causes misfortune.

Symbolism plays a big role in feng shui. Many symbols are used as remedies to a range of feng shui ills. The Chinese pantheon of symbols and deities provide practitioners with a large choice of images to incorporate into the décor of home and office. Amongst my absolute favourites for creating protective energy are images of ***Zhong Kuei*** (also spelled Chong Kuei) the *Deity that protects against bad spirit harm*. He is usually depicted carrying a sword in his right hand and a flask of wine in the other. He has a fierce countenance and loves to drink, but he is also alert and mindful to the quality of energy around him.

In my home I have two art images of Zhong Kuei, one I hang at the base of my staircase to prevent bad chi from going upstairs to my upper level where the bedrooms are located, and the other I hang near my front door. Zhong Kuei is said to be a powerful adversary of wandering spirits and merely having his image in your home or office is sufficient to chase away the *devils*! The Chinese use the word *devil* to describe people who would want to do you harm and cause you hurt. In other words, people who harbour secret ill intentions towards you, people you cannot trust.

Zhong Kuei is the deity that protects against spirit harm.

OTHER PROTECTIVE IMAGES

Other protective images are Fu Dogs, Chilin, the tiger or other fierce animals, and the powerful Door Gods. Wrathful deities like Kuan Kong, especially the five dragons Kuan Kong, also make excellent protector images. **Kuan Kong** is valued for the protection chi he symbolizes because he is said to protect both physically and spiritually. Kuan Kong also protects your wealth. For this reason, many politicians, business people, and even secret triad bosses display Kuan Kong prominently in their offices. There need not be any spiritual or religious connotations attached to the presence of these Chinese Taoist deities in the living or workspace. It is the chi they emanate that we want.

2 Dragons and Tortoises

Dragons and tortoises, phoenixes and tigers are the celestial protectors that feature prominently in the practice of feng shui. These are the **four celestial guardians of any yin or yang abode**; and anyone learning feng shui is advised to begin by understanding the role these four creatures play in achieving good feng shui. In the outer environment, they are said to represent the hills and mountains that surround a building. According to feng shui, when your abode is surrounded by the four creatures in an **armchair or horse shoe formation**, it is said to be under the shelter of these celestial creatures and thus protected from bad luck. Of the four, the dragon is the most prominent and significant.

Many people have asked me if these four creatures have any relevance inside the home, and my immediate reply has always been a resounding yes. Apart from the **white tiger**, which is best kept at a safe distance, the other three celestial creatures are powerfully propitious symbols in their own right. Indeed, dragons are the most auspicious symbol of all.

The dragon epitomizes the emperor, signifies heaven, and is the most celestial of all creatures. Having his image in the home always attracts good yang energy. Just note some ground rules. The image should never be too large for the house. Better to have a few small dragons in each room than to have an overly large one that dominates the house.

The Dragon Tortoise combines the courage of the Dragon with the steadfastness of the Tortoise.

Once I saw a really large nine-dragon embroidery that completely dominated someone's living and dining rooms. He was so proud of his nine dragons, I simply did not have the heart to caution him that the **nine dragons could consume him with over zealous ambition** – and perhaps cause him to make foolhardy decisions. This is not something easy to tell anyone. Alas, not long thereafter I heard he lost important positions in a corporate showdown.

Dragons are best placed along east walls of your living or dining room. Also place dragon images near water features to make them more powerful as prosperity energizers. If you like the *nine dragons* invest in a small cloisonné nine-dragon screen as they bring a range of great good luck. *You can learn to dot the eyes of the dragon as this empowers the image with greater energy.*

TORTOISES FOR PROTECTION

Tortoises are as important as dragons as protector images. If you can, I highly recommend that you keep live tortoises in your home. They are easy to clean and keep, and are simply so beneficial to have around. **Place the tortoises in the north and preferably in the back half of your house.** Do not place tortoises in the kitchen. Dragon Tortoises combine the two creatures and create the courage chi of the Dragon together with the protective chi of the Tortoise. It is a powerful combination. The Dragon Tortoise behind you when you work provides this excellent chi combination.

3 Place celestial guardians correctly

When you use symbols of protection in your home or office, make sure you place them in the correct locations. One of the key areas of the living or work space that requires maximum "protection chi" is at or near the entrance door. This is the *mouth* of the home where chi enters.

Here in the foyer just inside the door you might want to consider having a table 33 inches high on which can be placed a Kuan Kong image you like to invite home from one of your shopping trips.

With **Kuan Kong's fierce countenance** facing the door and looking directly at all who enter, it is said that even the most hardened ghosts and robbers get scared off! If you place a five dragon Kuan Kong here, either standing or seated, and if the Kuan Kong image is made of metal, it is also a very powerful cure for many Flying Star period-related afflictions. These Flying Star afflictions are usually associated with the earth element, which can be controlled effectively with the use of metal energy. So, a Kuan Kong image in solid brass or one which "looks" like brass would be very effective as a cure for bad chi caused by Flying Star feng shui.

A Kuan Kong made of metal is a very effective cure for many Flying Star afflictions. Also excellent placed in the living or foyer area and looking out of doors, offices and shops.

Near the vicinity of the main door is also a great place to hang an image of Zhong Kuei or images of Door Gods if you want something a little more esoteric.

It is at the door that Fu Dogs or Chi Lins are most effective in their role as protective guardians. Placed on either side of the entrance door, these celestials create excellent protection against harmful people, against being cheated and against petty burglary. Fu Dogs and Chi Lin can be placed on floor level or raised to higher levels. For apartments, they should be placed just outside, on either side of the door into the apartment.

This is crucial if your entrance door is facing the lift. You will definitely need the Fu Dog or Chi Lin to protect you from the symbolic *attacking tiger chi* that emerges from the lift shaft. For those of you living in apartments, if your entrance directly faces an elevator, you really should make an effort to have a pair of Fu dogs at the entrance to overcome the powerful negative energy coming from the lift shaft. If you worry your Fu Dogs might get stolen, use strong glue to fix them onto the floor. If you are really uncomfortable having them outside your apartment, then as a last resort, bring them inside, but make sure they stay in the foyer area looking at the door. Do note that having protective images inside is never as good as having them outside.

For bungalows and mansions, townhouses and semidetached houses, most of which have compound gates, the Fu Dogs should be placed high up on top of the gate looking out. This is a particularly powerful way of using Fu dogs since arranging them this way also attracts good fortune. Just make sure your Fu Dogs are large enough to stay in balance with the size of your home.

Refrain from overdoing things. Do not have too many protective symbols unless your space is very big. Always relate to the size of your space. **Balance is very vital**.

Select images that appeal to you. It is not necessary to have everything mentioned in this or other books. Using feng shui to make your interiors auspicious does not mean you throw good taste or personal preferences out the window.

Fu Dogs are celestial guardians that protect the home. Place a pair flanking the main entrance into your home. The male Fu Dog (playing with a ball) should be on the left of the entrance inside looking out.

Besides, effectiveness of symbols depends on how comfortable you feel with what you use in your décor. Let protective objects merge naturally into your space so the chi they create blends harmoniously with the energy of your home.

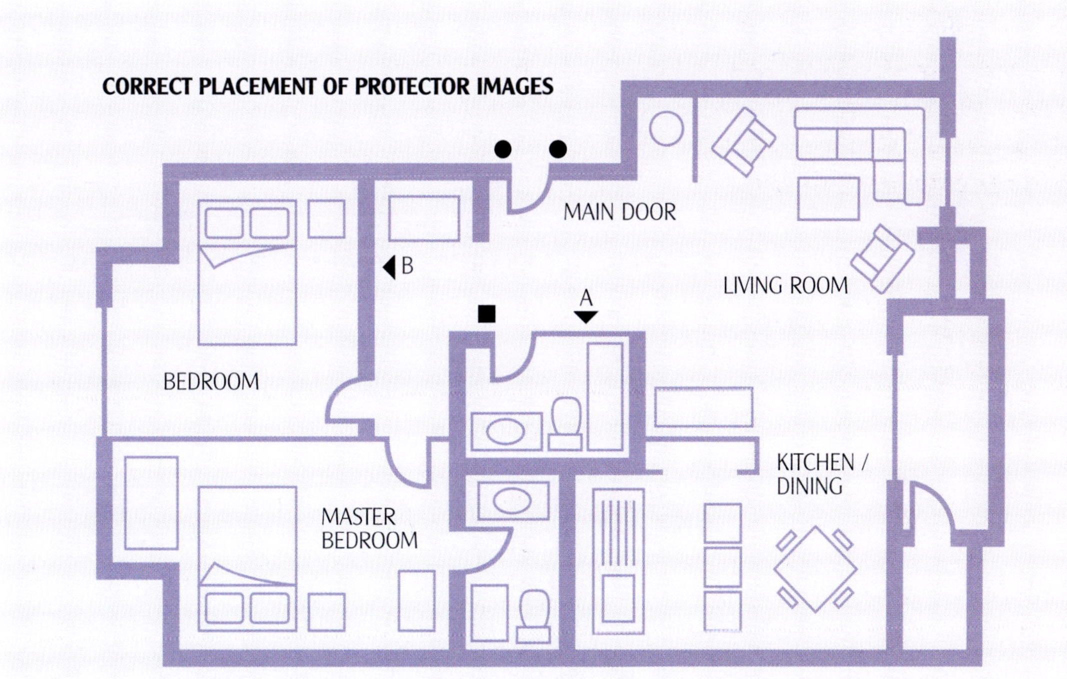

▶ Walls A & B : These are the best walls on which to hang protective art pieces of Kuan Kong.

● Place a pair of Fu Dogs or Chi Lin on either side of your main entrance.

■ Place a figurine of Kuan Kong in your main foyer area facing the front door.

4 Landscape feng shui

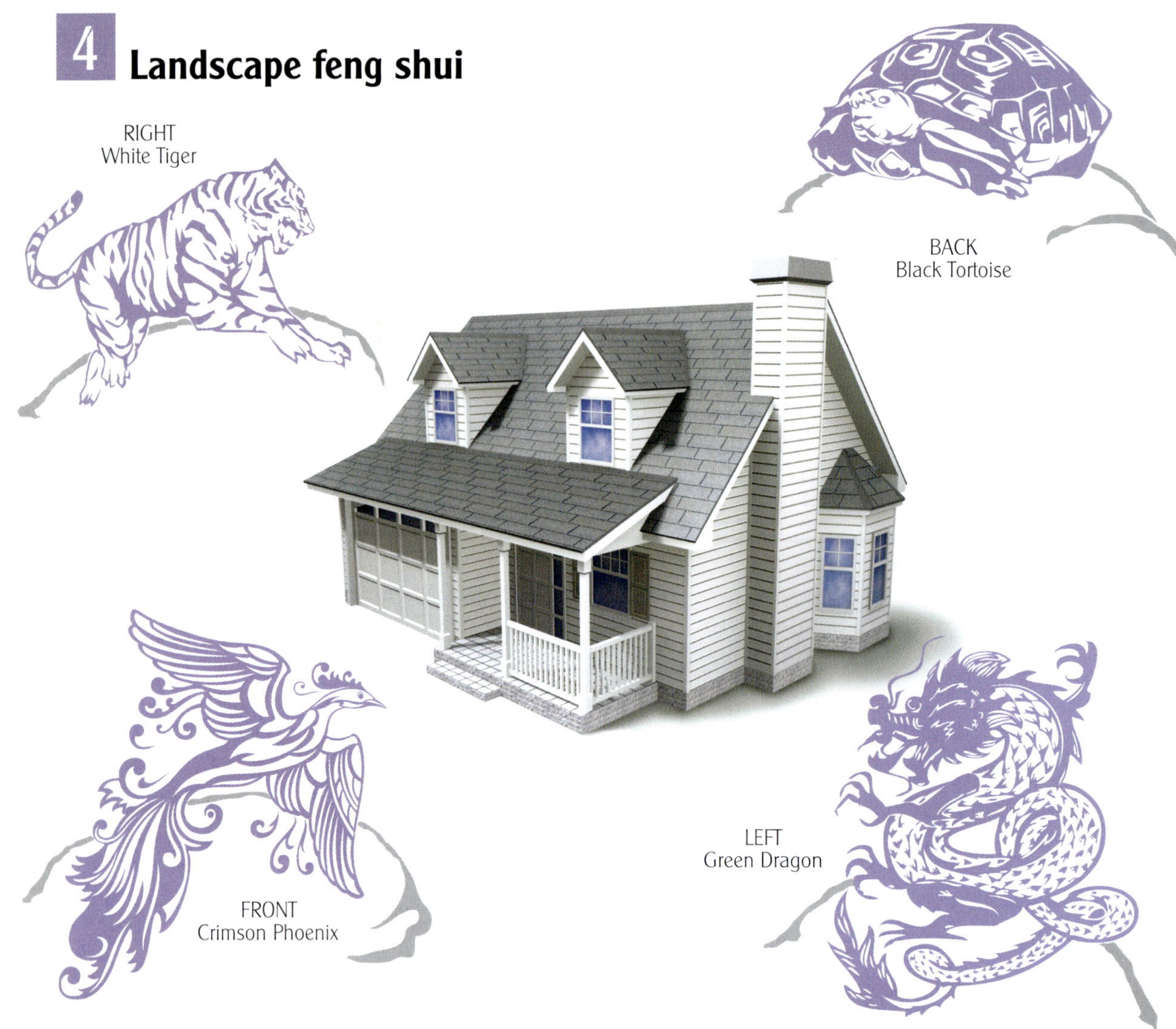

There are different systems of feng shui under which the analyses may suggest different remedies. In the outside environment, surrounding hills, elevations, rivers, roads, structures and buildings are investigated to determine the presence or absence of protector celestial creatures that may be "hidden" in surrounding hills and/or structures. This is collectively known as **landscape feng shui – the form school** that determines whether a home benefits from and is protected by its environment. Usually this feng shui is harder to correct manually, since the larger environment is usually impossible to change. The practice of interior feng shui offers greater possibilities for improvement, since here, everything is within our control. **Inside the home,** the practitioner can use different methods to determine the luck of compass directions and locations. This can then be effectively complemented with symbolic feng shui so that afflictions are corrected and good feng shui enhanced.

5 Clearing basic confusions

The prevalence of different systems of feng shui has led to some confusion in the minds of practitioners, especially in recent years when interest in feng shui has led to a veritable explosion of books on the subject. Confusion generally revolves around which feng shui method of investigation to use, as well as regarding issues such as how directions are taken under different system, what and how symbols are to be placed, and what advice to follow when confronted with contradictory recommendations. To sift through all the basic issues of contention that cause confusion, it is important to remember that feng shui is both a science and an art – sometimes requiring technical investigations and complex calculations and other times requiring an almost instinctive selection of options. Feng shui is mostly a diagnostic practice requiring judgement, experience and a good dose of common sense.

Using feng shui today means adapting classical and traditional practice to a modern environment. Theory alone is not good enough. Theory alone is an impractical approach. Unless feng shui theory is interpreted with an eye to the urban landscapes of modern city living, the practice of feng shui cannot bring meaningful results. So there is a need to interpret and adapt feng shui guidelines to suit modern day living and work spaces.

Some common issues causing confusion that need to be clarified include the following.

1 TAKING DIRECTIONS

When practicing formula feng shui, a proper compass should be used. Directions referred to in feng shui always mean directions as taken with a compass, not from the front door, not from where the sun sets or rises, and not from whether you live in the North or South hemisphere. Directions are always taken with a compass. It does not need to be the feng shui Lo Pan.

2 WHICH DIRECTION TO TAKE

To practice Eight Mansions, the direction of any door frequently used by you should be an auspicious direction as given according to your KUA number. When practising Flying Star feng shui however, judgement must be used on whether to use the direction of the main door or the direction of the whole house.

3 SUPERIMPOSING THE LO SHU GRID

When locating directions, draw a nine grid square over the floorplan to identify the compass directions of each corner of the home. For irregular shaped homes, the grid is still superimposed onto the home. Of course, there will then be missing and protruding corners. These corners are analyzed separately.

4 PLACEMENT OF SYMBOLS

When arranging the placement of decorative images that have some auspicious, protective or remedial impact, it is necessary to know the purpose of displaying the image before deciding where to place them. In placement, location is generally more important than *direction.*

5 SPACE & TIME DIMENSION OF FENG SHUI

The importance of both require the practitioner to make annual investigations that ensure the spatial feng shui of house and office doors and rooms are not hurt by harmful annual time afflictions. Thus some knowledge of the Flying Star formula is necessary.

6 Using the powerful formulas

I am often asked which of the feng shui formulas is best to use in the design of protective home feng shui, and my advice has always been to develop some familiarity with the powerful formulas. This ensures access to knowledge on protecting oneself and one's home from being hit by bad feng shui. It is sensible to **start by first learning the easy and simple methods** before graduating to the powerful formulas, since this way you will gradually become more sophisticated in your use of feng shui. But you should attempt to incorporate the powerful formulas into your practice as soon as possible. Amongst the many formulas, the three most powerful to use are summarized below.

1 THE EIGHT MANSIONS FORMULA

This is a personalized formula, which divides everyone into either EAST or WEST group. The formula states that based on one's *lunar year* of birth and one's gender, it is possible to calculate one's KUA number. Based on one's KUA number, it is then possible to know the following:

a. whether one is an East or West group person
b. which are one's auspicious and inauspicious directions
c. which is one's personal lucky trigram and lucky number

Knowing 8 Mansions enables you to practice very potent personalized feng shui. Armed with only a compass and the above information, you can select houses, rooms, directions and corners that bring maximum luck rather than harmful luck. You can also take steps to ensure that you are protected from inadvertently living in unsuitable houses, staying in inauspicious rooms or facing unlucky directions.

2 THE HOUSE TRIGRAM FORMULA (see Chapter Four)

Under the Trigram Houses formula, which is referred to as *Shuan Kong* feng shui, houses are categorized as one of eight types, with each type being named after one of the eight trigrams. This method is based on the sitting direction of a house. The *sitting direction* is defined as the direct opposite of the facing direction. The trigram of the house determines the chart of the house. This chart is then used in combination with the flying star annual and monthly charts to alert house residents of bad combinations of stars that bring illness and loss. This method is excellent for keeping up to date on killing chi energy created by the sheer passage of time. This method of feng shui is used in conjunction with the 8 Mansions formula to determine the compatibility of houses with residents based on their personal KUA numbers.

3. THE FLYING STAR FORMULA (see Chapter Five)

This formula reveals the transformation of luck from period to period. It identifies various types of good and bad luck in the nine palaces of any home including identifying illness and loss stars. It is based on the numbers of the Lo Shu square and involves numerology - knowing what the numbers 1 to 9 mean and what number combinations indicate. The nine palaces are the rooms in the home demarcated according to compass directions. When you read a Flying Star natal chart you will discover how effective feng shui can be, and when you design your space according to the information given in these charts, at the very least, you will definitely be protected from bad feng shui.

7 Updating your feng shui

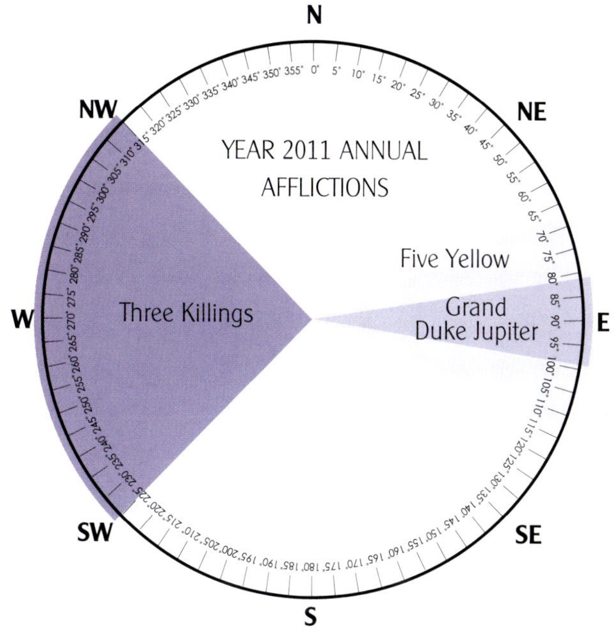

The annual afflictions change from year to year. In 2011, the 3 Killings is located in the West and the 5 Yellow is located in the East. To follow the annual changes of energy, log on to www.wofs.com

In **protective feng shui**, there is a branch of formula feng shui that adds an important extra dimension of analysis to the practice. These are the *annual afflictions*, which can be viewed as regular updates to protect your home against new problems brought to different parts of the home during each new year. Updating feng shui means knowing what special measures to take each new year to counter bad luck caused by annual "star afflictions" when these enter into *bedrooms* or affect the *main door*. Knowing about **annual (and monthly) afflictions** is what gives dynamic credence to your application of feng shui. In addition, there is also the period update, which is required every twenty years. The most recent update was February 4th 2004, when Period 7 changed to Period 8.

There are three important annual afflictions you must take note of each year. These are the ***Grand Duke Jupiter***, the ***Deadly Five Yellow*** and the ***Three Killings***. Shown here is the compass map for year 2011. A new map is needed for each new year, as each year, the location of these 3 afflictions change, and the basis of this change differs for each one of these afflictions. So updating your feng shui each year requires you to know the location of these annual afflictions in each new year. This is what feng shui masters focus on when they undertake their annual updates for their clients. In Hong Kong, many businesses take the annual update feng shui advice very seriously. Otherwise the afflictions could be serious enough to cause sudden loss and bankruptcy of the business. Sometimes annual afflictions can also cause terminal illness to strike.

Note that each of the three afflictions **occupy different angles in terms of degrees** – the Grand Duke occupies only 15 degrees, the 5 yellow occupies 45 degrees and the three killings occupies 90 degrees. So the extent of their impact on the floor area of houses and buildings will differ.

There are antidotes for controlling afflictions depending on where they are each year. There are also safeguards that can be used according to locations afflicted. To ensure protection from the ill effects of these afflictions, **the first thing** to take note of is their location from year to year. **The second thing** to note are the taboos – what you simply must NOT do so as not to incur the wrath of the afflictions. The 5 yellow brings major financial loss and severe illness, the 3 killings brings three kinds of bad luck associated with relationships, while the Grand Duke brings defeat and failure. Knowing about these afflictions will help you to evade their ill effects.

8 Do not offend the Grand Duke Jupiter

The Grand Duke Jupiter (also known as the Tai Sui) is an annual affliction that affects fifteen degrees of space that corresponds to the direction of the animal sign of the year. This means the fifteen degrees that represents the direction of the animal sign is where the Grand Duke resides in in that particular year. So all the taboos with respect to the Grand Duke apply to the direction of the year's animal sign.

Firstly, no one should sit directly facing the direction of the Grand Duke, since this is interpreted as challenging him. When you confront Tai Sui, you will lose, you will be defeated and you will get sick. Instead, you should sit with the Grand Duke behind you. This way, you will get his support.

Secondly, you should not disturb the peace and quiet of the Grand Duke's palace. This means that you should not play loud music in the direction of the animal sign of the year. You should not quarrel there and you should not undertake renovations, banging, digging or demolition work there. If you do, the result will be loss, bad luck and illness. This vital taboo applies if you are planning to undertake spot renovations in the home. So each year, you must take note of the parts of your home where you should not undertake any renovation work.

Shown in the diagram on the facing page are the directions of the Grand Duke indicated for the next 12 years. Once you know where to find the Grand Duke each year, it is easy to observe the taboos associated with him.

To cure this affliction, place the celestial protector the Pi Yao in the Grand Duke's location. This means the direction of the animal sign of the year. The animal opposite the animal sign of the year should able to be more careful and should carry the Pi Yao as an amulet to appease the Grand Duke and to control his wroth.

Note that those born in the animal year directly opposite to the ruling animal are said to be in direct conflict with the Grand Duke. People in conflict with the Tai Sui should protect themselves by having a pair of **Pi Yao** or **Pi Xie** in the home; these celestial animals are said to appease the wrath of the Grand Duke.

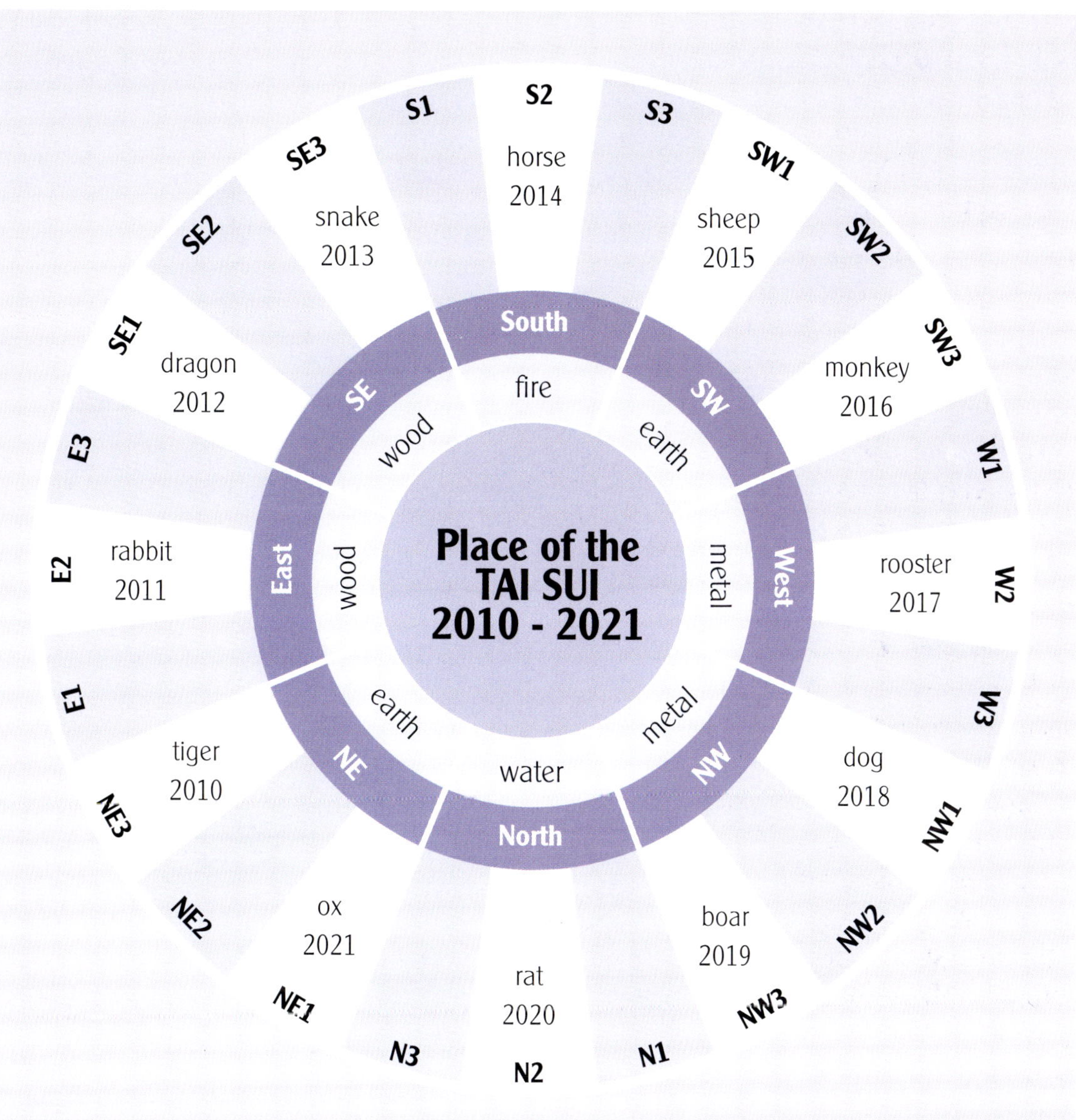

This circle chart here shows the Astrology Wheel. It marks the locations for each of the 12 animal signs of the Chinese Astrological System. We have also indicated the years which correspond to the 12 signs and this also indicates the location of the "Tai Sui" or Grand Duke Jupiter. The feng shui connection here is that one must never never confront the direction of the Tai Sui! This means that for the year in question do not ever directly face the place of Tai Sui when making a dining, even if that direction is auspicious for you under Mansions Kua Formula.

9 Grand Duke and renovations

Once you know about the Grand Duke taboo, commit it to memory and bear it in mind in your practice of feng shui. Remember that while one of the best things you can do to maintain good fortune luck in your home is to constantly revitalize the energy of your home through periodic repainting and renovations, it is very important that you observe the renovation taboos imposed by the Grand Duke's location.

Each year there will be parts of the home which simply must not be disturbed or renovated. You should **refrain from knocking, banging and digging in those areas**. The worst thing you can do to activate the negative side of the Grand Duke affliction is to undertake demolition work in the part of the house occupied by him.

EXAMPLE:

See the apartment laid out below. In 2011, using a compass to get my orientation of this apartment, I found that the Northeast (the part shaded in grey) was occupied by the toilet. So if I wanted to upgrade my toilets – e.g. retiling or repainting, then I COULD NOT do it in 2011.

Still using the example of the apartment, if I want to upgrade the kitchen, then I must find out in what year the Grand Duke will be occupying the Southeast because this is where the kitchen in this apartment is located. By checking the chart given in the previous tip, we will discover that the Grand Duke will be in the Southeast in the year 2012 and 2013, so I have plenty of time to undertake renovations in the kitchen area.

If I wish to make changes to the interior design of the main bedroom however, it is important to either do it these 3 years. Otherwise I will have to wait until 2015 since in 2014 the Grand Duke will be flying into the South.

All of the above notwithstanding, IF you are undertaking **renovations to the whole house** then you only need to make sure that you do not **start or end** your renovations in the place of the Grand Duke.

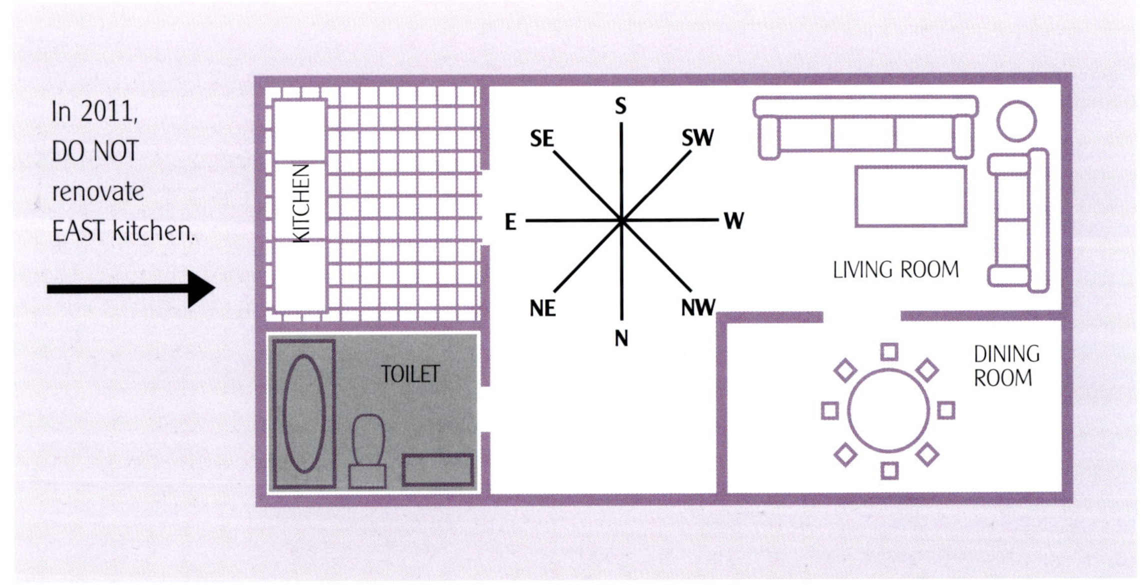

10 Beware the deadly Five Yellow

The Five Yellow is the most deadly of the three annual afflictions, especially in years when it flies into Earth and fire element sectors. This happened in 2010 when it flew to the Northeast, a fire element sector. This will also happen in 2014 when it flies into the South, an fire element sector. In these two sectors, the Five Yellow, being an earth element affliction, will have its evil essence considerably strengthened, making it deadlier. It brings severe illness, financial loss and obstacles to success.

The Five Yellow is at its deadliest when it afflicts the main door or your bedroom. This happened to me in 2001 when the Five Yellow flew into the Southwest. Both my main door and my bedroom were afflicted. In that year, I discovered I had high blood pressure, diabetes, a malfunctioning thyroid, water retention, arthritis and a cyst in my womb. These health afflictions jolted me to check my own feng shui. That's when I realised I had hung 6 windchimes at my door but had forgotten my bedroom was also in Southwest. I lost no time in quickly placing windchimes there. I also flew to California to consult with my spiritual guru who arranged for special puja prayers. It was a worrying time for me and my family.

In February the following year, my doctor was amazed when blood tests indicated I had recovered. My diabetes, water retention, thyroid and blood pressure had amazingly become normal again The bonus was losing weight and in the process getting trimmer!

My own experience and very lucky escape has really strengthened my confidence in my spiritual practices and in the Flying Star system of feng shui enormously. Combining my two passions – feng shui and Buddhism – really helped me regain my precious health. Today I feel fitter and stronger physically. I am using this personal example to pass on an important tip regarding the danger of being affected by the Five Yellow. If you take the attitude that feng shui is a living skill, like cooking or interior design, you will share my realisation that there is nothing to lose and everything to gain by having good feng shui knowledge and applying it to make our lives and the lives of our family better, safer and healthier.

The five element pagoda is one of the most effective cures for the Five Yellow and it is also beneficial when worn as a pendant.

Do not take the ill effects of the Five Yellow lightly. It can be deadly when it hits you. Thus try never to occupy rooms afflicted by the Five Yellow. If you cannot help it, then make sure you use remedies to overcome its pernicious effects. **Do not undertake renovations in your home if the Five Yellow is at your front door.** And you must not cut, dig or demolish any part of the home afflicted by the Five Yellow. Take these warnings seriously because I have seen how businesses have been ruined by the Five Yellow, and how peoples fortunes have taken a severe tumble because of it.

11 Subdue with the Five Yellow

There are different ways to counter the ill effects of the Five Yellow. One method is to hang 6-rod metal windchimes. The rods should be hollow and the windchime should be made entirely of metal. The sound of metal caused by metal on metal in sectors occupied by the Five Yellow is a very effective cure because the metal chi exhausts the earth chi of the Five Yellow. **Feng shui masters always recommend using the exhausting cycle of the five elements rather than the destructive cycle to control the Five Yellow affliction.** Windchimes are an excellent antidote because it engages the power of the winds, but if you like, you can also place six metal coins above the doorway, or six coins on either side of the door to exhaust the power of the Five Yellow.

An important point about the Five Yellow is that wherever it occurs in any home or building, it is important to keep the lights there dimmed. This is because fire chi will strengthen the earth energy of the Five Yellow. If you have spotlights in the sector of the house where there is the Five Yellow for instance, this signifies fire chi strengthening the Five Yellow, thereby making it even more deadly. This is exactly what happened to one of my UK Publishers in 1999. Publishers ELEMENT Books forgot to turn off the bright lights they had installed in their South entrance. I had told them in 1997 to install the spotlights at their South entrance to bring them recognition, fame and success. This was exactly what they achieved and ELEMENT as a Publisher was widely respected in the Trade then. Alas, when the Five Yellow flew into the South in 1999, ELEMENT found themselves overstretched and with cash flow problems. It was to be a setback from which they would not recover. The following year they went into voluntary liquidation. The ELEMENT imprint was eventually sold to Harper Collins.

Six metal coins energised with red string can be used to suppress the ill effects of the Five Yellow.

Do not undertake renovations, digging, cutting or create noise in sectors occupied by the Five Yellow, otherwise you will inadvertently activate it. Let the corner of its occupation stay undisturbed all through the year. And if there are bright lights there, keep them turned off.

In 2010 the 5 yellow is in the Southwest

In 2011 the 5 yellow is in the East

In 2012 the 5 yellow is in the Southeast

In 2013 the 5 yellow is in the Center

In 2014 the 5 yellow is in the Northwest

In 2015 the 5 yellow is in the West

In 2016 the 5 yellow is in the Northeast

In 2017 the 5 yellow is in the South

In 2018 the 5 yellow is in the North

12 Overcome the Three Killings

Never sit with the Three Killings behind you. Rearrange furniture in your home each year to ensure you are not affected by the Three Killings.

The last of the three annual afflictions that needs to be updated at the start of each lunar New Year is the **Three Killings**. This is an affliction known as the *sarm saat* in Chinese.

Unlike the Grand Duke Jupiter, which must never be confronted, the Three Killings must always be faced up to, head on. Having the Three Killings behind you is **asking to be stabbed in the back**. So you must always rearrange your furniture each new year so you do not inadvertently have the *Three Killings* behind you. The best solution is to arrange the furniture in your home such that you never sit facing the Grand Duke. Nor should you have the Three Killings behind you. This is usually not difficult to achieve, since the Three Killings is usually the direction opposite the Grand Duke.

When planning **house repairs and renovations**, make sure you do not undertake such works in sectors of the house occupied by the Three Killings. This is a troublesome taboo to observe, since the Three Killings can occupy a very large part of the house – this is an affliction that covers 90 degrees of the compass. The reason for this is because the Three Killings only flies to the cardinal directions and never into the secondary directions.

CURES FOR THE THREE KILLINGS

In the years of the Ox, Rooster and Snake, it occupies the **East**. The cure here is to shine a bright light or hang a metal windchime.

In the years of the Boar, Rabbit and Sheep it occupies the **West**. The cure here is to place open water in this corner, or shine a bright light.

In the years of the Monkey, Rat and Dragon, it occupies the **South**. The cure here is use crystals or place open water here.

In the years of the Dog, Horse and Tiger, it occupies the **North**. The cure here is to place a strong plant or use strong earth energy in the form of crystals.

13 Protect your main door

A main door with a small outdoor patio like this is auspicious.

In the practice of feng shui, the main door features prominently on the list of significant things to get right. Every school and system of feng shui offers advice on how this all-important entrance into any home or building should be angled, positioned and designed to ensure maximum good fortune for the rest of the household. In this chapter on protective feng shui, we are focusing on protecting the door itself. The impact of surrounding features, rooms and other structures are dealt with in Chapter Two which looks at the entrance on the outside and on the inside.

MAIN DOOR SHOULD HAVE A ROOF

It is important that the main door is protected, even if only symbolically. This suggests a small roof above the main door. If you look at the architecture of old homes and inside the palaces of the Forbidden City you will find that all main entrances have this protective feature. In modern homes, a popular adaptation is shown in the photo here. If your door does not have such a protective roof you might want to consider having a canopy made to simulate a roof cover.

MAIN DOOR SHOULD BE SOLID WOOD

Main doors should be made of solid wood with some metallic trimmings. The stronger the door, the better it is in terms of protecting the home. Glass doors afford little protection. Gold or brass decorations on doors are excellent. These can fine-tune the compass direction chi of the door itself. You will find the presence of metal studs or lion door knockers can change the direction of the compass reading near the door by a few degrees. This used to be a secret and efficient way to adjust chi direction near the door.

MAIN DOOR SHOULD OPEN INWARDS

When the main door opens inwards, chi is welcomed into the home. It is easy to adjust this if your doors are opening outwards. It is not a good idea to have sliding doors as the main entrance. Should you place a mat at the entrance, make sure the mat is outside and not inside the house. Never put your name on the mat. You don't want to get stepped on, do you ?

MAIN DOOR IDEALLY HAS TWO LEAVES

Having a pair of doors is better than having a single door, since this looks grander and more inviting. Mansions and palaces always have this feature. If you have aspirations to live well, then it is a good idea to start at the doorway. Ideally, the two doors are of the same size, but if one is larger than the other, use the larger of the two doors more regularly.

14 Mirror reflections

Mirrors are powerful feng shui tools and they can do wonders for doubling your wealth, your good fortune and your happiness. But mirrors can also bring havoc into your life when they are inadvertently placed in the wrong places. Whether mirrors bring good luck or bad depends very much on **what they are reflecting**. So the mirrors inside your home must never reflect anything that suggests wealth flowing outwards or worse bringing danger into the home.

MIRRORS REFLECTING THE MAIN FRONT DOOR causes wealth and good fortune to come in and then instantly flow out again. This is because the mirror is reflecting the outside of the house each time the door opens. I know several successful people who have suffered major losses as a result of having a large ornate mirror directly facing the front door. Do note however that if your mirror does not reflect the door, it is not harmful.

MIRRORS REFLECTING THE BED inside the bedroom causes the marriage to get crowded. Feng Shui masters warn against mirrors doubling the yin energy inside the bedroom, creating problems with sleeping. Mirrors that reflect a sleeping couple can cause one of them to have a sexual liaison with a third party outside of the marriage.

MIRRORS REFLECTING THE STOVE or cooker are also bad news. It is dangerous to reflect a naked flame as these can cause accidents. Reflecting the food being cooked is not the same as reflecting food being served in the dining room.

The round wallmirror here faces the entrance into the home. This causes wealth that flows in to flow right out again. Avoid hanging a mirror that reflects your main door.

A typical garden in Suzhou, China demonstrates clever use of landscape design to force chi to gently meander.

15 Chi moving in a straight line

This is a classical feng shui affliction, which was strictly avoided in the old days. If you take tours to old mansions in any of the cities of China, you will see that pathways and corridors of these old houses always meander. Sometimes the meandering is curved and other times it looks like a *zig zag* pattern. The picture above shows a typical garden of a home in Suzhou. The garden pathway meanders from one courtyard to the next and even the pavilions are connected by zig zag walkways. The idea is to **slow down the flow of chi** ensuring it does not gather speed and take on killing energy that harms residents.

Inside the home, it is important to plan the layout of rooms and placement of doors in such a way that reflect this kind of meandering flow. **Straight flows must be avoided at all costs**. Use low furniture, plants and room dividers like sideboards and screens to achieve this meandering flow. If you encounter three doors opening in a straight line, it is a good idea to reposition the middle door. Or place a small piece of furniture to divert the flow of chi. I find that many people have this straight-line chi affliction without realizing it; so you really do have to consciously look at your home to map out the flow of chi inside the home. When you have corridors and cannot do anything about it, slow down the flow of chi by decorating the walls with auspicious art, or keep the corridors well lit at all times. You can also use a clever mixture of wall colours, plants and other images to slow down the flow.

The two floor plans shown here highlight rather dramatically the flow of chi. At first glance, the floor plan of both houses do not seem to tell very much, but when you begin to analyze how the chi moves from one room to the next, you will begin to realize how the positioning of doors plays such a crucial role in determining the quality of your feng shui. The yellow spots are the potential trouble spots. Be creative in your solutions. Always let the chi meet with an auspicious object as it moves through your home.

THE FLOW OF CHI

Inside the home, the flow of chi reflects the flow of traffic as well as the way luck permeates the space. The idea here is to slow down the flow so that good chi has a chance to settle and accumulate. Simply following this golden rule of allowing chi to meander will improve your feng shui considerably, both indoors and outdoors!

Leafy potted plants can be used to re-orientate the chi in your home to ensure it meanders gently and does not flow in straight lines.

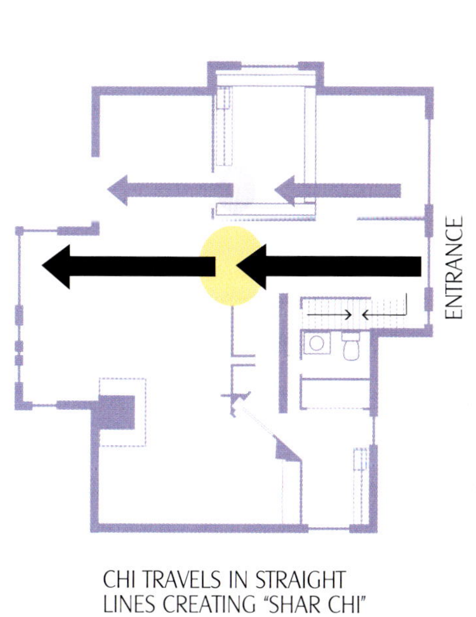

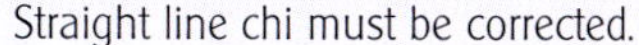

Straight line chi must be corrected.

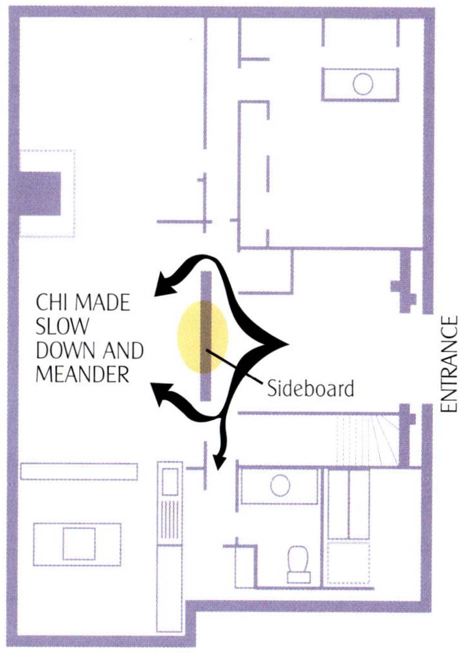

Chi meanders due to strategically placed sideboard.

Yin water that is still is one of the best cures for quarrelsome energy when you also place a light inside.

16 Bad vibes from neighbours

I have often been asked to suggest ways of dealing with unfriendly neighbours, or neighbours with noisy children, or neighbours with insensitive feelings and worst of all neighbours who are downright hostile. This last category of neighbours can either be very quarrelsome or they may hang Pa Kua mirrors above their doors that are aimed directly at you. In such cases what can you do?

Problems with neighbours are especially trying when you live in link houses or in apartment blocks with thin walls. Then the wailing of children and noise can sometimes be so trying as to unsettle you hugely. And when they resort to using feng shui against you it can even cause you to have bad luck.

One of the most effective cures to calm down noisy and quarrelsome vibes in the air is to place **a large surface area of water as shown here**. The water should ideally be still rather than bubbling. So it is *yin* water. Then place a light inside the water and try to create life as well. This brings in the yang energy. This can take the form of a plant, or you can have a few small fish inside. Place floating candles or lotus decorations to create purity of motivation. Place this feature near the wall that you share with the neighbour. It will absorb all hostile vibes. It is also excellent for absorbing bad chi caused by Pa Kua mirrors hung across the road, or above the door of the neighbour opposite. Let your water feature "receive" the bad chi and then transform it. This type of water feature is also an excellent cure to overcome the hostile flying stars 3 and 2 where they occur.

17 Beams and overhead fans

Feng shui taboos regarding the presence of anything heavy or threatening above can be a bane to modern interior design enthusiasts who love incorporating design beams as well as decorative lines on ceilings. If you wish to incorporate designs in the space above you, try to do it skillfully such that *auspicious* objects or lines can be incorporated into the designs above e.g. using the auspicious **trigram *Chien***, which comprises three straight lines. It is better not to have heavy beams criss-cross the space above, as this makes it difficult to place furniture below. When these heavy structural beams are positioned directly above sofas, chairs and beds, they tend to cause illness to those seated or lying directly below, usually manifesting as severe migraines, headaches and general stress and fatigue.

Right: Heavy chi emanating from ceiling beams presses down on those seated below.

Left: Overhead fans can have the same effect. I prefer stand fans to ceiling fans, except in instances when the chi of the room benefits from having a fan to keep the chi moving.

A sweeping curved staircase causes energy to meander gently. Do note that while corkscrew type staircases are bad, gentle curved stairs like this one here are auspicious.

18 Slow down the chi

The easiest way to protect your home against bad feng shui, and to enhance the chi within is to ensure that all energy inside the home never moves too fast. This implies making an effort to slow down the movement of chi throughout your home. Try achieving this in different and innovative ways, thereby bringing your own ideas into your practice of feng shui. There is room for creativity in the practice of feng shui – don't let anyone convince you otherwise.

Working with decorative objects such as auspicious art objects and paintings as well as plants will allow your creativity to work magic in your home space. Remember that when chi slows down, the spirit of the home benefits from its benevolent energy. This encourages the chi to accumulate and gather strength, bringing good feelings into the household. You can use lights along narrow spaces, staircases and corridors to create yang ambience, which also ensures that chi never gets stagnant. You can place auspicious objects to distract the chi enticing it to settle. Your intention should be to **prevent the flow from moving too fast up** the stairs and from room to room. So interconnecting areas must always be attended to.

WAYS TO SLOW DOWN THE CHI

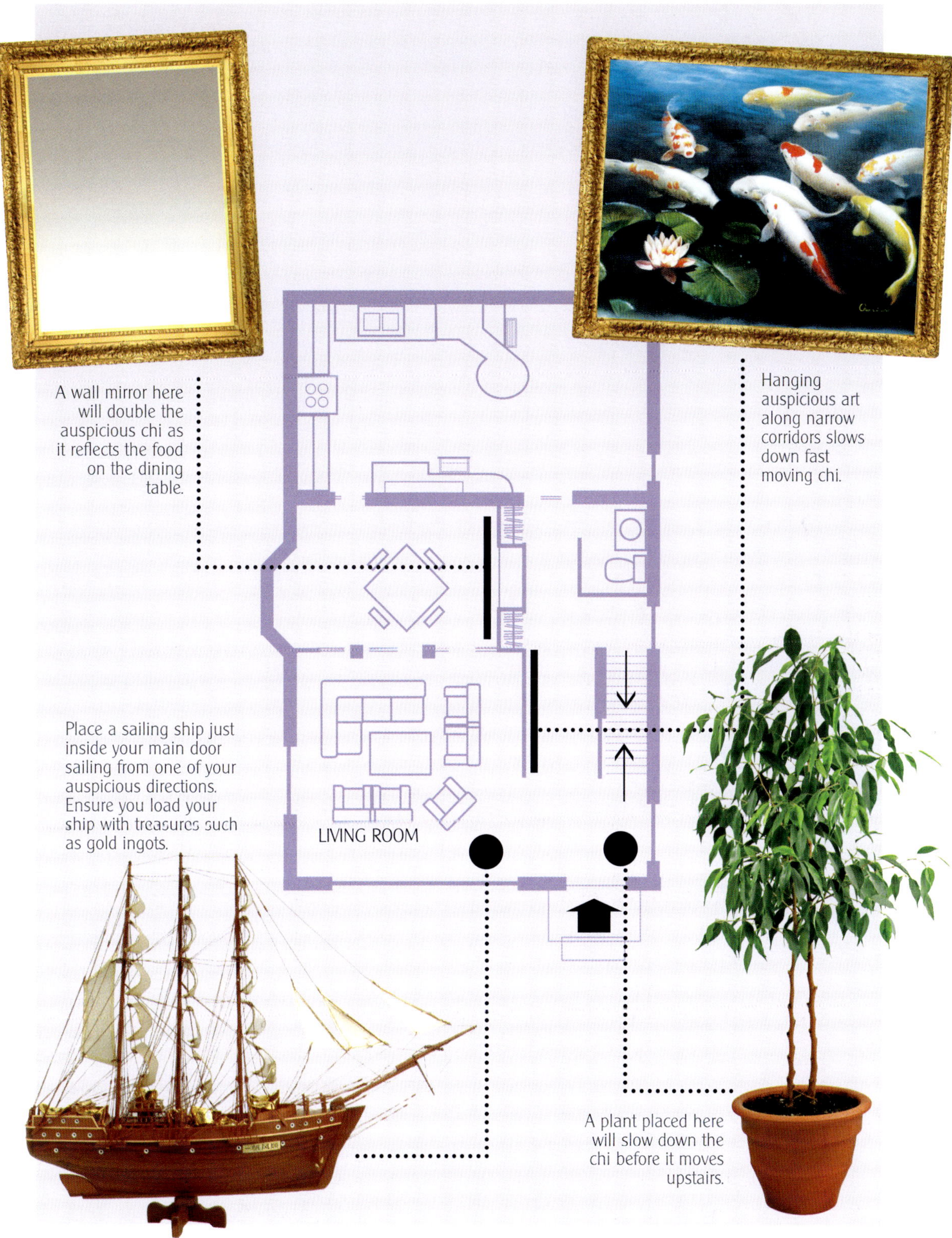

19 Inconvenient toilets

Unfortunately, toilets and bathrooms, which are places where we can relax after a long and hard days work, tend to be places where bad chi is created and accumulated. Each of the Pa Kua's eight directions superimposed onto a living space indicates a specific kind of luck which is afflicted if a toilet or bathroom is located there. Hence toilets anywhere INSIDE the home are a source of problems. Consider the following rules about the placement of toilets and you will realize that these modern conveniences seem to be a real inconvenience when we want to practise feng shui. Bad feng shui or not, we all need and want these modern conveniences, so take note of the cures and remedies:

- A toilet in the South causes harm to your reputation, makes you unpopular and when compounded by other bad indications, can even lead to legal entanglements and imprisonment. Place a jug or urn of yin water (i.e. still water) to counter this toilet.
- A toilet in the **North** afflicts your career and slows down your upward mobility. Place a plant inside the toilet to counter the afflicted chi here.
- A toilet in the **East** afflicts your health and limits your growth. Place a red lamp in the toilet or hang a tiny curved knife (about 3 inches) to slice through the afflicted chi.
- A toilet in the **West** afflicts your descendants luck and your children. Place a red lamp or a bowl of yin water to control the bad chi.
- A toilet in the **Southwest** afflicts marriage and marriage opportunities. Overcome by placing a plant inside the toilet or by hanging a 5 rod solid windchime.
- A toilet in the **Northeast** afflicts education and examination luck. A plant here will take care of the affliction.
- A toilet in the **Southeast** afflicts your family fortune causing loss of wealth. Place a small curved knife or have a bright light inside the toilet.
- A toilet in the **Northwest** causes loss of patronage luck. It also has a negative effect on the luck of the family patriarch. This is a serious affliction and the best way to overcome it is by having the toilet well lit and having an urn of water.

In addition to the afflictions listed above, it is also unlucky when toilets directly face the main door, or doors into bedrooms and dining rooms. In such situations, hang a wall covering to visually block the toilet. Placing a door mirror on the toilet door (on the outside) or painting it bright red are also good solutions. These strengthen the yang chi around the toilet. If there is a toilet on the upper floor above the main door, keep the entrance foyer or dining room well lit. This has the effect of pushing the chi upwards.

20 Pillars and corners

Round pillars are always preferred over square pillars. But too many pillars inside a residential home is not advisable if the home is small.

As a general rule, round pillars are preferred to square pillars. These signify earth chi moving upwards and brings the promise of abundance. In modern homes, **high round pillars** can transform a home into a palace, thereby creating the chi of abundance and prosperity. If you live in an apartment building, the presence of round pillars has the potential to transform your building into an auspicious and abundant abode.

However, it is important never to overdo the presence of these soaring pillars. When there are too many soaring pillars, something auspicious can transform into excessive yin energy. There is also the question of balance. If yours is a modest home make certain the size and height of pillars blend harmoniously. Never allow pillars to dominate your living space or your entrance. When balance goes out of sync, the chi will no longer be in harmony.

Note how soaring round pillars lend an air of abundance to this **very large home**. Being round, they do not have sharp edges that emit killing chi. Instead, the circular energy created is conducive to a good flow of chi making its way through the home.

21 Irregular shaped rooms

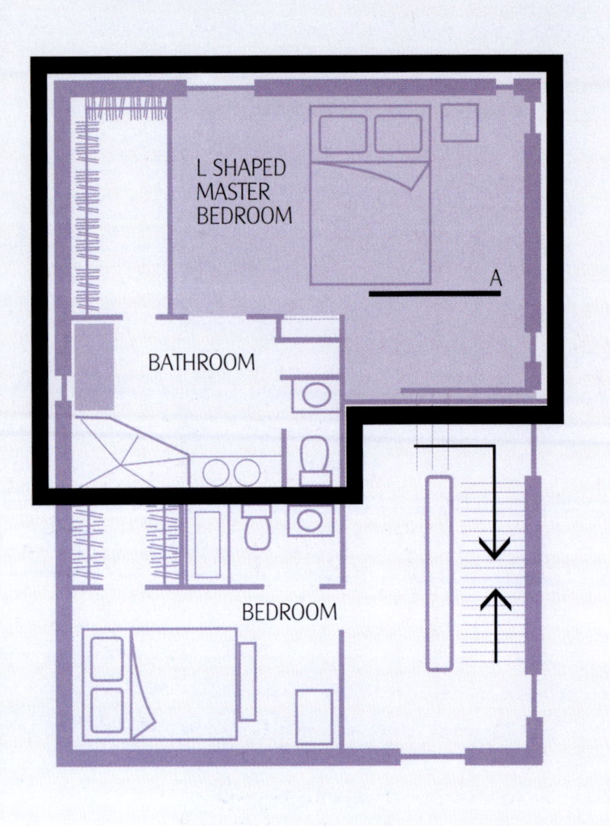

This master bedroom would benefit from some kind of divider at point A, as this would regularize the shape of the sleeping area. The attached bathroom and closet should thus be treated as separate entities of space.

Every feng shui enthusiast knows and appreciates the value of regular shaped rooms. Square and rectangular rooms suggest balanced feng shui and are easy to enhance. **Irregular shaped** rooms on the other hand present something of a challenge. Not only are such rooms unbalanced and have missing corners, they are also difficult to assess and to enhance. It is difficult to superimpose the Lo Shu square onto irregular shaped rooms, thus making it difficult to make Flying Star feng shui assessments of the space. It is also harder to use the Pa Kua eight directions to identify lucky and unlucky corners according to the various schools of feng shui.

The most common of irregular shaped rooms are those that are **L shaped** – and these are usually bedrooms with attached bathrooms. L shaped rooms are easy to correct since all that is needed is the placement of some kind of barrier – screen, side board or curtain – to create a visual separation. This has the effect of demarcating the sleeping area, which then makes it easy to position the bed and other furniture. If the missing corner of the room houses the bathroom, then introducing the correct cure for the bathroom should bring things back into balance.

Triangular shaped rooms are more difficult to deal with, as shown in the illustration on the facing page. Here the placement of the bed will pose a challenge indeed due to the placement of the two doors into the bedroom. Placing the bed against the wall, which has washbasins on the other side, will create incredibly bad feng shui for the sleeping residents. So here the best thing to do is to close one of the doors, perhaps the one going to the garden terrace, so that the bed can be placed against this wall.

In any case, triangular shaped rooms are very unsuitable as offices or bedrooms, and it would be advisable to look for an alternative room to work or sleep in. If you have no choice, the way to deal with such rooms is to use furniture or curtains to cordon off a corner behind which you can place clothes, suitcases and so forth. Yes, this drastically reduces the size of the room, and yes, you should treat that part of the room which has been "discarded" as a storeroom, as this clearly demarcates the room visually and mentally. This is one way to regularize the shape of the room. You can then treat the regular shaped area just like any regular bedroom.

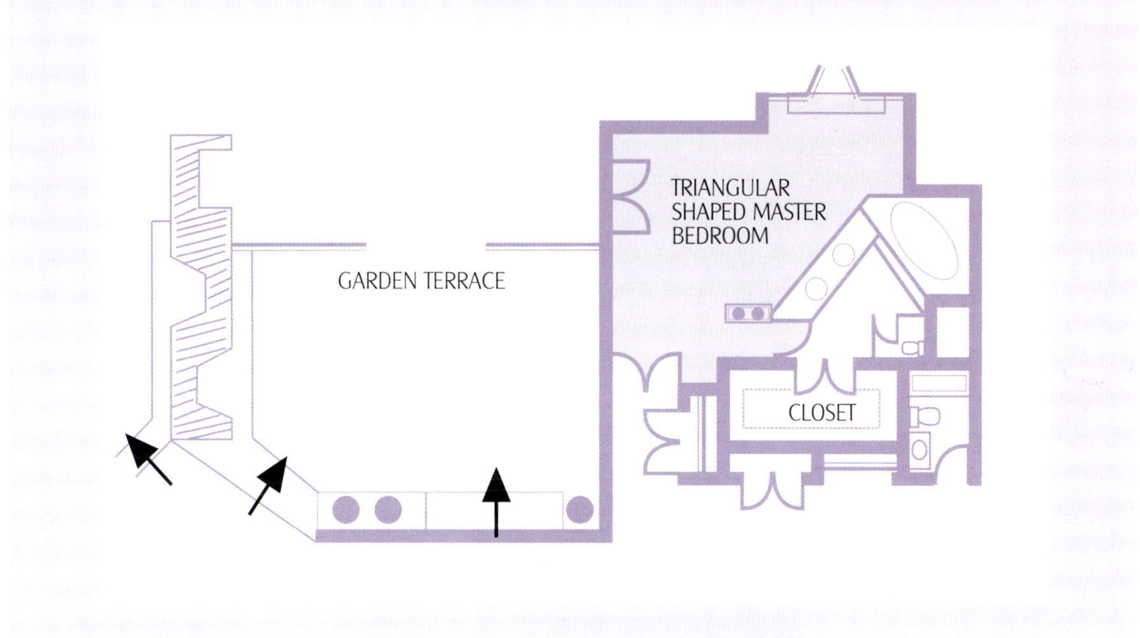

Above: The attached bathroom here causes the main bedroom to have an awkward shape, making it very unbalanced. This is not advisable.

Left: Cabinets and shelves like these behind the bed are not recommended. These signify hidden poison arrows causing bad dreams and unbalanced sleep. It is a good thing that the headboard is big, offering some protection.

22 Staircase suggestions

The staircase in your house or apartment is basically a conduit of chi. It is where chi moves from one level of the home to the next. When your staircase has good feng shui, it distributes good fortune to the rest of the home. When it is flawed from a feng shui perspective, it spreads harmful energy causing illness, robbery and loss. A staircase that conducts afflicted chi is really bad news. So do take note of the several ways to assess your staircase. Try to incorporate the general guidelines that ensure good staircase feng shui. This requires good staircase design and location. The former is based on the form school. while actual location of the staircase is best assessed according to the Flying Star chart of the home or by using the Pa Kua eight directions.

CURVED STAIRCASES ARE BEST

Broadly curving staircases are the most conducive to an auspicious flow of chi. **Spirals** are not the same as curved staircases and are not encouraged for indoors, but if you really like a spiral staircase that leads up to a mezzanine floor, use wood rather than metal. **Straight and steep** staircases cause chi to move too fast. When you have a steep and straight staircase, they are less harmful when placed by the side of the home. When they are in the center of the home they can be the cause of severe afflictions that result in loss and illness.

STAIRCASES SHOULD NEVER FACE A DOOR

If your staircase directly faces your main front door, place a screen or divider between the stairs and the door. If you cannot do this, try to turn the last three steps of the stairs and if you cannot do this then install a very bright and elaborate light fixture in the space between. This will cause the chi entering the house to slow down before making its way up the stairs. A crystal chandelier is best for this purpose. Upstairs, the same rule applies. Try not to let the top of the staircase directly face the bedroom door. If it does, once again, a bright light here will remedy the situation.

STAIRCASES SHOULD NOT HAVE "HOLES" IN THE STEPS

The holes in between the steps suggest a "leak" in your wealth. Even if you have rented an apartment with this feature it really is worthwhile to close up the gaps with carpet or plywood. When the staircase looks solid, the flow of chi between house levels is also firm and strong. Note that wooden staircases symbolize growth and are to be favoured.

Be careful what you have under your staircase. A TV is fine but not books or other auspicious objects. A curved staircase is excellent. Solid steps are always better than steps with holes, and do be wary of red carpets on staircases. This is not a problem when the staircase is by the side of the home, but a staircase with red carpeting in the center of the home can be dangerous.

23 Staircase protection

Staircases that are excessively narrow are best kept lit through out the day. Like corridors, these are conduits of chi. The staircase brings the chi which enters the home into the inner sanctum of the home. So it is always a good idea to keep them bright and attractive. In addition, it is also an excellent idea to create **staircase protection** so that bad energy does not move up the stairs into the sleeping quarters of the home.

The best way to ensure this is to hang a painting of a "Protector" image. The Chinese believe in protector images such as *Zhong Kuei* and ***Kwan Kung***. Paintings of these deities can be hung at the base of the stairs to create protective chi here. Another method is to place two small images of ***Chi Lin or Fu Dogs*** by either side of the stairs. A third method is to have a very bright light at the base of the stairs so that good luck chi is encouraged and enticed to travel upwards.

Do remember that steps in the staircase must be solid and it is worth the inconvenience and extra expense to make them so. Also try not to keep the spaces below the staircase empty. Put this space to good use by converting it into a storage area. But never place things that represent family wealth in this area. Nor should you keep text books or anything else that symbolize your aspirations since you really do not want to step on your own aspirations. Another useful point to note is that **water under the staircase hurts the second generation**. Thus do not place a water feature or a decorative pond under the staircase, as this will afflict the success potential of your children.

Staircases can be made of wood, metal or concrete to simulate these three solid elements.

It is important to keep staircase chi moving, but the chi should not move too fast. Keeping staircases well lit will encourage the chi to flow upwards. Art on walls also serve to slow down the chi so that its movement upwards is both benign and benevolent.

Use the productive cycle of the five-element theory when choosing which type of staircase. **Wood staircases** work best when the staircase is in the South, **metal staircases** are best in the North, while **concrete staircases** work best in the West and Northwest. Try not to have staircases in the center of the home or too near or directly facing the front door.

24 Cramped spaces and narrow corridors

One of the most important things to look out for in interior feng shui are dark corners and cramped spaces in the home. This is because **stagnant chi accumulates** and this creates stale energy that can cause illness, lethargy, fatigue and general apathy. Cramped spaces suggest that life does not flow smoothly. There is little room to move, so chi stagnates. This reflects into your life, your work, your business and your relationships. You will feel there are obstacles to the smooth flow of life and work.

Cramped spaces are the result of low ceilings and small dimensions in room size. Narrow corridors and tight staircases are also the cause for this affliction.

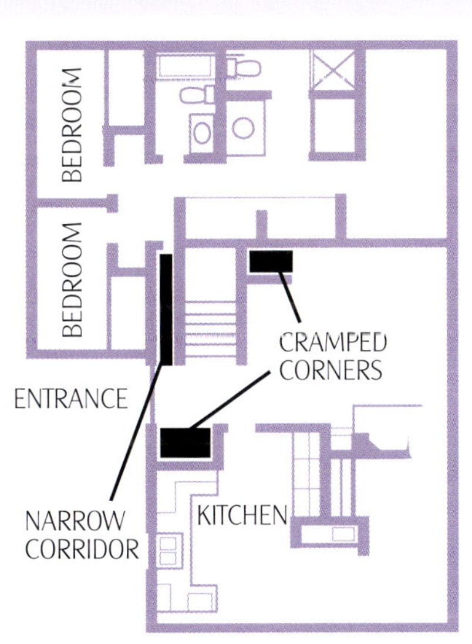

Here the corridor that connects the foyer to the bedrooms is too narrow such that chi here will tend to stagnate unless the corridor is kept brightly lit at all times. Since corridors are conduits of chi, they must not be ignored. In addition to lights, it is a good idea to hang pretty pictures and even a wall mirror to visually improve the space.

Narrow and long corridors should be well lit for chi to flow. Hanging paintings on the walls is also a good idea.

The best antidotes for cramped spaces are cleanliness, white paint and lights. Take stock of your home and see if there are corners in your home where stagnant chi accumulates. If there are, then organize a major cleaning of the space. If the corner feels stale and "dead", revitalize with sound and incense which will make the chi come alive again. Then go out and buy a can of light-coloured paint.

White is the best colour as this is a very strong yang colour that complements all other colours. Cramped spaces that are painted white instantly look better, brighter and lighter. The energy improves almost instantly.

To ensure that tight spaces never feel cramped again, install soft warm lights that will further improve the flow of energy. Keep these lights turned on all through the day if necessary. The flow of chi will likewise improve and all the obstacles you might have been experiencing will dissolve and start to move again.

25 Kitchen woes

The kitchen of the home where food for the family is cooked also benefits from feng shui treatment, although generally there is no need to activate the chi of the kitchen. Instead, what is more important is to take note of the feng shui taboos to observe.

Although this kitchen looks stylish, it is better not to use a red colour scheme in the kitchen, as there is already enough fire energy here.

KITCHEN TABOOS

1 **Do not hang family portraits, mirrors or pictures** of fierce animals inside the kitchen. The fire energy here is much too strong and we do not want it magnified. Animal pictures should also not be placed here since the animal realm generally offers protector images in feng shui. Setting them near fire causes disturbance of an auric nature within the home. Energy generated in the kitchen can then become harmful.

2 **Do not have a colour scheme** for the kitchen that is dominated by red. There is already enough fire here. Excessive yang energy always poses a real danger so turn to pastel colours instead.

3 **Do not have the kitchen located in the Northwest** of the home. This suggests "fire at heaven's gate" and is regarded one of the danger indications in feng shui. If you do have your kitchen already located here, place an urn filled with still water. This uses the YIN WATER cure, which serves to absorb the fire without causing damage. Inside the kitchen itself, do not place the stove or oven used for cooking in the Northwest corner of the kitchen. Naked fire in this corner can be dangerous, especially for the patriarch of the household.

4 **Always keep the rice urn covered** and treat it as a repository of the family's assets. The rice urn should not be made of plastic. Earth energy is the best (e.g. rice urns made of ceramics, clay or porcelain are most auspicious).

5 **Try to position the cooking direction** in such a way that the cook does not have his/her back to the door. This brings bad luck into the kitchen.

6 **Try not to position the sink or refrigerator** directly opposite or next to the stove. This brings the two elements – fire and water – into direct conflict with each other, and accentuates the clashing elements of the kitchen area. If you do not do much ethnic cooking, it is a good idea to have a dry and modern kitchen, which does not use open naked fire. Ovens, microwaves, steamers and rice cookers that do not use open charcoal fires guards against fire energy getting out of control.

7 Finally, try not to **position the kitchen in the center** of the home. If your kitchen is already positioned in the center of your home, try to keep cooking with a naked flame to a minimum.

OVEN TIP

Do not have the sink located directly next to the main oven. This causes a clash of elements.

KITCHEN TIP

Never have the kitchen door directly face the main entrance door into your home.

26 Seeing the big picture

The best way to practice feng shui is always to start by seeing "the big picture". This means looking at the place being analyzed as a whole entity. Look at the overall impression and examine external surroundings before going into the details. Begin feng shui practice by using a camera to snap a roll of film that shows you the home or apartment from all angles. You will be surprised at what the camera captures which your naked eye has missed. For instance, if you stand at your main entrance and position your camera such that it snaps the view directly facing your main door, you would be able to identify obstacles and physical afflictions immediately. The best view would be a **flat field or open ground** of some kind. When you detect harmful hostile objects outside, always create protection for your door by blocking the view or reflecting it away.

Next, never do the feng shui of any home without **referring to a floor plan**. You need the floor plan to give you a snapshot of where each room is placed in relation to other rooms.

You also require a good layout plan to see how energy flows within the house. When energy can move smoothly and without obstruction, winding its way through the home, chi of the home is said to be benevolent. When chi moves in long straight lines, it is said to become harmful. Straight lines of flows must be made to slow down using the strategic placement of furniture and decorative items. Because of this, feng shui is sometimes known as the art of placement.

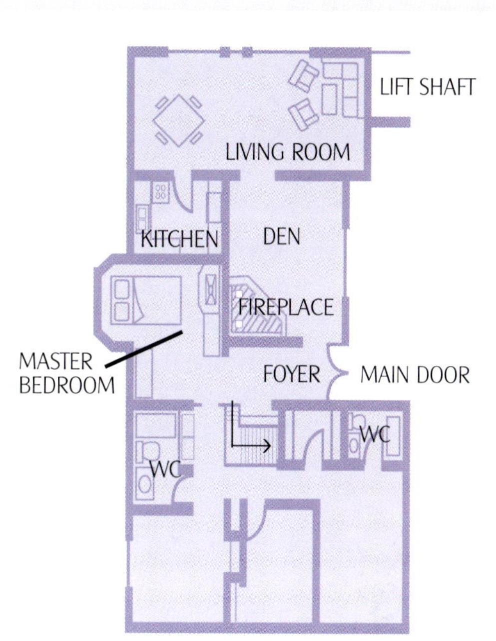

In the layout plan here, see if you can find the following observations that need some feng shui improvement.

1 The **chi flows straight** into the master bedroom. This causes residents to suffer from straight energy, which is fierce and hostile. The best thing to do is place paintings on the wall of the small corridor.

2 The **master bedroom shares a wall** with the kitchen. This is not a desirable arrangement. In this case however, the oven is placed on the opposite wall, so the fire energy does not disturb the master bedroom.

3 **Notice that the fireplace** is located against the wall which is also shared with the master bedroom. This is not advisable, as fire energy so close to the bedroom causes yang disturbances to the residents of the bedroom.

27 Creating an energy field

One of the most powerful protection for one's living space is the creation of a defensive field of guardian chi. This is like building an **invisible shield** that defends the home so that its energy will not succumb to attacks from hostile chi. This is done by developing the capability of focused mental imaging. Everyone has this ability, which involves concentration to mentally create powerful visualizations in the mind. The images you build have a mysterious power and this can be channeled towards creating a force field of energy that protects the home. This force field defends the home in different ways. It can prevent hostile chi from penetrating the natural aura of the home. It can stop people who have hidden bad intentions from even entering the home. It can also act as a kind of **invisible barrier against wandering spirits** which coexist with us in a different realm. How powerful the force field that you build will be depends on the strength of the concentration you use to create it. I have found that even a novice practitioner new to the concept of mental visualizations can use mental imaging with some degree of success. The **imagined force field will actually reduce killing chi** and hostility of evil intentions from coming into the home. So those of you new to this concept can try using it with some confidence.

Generally, the more attuned you are to the energy of your home, the closer you will be to its spirit and therefore the more empowered your force field will be. An affinity with the spirit of your home empowers your visualizations with tremendous strength. Empowerment of this kind can never be used to harm people and works best when the motivation is pure. Thus for instance, in the case of parents who are motivated to protect their children, their **mental visualizations carries enormous strength**. This is because the energy behind the mental image is unconditional love, the spirit of which has great power.

Those of you familiar with creative visualization or have done some meditation will find it easy to mentally create the force field which is like a shield.

Firstly, stand in the center of the room. Raise both arms high in front of you with palms open facing outward. Take a deep "in" breath as you raise your arms, then gently let the palms of your hands lower a few inches. Breath out. *Do this three times to awaken the chi.* Visualize receiving energy in the form of golden light from the Universe.

Hold your hands palms open and facing the sky as if to receive this energy from the Universe. Feel the chi by tuning into the palms

Mentally creating a protective cocoon of light around the home can create a protective shield against any harmful energy.

of your hands. Stay like this for a few minutes. When you feel a tingling sensation on your palms slowly turn your palms to face each other. Your hands are still high above your head. Slowly lower your hands and imagine holding a transparent sphere of protective blue-ish light between the palms of your hands - hold this sphere of bright intense energy.

Next move your palms very slowly away from each other and imagine the sphere of light getting larger and larger. Now visualize the sphere of light energy getting brighter and bigger until it becomes bigger than you, bigger than the room, bigger than your house., your apartment... soon it surrounds the whole house or the whole apartment building in its protective light. Nothing negative can penetrate the force field created by this sphere of light.

Focus on this protective aura around your home strongly. Be convinced of its power. Now gently close your eyes and visualize the blue light completely cocooning your house, apartment, or simply your room. Think, "This is the energy field of my space/home/room. Nothing harmful can penetrate this energy field".

Think of this cocoon of light as a protective halo around your home.

The first way is to visualize a protective **aura of pale ethereal blue light** around the home as shown above. Or you can also visualize a halo of blue light above the home sending protective beams of light below. When you undertake this meditation on a regular basis, your home will enjoy the harmony of being one with the cosmos. This is because you are actively drawing vital energy from the Universe and channeling it into your home, making it vibrant and filled with strong yin yang chi, which is also the universal tai chi. Do this mental imaging exercise regularly. With practice, you will be astonished at how good you become after just a week of visualization exercises.

If you live in an apartment, you can imagine the cocoon of blue light encasing the whole building so that everyone residing within (i.e. other fellow apartment residents) also enjoys the benefits of your wonderful visualization. Stand in front of the apartment building and soak in a picture of the whole building into your subconscious mind before doing this meditation.

Practise with a determined and focused concentration when you do this exercise. Remember that you are **not** using your own energy to empower your home with protective chi. You are using energy drawn from the cosmos. So you need never be afraid of ever becoming exhausted with this exercise. At all times, make certain you are not tense. The great secret of success in visualization work is the ability to generate a relaxed awareness.

2

ENHANCING ROOMS & CORNERS

One of the most potent systems for activating energy inside homes is the Pa Kua Eight Aspirations method of feng shui, which offers a simple way for you to start activating the corners of your home. You can use this easy method to improve your feng shui in any room within your home that you use frequently in order to attract any single one of the eight kinds of luck. To be effective it should be a room that you use often. The result of enhancing rooms and corners using the element associations of the Pa Kua is often pleasantly surprising. Good fortune associated with the kind of luck you are activating will manifest, sometimes in ways you least expect. Many of my readers and students using only this system of feng shui have experienced amazing results. Applying this particular formula to rooms and apartments is based on understanding the big & small tai chi. This is what helps you use the Pa Kua formulas with ease and effectiveness.

This bedroom has beautiful warm light which is both energising and restful at the same time - so perfect for a young couple.

The Pa Kua of Eight Aspirations

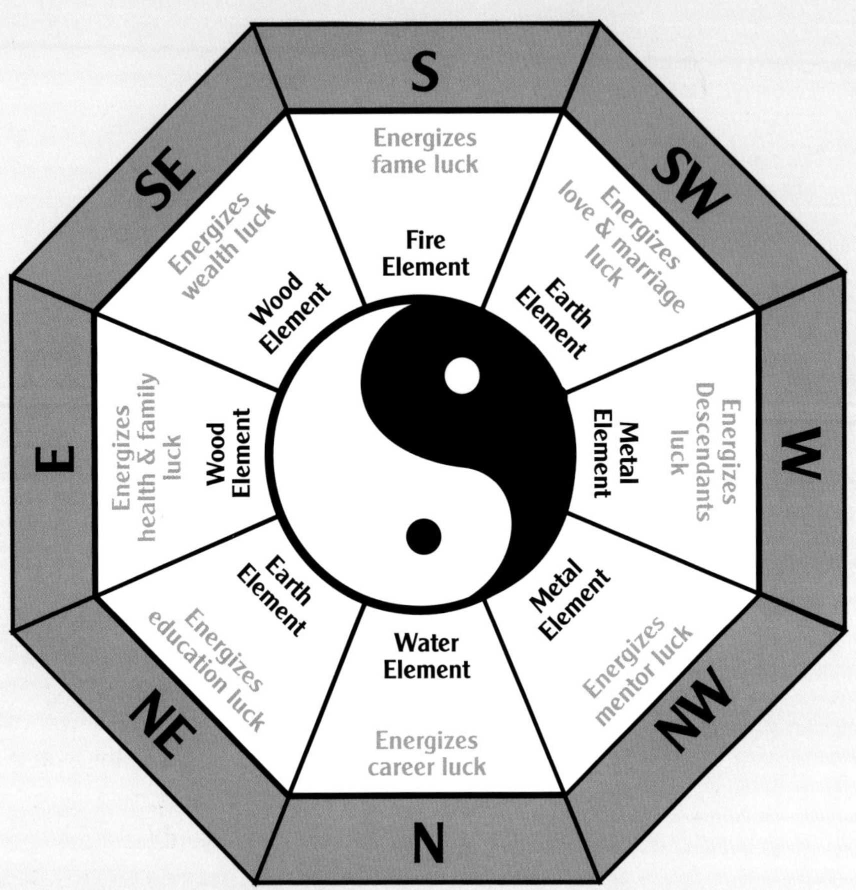

The Eight Aspirations Formula is one of the easiest ways of energising chi in various corners of the home, easily bringing dead energy to life and generating fresh new ideas. Depending on what compass location the corner is located in, different emanations of luck takes place. The Pa Kua illustrated above summarises the aspect of luck generated, and these categories of luck are based on the trigrams placed around the Yang Pa Kua - which is also known as the Later Heaven Pa Kua.

28 Big tai chi of the whole house

The tai chi symbol is the yin and yang symbol. Yang is the white part of the symbol and yin is the black part. According to Chinese texts, this symbol theoretically signifies all that makes up the Universe, and so it encapsulates the fullness of heaven, earth and man in all their varying manifestations. In accordance with feng shui theory, the **tai chi applies to every microcosm and every macrocosm of space that exists**. The big tai chi refers to the larger picture. This can mean seeing the symbol as representing the whole world, or a continent, or a country or a city or a district or a whole house ... So *bigger* or *larger* is to be viewed in a relative way.

What is big in one context may be small in another. Thus when we describe the bigger tai chi in a feng shui context, we can refer to the tai chi of any space according to how we define the space. So we can refer to the feng shui of the whole house as being the **big tai chi**. At the same time, we can also be referring to the tai chi of an entire office building or an apartment block. Master practitioners of the old school generally begin by working with the big tai chi, so they define the parameters of the space they are working with.

The big tai chi means looking at the whole house as a single space entity, and the Pa Kua of Eight Aspirations is then superimposed onto the floor space of the whole house. Implementation of energizers and enhancers must therefore be undertaken in the light of the big tai chi. The Pa Kua of Eight Aspirations should be superimposed onto the house layout plan according to orientations determined with a compass.

In this example, the door is facing North, so the North side of the Pa Kua is placed where the door is. Looking at the diagram, we know that the wealth luck of this house resides in the master bedroom, while the love and relationship luck is near the kitchen. Career luck is near the entrance door, while mentor luck is in the Northwest, which falls in the living room. The layout of this house seems to facilitate the application of feng shui enhancement techniques. Notice the Pa Kua is stretched lengthwise to accommodate the rectangular shape of this house. This is done because the tai chi symbol is not static. It is a flexible symbol that can be stretched to facilitate application of its many layers of secrets.

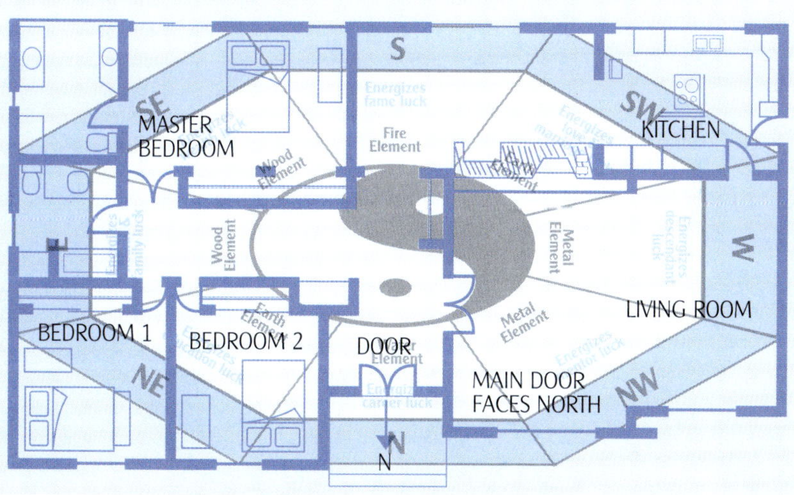

Note how the Pa Kua with all its attributes can be superimposed onto floor plans for ease of implementation. Note also how the Pa Kua can be "stretched" to fit a room that is not perfectly square.

29 Small tai chi of each room

Space can also be manipulated within the confines of separate rooms. This acknowledges that a living abode is made up of several small areas signified by the ***small tai chi***. Thus all living abodes comprise the manifestations of energy as symbolized by the small tai chi. This implies that the Pa Kua of Eight Aspirations luck can be applied onto single rooms.

Look at the example illustrated here. I superimposed the same eight aspirations Pa Kua onto the living room of this home. Once again I use a compass to determine my orientations in this room. Since this house has a Northeast facing entrance I have placed the Northeast side of the Pa Kua near the door. From this I am now able to identify the career corner in the living room, the wealth area, the love area, the family area and so forth. I do this by simply looking at where these sectors are as shown by the Pa Kua. By doing this, **I am using the living room to energize the small tai chi luck of the living room**. So if I want to activate for career luck, I will make sure I install a decorative feature in this north part of the living room with an element that will "produce" the element of this corner. Since the element of north is water, I know from the cycle of five elements that metal produces water. Thus to give myself a dose of career luck I will place an auspicious **career symbol** made of metal in this corner. This can be a windchime, a metal painting, a **gold plated ru yi** and so forth. I can also use water itself to strengthen this corner. In the same way that I activate this career sector, I can also systematically start to think of activating all the other corners of the living room using the Pa Kua's eight trigrams which manifests the 8 Aspirations, as a guide. To get the most out of what you have done it is important that you use the living room of the home frequently. If you do not spend time here, you will not be able to benefit fully from the feng shui enhanced living room.

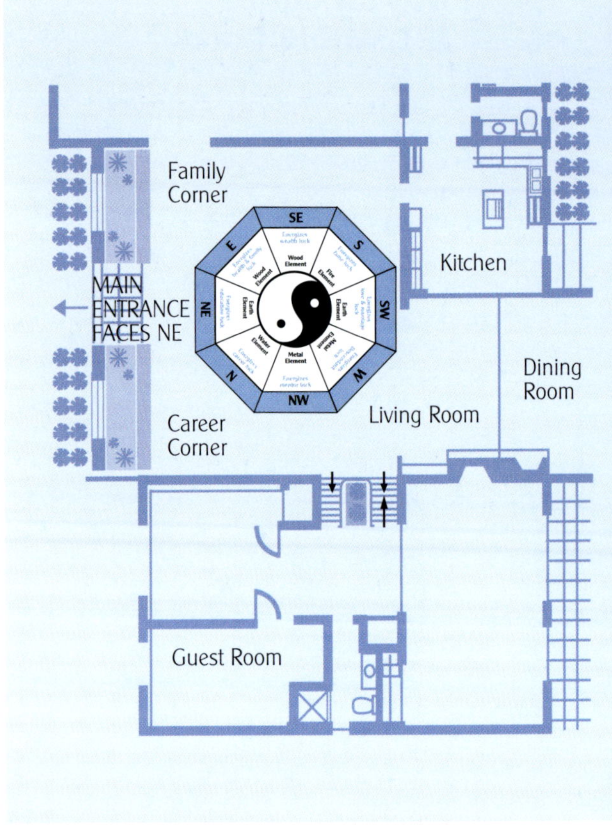

Use the principle of big and small tai chi to define the space to work with. This is a concept that is useful to bear in mind since it holds true also for all the compass formulas of feng shui. As an example, note that you can activate the Southwest of your living room or your bedroom to attract love luck IF the Southwest of your home is missing or if there is a toilet pressing down on your love luck in the Southwest of your whole house. When it comes to love, work with your bedroom space. It is where you spend a great deal of your time!

30 Eight aspirations of the Pa Kua

Happy space can be made auspicious when you factor in the hidden meanings of the Pa Kua. There are thousands of secret symbols contained in this powerful feng shui tool. The Pa Kua is an eight-sided object, empowered by its trigrams. These three lined symbols (made up of broken and unbroken lines) are placed on each of its sides in two different arrangements, generally referred to as the **Early Heaven** and **Later Heaven** arrangements. Feng shui is the skill of deciphering the meanings of these arrangements of the trigrams under different situations.

The Eight Aspirations method makes use of the Later Heaven Arrangement of the trigrams around the tai chi symbol. It is from these trigrams and what they stand for that we are able to decipher the chi of each corner. There are eight root trigrams and eight sides to the Pa Kua. We can thus divide all rooms, and all spaces into eight sectors with a center sector, thereby making a total of nine sectors. This way of looking at rooms (or space) is intrinsic to the practice of feng shui.

The illustration here summarizes the trigrams and indicates the type of luck each side stands for based on the trigram. Each of the sides can then be identified according to their compass directions. Use a compass to identify the "side" you wish to activate. You may, if you so wish, activate all eight sectors of all your rooms.

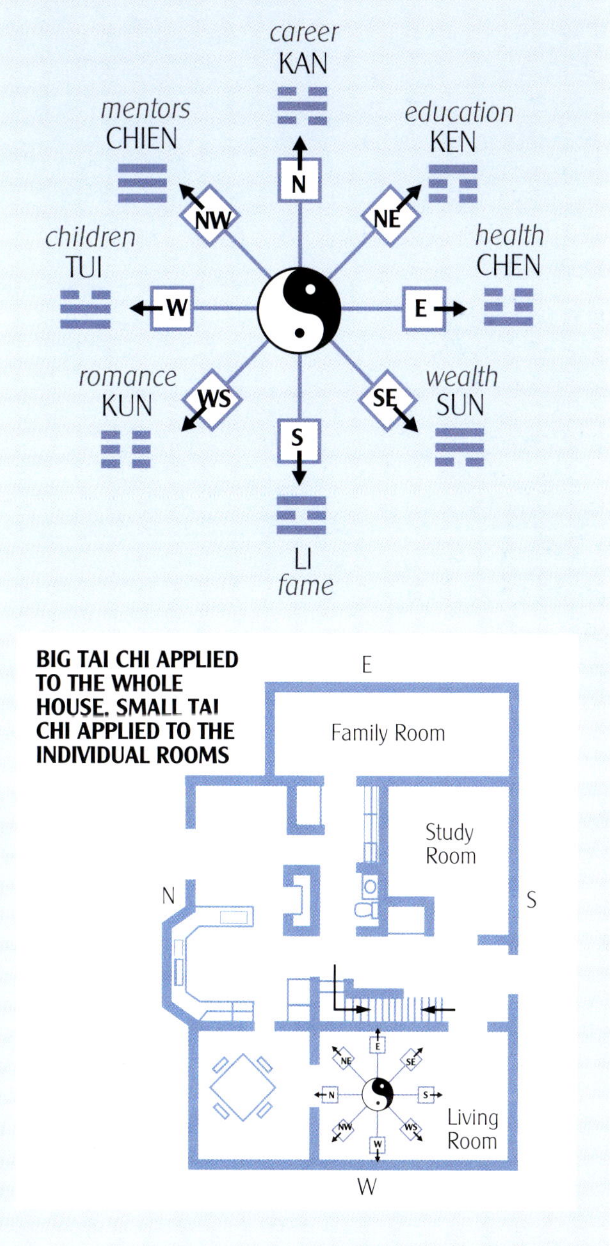

In the example here, you can see how the Pa Kua has been fitted into the living room. Each of the eight arrows point to the respective corners that stand for career (North), education (Northeast), health (east), wealth (Southeast), fame (South), romance (Southwest), children (West) and mentor (Northwest) luck.

31 Creating happy space

Once you have developed the ability to superimpose the Eight Aspirations Pa Kua onto the different rooms of your home and also onto your whole house, you have at your fingertips a certain flexibility of application. You can choose which corners and which rooms you want to activate, and concentrate your efforts on corners and rooms you use most. It is you who must be the one to make judgements as to where and how you want to activate the big tai chi and where you can more efficiently activate the small tai chi. There are no simple answers to these choices, since there are usually localized factors to take account of. Every person is also different with respect to tastes, attitudes and what they want out of life.

PERSONAL ASPIRATIONS AND TASTES

In feng shui, as with everything else, personal creativity and taste, as well as individual priorities, must be factored in to obtain maximum results. So do listen to yourself. Do not use anything, paint any colour or place any piece of art or object, that you yourself do not like. **You must respect yourself and your own inner voice**. This is the best way to ensure that your personal chi blends with the way you decorate and arrange your rooms. Unless you have a positive interaction with all the objects you place inside your home, they will not have as much power to actualize

Use fresh flowers and pleasing scents to invigorate the chi inside your home.

Side tables that are portable, make it easy to move things around as time dimension feng shui requires.

good luck for you. For example if you absolutely hate the colour pink, then no matter how good this colour may be for attracting love into your life, my advice is not to use it. This is because your dislike of the colour is related to your own auric field at some unconscious level. So respect that!

Also, as we grow older, our tastes and aspirations will change. So you can change your tastes as often as you wish. You can re-arrange your room, furniture and the decorative objects you use to activate your corners as often as you like.

I change things around all the time. Nothing makes me happier than to revitalize my rooms. In addition to creating beneficial movement of chi, this also ensures that the energy of my home never gets tired. **So my life never stagnates**. Each day and every day, something new manifests. I never forget that in feng shui there is always an alternative way to go.

HOW OFTEN TO MOVE FURNITURE AROUND?

As a rule of thumb, I rearrange my living room furniture every year, just before the start of the lunar New Year, and I change my bedroom furniture around at least once every three years. This is to prevent the energy around me from ever growing stale. This reflects my approach to feng shui and also my approach to life. I view life as a dynamic process of new opportunities and new experiences. To me, feng shui has always been the science of enhancing my personal space, so I make sure that wherever I am, whether at home or in a hotel room, I am always surrounded by **fresh invigorating chi**. It may be something simple like displaying a bouquet of fresh flowers or spraying the room with my favourite perfume. Or it can be **happy music** played loud to raise my spirits. I use whatever is easy and near at hand to energize my personal space. Let me share these secrets of happy space with you. Think in terms of what makes you feel energized, then do the same for your space. Every corner of your room will benefit from attention. When the corners of your room are made happy, they will attract, store and accumulate tons of good luck – all for you!

32 Applying the five element theory

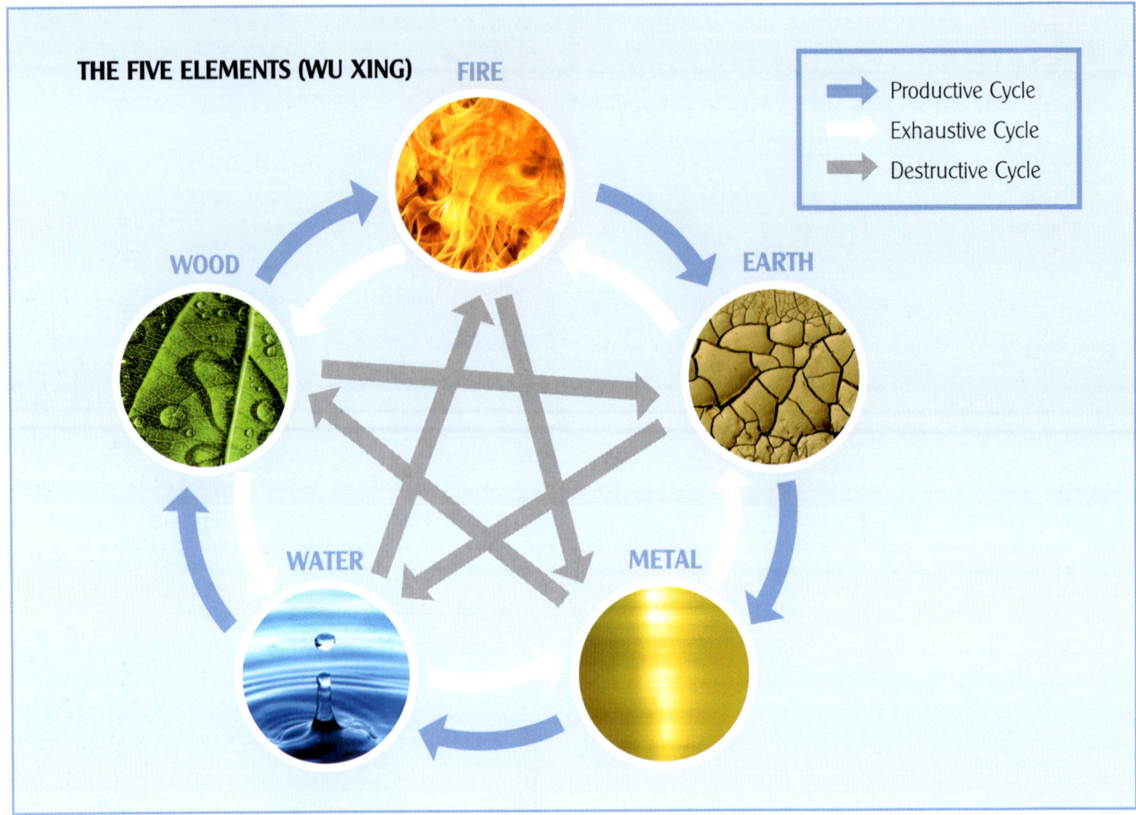

A core concept in feng shui practice is the theory of the five elements. If you understand this concept (also known as *wu xing* in Chinese), you will become adept in feng shui and also gain a firm grounding in the fundamental philosophy of Chinese thought. Many things Chinese are based on ***wu xing***, from fortune telling, to medical cures, healthy living, chi kung exercises and fighting martial arts. The five elements theory is the foundation of all these esoteric skills. In feng shui, knowledge of the five elements and its three cycles – Productive, Exhaustive and Destructive - offers invaluable insights to the cures, remedies and energizers recommended by feng shui masters. It is thus an extremely good idea to commit the three cycles of the five elements to memory.

To use the theory of the five elements, you need to understand the relationship of each of the elements – **fire, wood, water, metal** and **earth** to each other. There are three relationships and these give rise to the three cycles.

USING THE 3 CYCLES

- To energize or enhance corners use the productive cycle to strengthen.
- To install remedies and cures for afflicted chi, use the exhausting cycle.
- To overcome and control killing chi, use the destructive cycle.

33 Two demarcation options

There are two ways to demarcate space to apply the Eight Aspirations method of feng shui. This means that to identify the actual corner of the room or home where we wish to activate for any one of the eight types of luck, we can use either the *pie chart* or the *Lo Shu grid* method of demarcation. It is up to you which method you prefer.

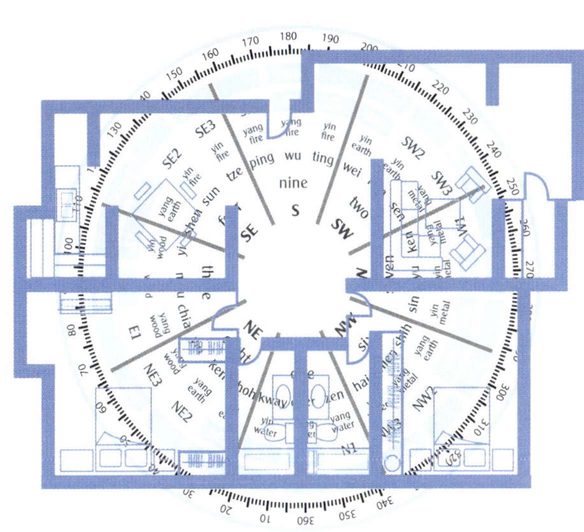

PIE CHART METHOD OF DEMARCATION

THE PIE CHART METHOD means superimposing the circular compass onto a space and demarcating the space according to the circular method. The use of the circular compass shows chi radiating outwards from the center. The demarcation of space this way suggests that the distribution of chi comes from a center point in the room, or the home.

Each sector is shaped as a triangular slice of cake. This method is widely used by the Cantonese feng shui masters of Hong Kong. They base their preference for this method on their belief that chi revolves around the compass and that inside any space, this is the way chi is to be measured to have meaning. Greater emphasis is thus placed on the 360 degrees of the compass.

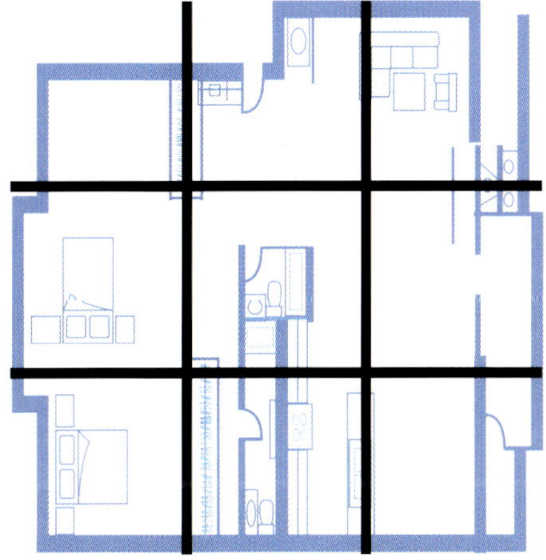

LO SHU GRID DEMARCATION

THE LO SHU GRID METHOD is the other method used. Here the compass is used to read the compass orientation. But in addition, the square Lo Shu grid is used to define the parameters of the space under investigation.

Both methods require the compass to define the directions. The difference lies in defining the space that falls into each direction sector.

Personally I prefer to use the grid method, as I find it easier to work with a regular square or rectangular shape.

34 The South brings recognition

In the year 1999, an English friend of mine passed by Kuala Lumpur and invited me to lunch. I had known James and his wife during the late Eighties in Hong Kong when he was an investment banker and I was running my department store. He was thrilled I had changed careers yet again and we spent time catching up. In the course of that lunchtime conversation, he brought me up to date on his life. He told me everything had been going well for him until recently – when everything seemed to be going wrong. At work, all sorts of problems were surfacing. At home, his wife Sally had taken seriously ill having just been diagnosed for cancer, and his son sustained serious injuries in a freak accident. He invited me to spend a weekend with them at their home in the country the next time I was in the UK. "Maybe you can set us right," he smiled weakly.

Well, I did visit them quite early in the following year and indeed they have a lovely home in Kent, with beautiful feng shui, except that their front door faced South, which of course immediately explained the awful spate of bad luck of the previous year. **In 1999, the South was seriously afflicted by the annual flying star 5 yellow bringing accidents, loss and illness.** I reassured them that from my visit onwards, their luck would improve.

I noticed the brightly lit chandelier in the foyer of their home just in front of the main door. I advised them to keep the light on for as long as possible, even through the night, since this would activate the fire energy of the South, bringing James the luck of recognition and even some measure of fame and honour. And because the South was also where the main door was placed,

A brightly lit chandelier in the South sector activates recognition luck.

this would serve to "activate" the chi of the South even more. The light and the door being there also explained why they had had such bad luck and illness in the previous year. Energizing fire energy that year by simply turning on the light had inadvertently strengthened the five yellow causing bad luck to turn worse. Now that the 5 yellow had moved on to another sector, it was safe to activate the South once more.

In addition to lights, I also advised placing their porcelain horse in the foyer. This is because horses also belong to the fire element. By the time I left Kent, Sally had really got hooked on feng shui – and later I was to find out how she changed her curtains and carpets to energize her living room using the productive cycle of the element colours of each corner. To make a real statement, she even painted her entire foyer a bright red! I am glad to report she must have got it right, because James and Sally are now Sir James and Lady Sally. She recovered and their son graduated with first class honours from Oxford University. **Activating the South with red walls had brought health, happiness and a knighthood to the family.**

35 The North is to generate career luck

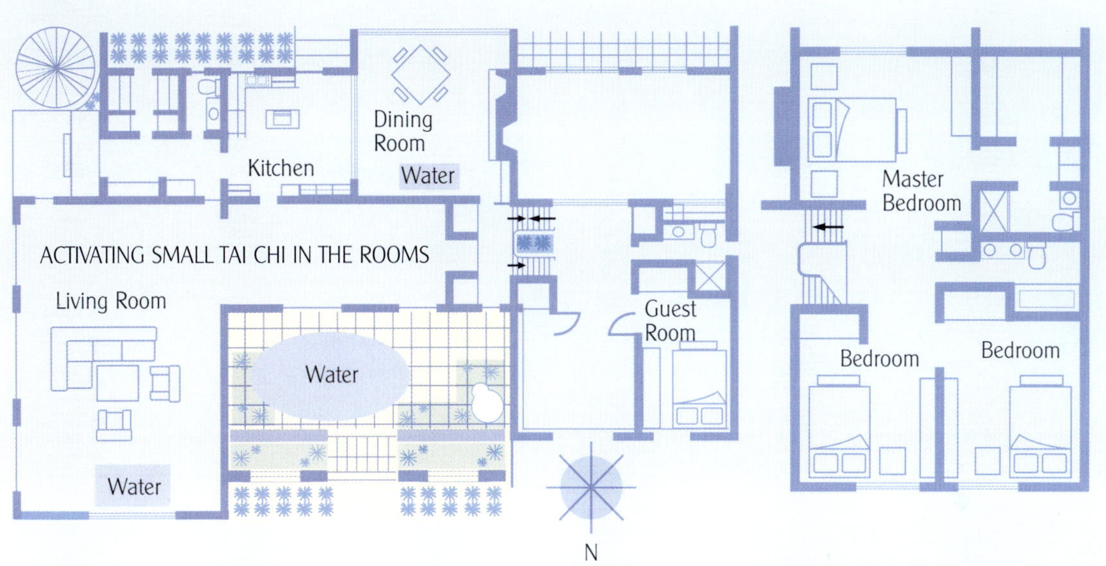

When you use water to activate the North of your whole house, you will see the fastest results in the area of your career and business. Shown above is a house, that faces North, so the North sector of this home is basically the area marked yellow, It is important to use a compass to determine where North is. Here the compass shows the house facing North, so the North sector is the front middle part of the house. **The placement of the *koi* pond just in front of the living room and foyer area is thus an excellent way of activating for great career and business luck.** In addition, note that there are several doors and windows from the house into the landscaped area (marked in yellow) thereby allowing the water drenched chi to enter the home bringing career luck. Since water also stands for wealth, the strategic placement of water here is excellent. Note that this pond here activates the big tai chi of this house, so it benefits the entire house and all its residents.

In addition, note that it is also a good idea to place smaller water features to energize the North sectors of the individual rooms. Thus the North side of the dining room as well as the North side of the living room can be activated with symbols of the water element, such as a painting showing water or an aquarium with live fish. You can also paint the North wall blue (or deep purple) because blue stands for water. **Do not use black, as this would be too yin**

ACTIVATING WITH THE PRODUCTIVE CYCLE

Because metal activates water in the Productive cycle, you can also use metal energy to activate the North sectors. You can paint the North wall white/silver/gold. Or place **white/silver/gold** curtains, carpets, and have your metallic stereo systems here. You can be as creative as you wish. Just remember that to benefit from your feng shui efforts you must use the rooms that you energize. And any water feature that is created outside the home must face a door or window for its benefits to be felt.

36 The East is the place of the Dragon

The element of the East is wood and the trigram of this sector is Chen. In feng shui, the East is a very important direction because this is the place of the celestial dragon. This is the direction that is filled with the most amount of sheng chi – also translated as growth chi. Because of this, the East is the ideal part of any home for the sons of the family to have their bedrooms. In fact, in the palaces of the Forbidden City in Beijing, all the young princes of the realm had their quarters on the East side.

Activating the East always means placing the **image of dragon** and one of the best of such images is this one here where the dragon holds a symbolic rotating pearl and spouts water. I have been asked many times how many dragons to place here to generate maximum luck for the family and my reply has always been as many as you wish, but make sure you have the karma to carry the number of dragons you display.

For example, not everyone has the "hei" to sustain the tremendous yang energy of nine dragons. Thus even when dragons bring much good fortune, it is better not to be too greedy if you cannot sustain them. A single celestial creature is therefore quite sufficient. Unless you are born in the year of the dragon, or you already hold a high position such as a Minister or as head of a large organization or company. Otherwise it is better not to be too greedy. Place your dragon image near or inside water – let it not be too large nor too small.

A dragon activated by water symbolises the thirsty dragon whose thirst is quenched, a very powerful symbol indeed. But do not make sure your Dragon does not overpower your house.

37 The East brings good health & longevity

Live plants placed in the East corner of any room enhance for good health for the residents.

Activating the East brings good health, longevity and descendents luck. It also creates the luck conducive to the accumulation of wealth assets for the family. Wood element energy grows upwards and outwards, sending many branches into the sky. The symbolic meaning of this is amazing good fortune if you place the symbols correctly. Choose from the many decorative objects that are suitable for this part of your home. If you prefer natural objects, make free use of plants. Live, young plants with broad leaves are excellent for accumulating wealth chi. Fill your East side with such plants and grow rich!

While I love live plants, I also like the wealth trees made of semi precious-stones such as citrine and aventurines. Choose trees with solid trunks to ensure a firm foundation. And tie special coins with red or gold ribbon to simulate the money tree. Placed in the East of your living room, these crystal trees bring excellent energy into the home. If you are thinking of getting a crystal gem tree, do make sure the tree looks abundant. You can also "empower" such trees with empowering mantras if you so wish.

Artificial trees made of semi precious stones such as citrines are great wealth energisers.

38 The Southwest for marriage

Above: Happy photos of couples in the southwest ensure the relationship is strong.

The Southwest is the place of KUN, the matriarchal trigram that enhances the **luck of relationships**, bringing with it the promise of romance, love and the start of a new phase in the lives of people of marriageable age. To the Chinese, there are three major happy occasions in life, what they call the "*hei see*" or happy occasions. Of the three (**a birth, a marriage and a longevity birthday**) it is marriage, which is regarded as the most significant of the double happiness occasions. So the word double happiness has come to symbolize the marriage union and placing this symbolic image in the Southwest makes for a most powerful talisman to create the luck of marriage. I have personally seen the powerful effect of the double happiness symbol work wonders with confirmed

Below: Mandarin ducks with peonies together are one of the potent symbols of love and marriage.

bachelors, especially when it is placed in the Southwest. I have also seen the negative effect of a **missing Southwest corner in the home** – this usually manifests as a total absence of marriage prospects for the beautiful daughters and eligible sons of families.

In my own home, there was no such danger, since I activate the Southwest corner of every important room with many different symbols – from mandarin ducks to red peonies (said to attract wonderful husbands for eligible young ladies) to crystal balls and the strategic placement of lights and faceted glass hangings that invite in rainbow rays of sunshine. I also have a beautiful dragon and phoenix image, the other powerful marriage enhancer.

As I believe strongly in the power of feng shui, I have enhanced the living space for my loved ones for years. I am glad to say that my daughter Jennifer married the most wonderful guy.

I like to think feng shui played at least a small part in Jennifer finding such a delightful young man – someone who obviously adores her. Leaving nothing to chance, I observed the most important marriage rituals during her week-long wedding celebrations including having five lions perform the marriage dance at her wedding banquet that culminated in their bringing a long stalk of sugar cane for her (to ensure a very sweet and long life). In my home, I hung a **hundred double happiness lanterns** and other auspicious hangings to attract in the powerful yang chi. At the wedding banquet, we gave out specially designed souvenirs of auspicious *endless knots* for undying love, the *wu lou* for good health, the lotus for purity of motivation and *ingots* for prosperity – all carved in jadeite. This is to multiply the good yang energy for the evening.

When the groom came to fetch the bride, we made sure she left sheltered by a **red umbrella** held by her father to signify an auspicious new beginning in her life, and we threw rice in front of her to ensure her new life would be prosperous. I wore an auspicious outfit **embroidered with 100 children** to signify plenty of grandchildren.

Having a picture of the family with happy smiling faces on a Southwest wall in the living room is exceptionally good feng shui as it ensures the family will always stay happily together and will be close.

39 The West protects family luck

In traditional feng shui lore, the West has always been identified as the place of the white tiger, which is also the symbol of protection. In the Later Heaven arrangement of the trigrams, the West is home to the trigram of joyousness – TUI – also known as the river or lake trigram. Thus the West has been designated as the space where happiness arises as a result of a happy family. When the chi in the West part of the home is protected and energized, the family stays together and remains healthy and strong. All the older members of the family – those of the older generation – will live a long life. Both the patriarch and matriarch whose luck theoretically resides on both sides of the West – the Northwest and Southwest respectively will enjoy increasing happiness and good fortune through the passing years. It is thus vital to keep the chi of the West side of the home moving smoothly and in harmony.

The West belongs to the element of metal. The colour here is white. It is not necessary to place the image of the white tiger, since not everyone is able to sustain the "presence of the tiger" in the home. Instead, it is better to activate the element of metal OR the element of earth, since earth gives birth to metal under the producing cycle. The best activators of chi for the West are the vast variety of gold coins that are now coming out of China and Taiwan. Truly, the research being done in these countries to copy many of the ancient antique coins of the golden ages of past dynasties is amazing. I am thrilled to have come across many of these wonderful coins. In addition, I also really like the gold ingots, which are stunning energizers not just to attract prosperity into the home but also to act as powerful talismans and amulets. Gold or gold colour has powerful wealth-creating energy.

Coin Swords are excellent energizes for the West. Hang it with the "blade" pointing downwards.

If you like, you can look for the powerful coin swords made with coins. These are very effective in **warding off jealousy and envious eyes**.

I rather like the real antique swords I see in the museums in Shanghai and Beijing – it seems that in China great reverence is accorded to antique swords that belonged to the heroes of another time. The wonderful movie – *Crouching Tiger, Hidden Dragon* – was about a sword said to possess mysterious attributes. Alas, I do not have the courage to display a real metal sword inside my home, although Taoist Masters believe that **hanging a sword inside large halls** and temples, and hung on the West wall can create the most **powerful protective auric field**. I am quite happy sticking to coins, ingots and my special metal fan and bat amulets. Fans are especially powerful protectors and bats bring the luck of magnificent abundance. In addition, hanging three coins tied with the endless knot is another great energizer. These can be displayed in the West part of your living room. Note that these metal activators double up as talismans. Using them combines the practice of feng shui symbolism with compass feng shui.

40 The Northwest for mentor luck

The Northwest is the place of the Patriarch. Here the trigram is *chien* – the heaven trigram that signifies the luck of **powerful and influential benefactors**. If you want help from mentors and support from your bosses, this is the corner to activate. If you want your patriarch to flourish and become prosperous – and this can be your husband or your father – then this too is the corner to focus your feng shui on. The Northwest is therefore a very important part of the home. The element of this corner is metal and in Chinese, **metal also signifies gold**. So the Northwest is the source of a family's wealth – the kind that is supposed to last through many generations. If you make a **wealth vase**, and you keep the vase hidden somewhere in the Northwest corner of your home, it will benefit the patriarch of the home. If you have a garden and you bury a symbolic wealth box in the Northwest of your garden, this too will benefit the patriarch.

There are many different ways to activate the Northwest. In essence, it is objects that are made of **metal** that are most effective.

Ingots and coins are perennial favourites, as are cloisonné objects d'art, such as the nine dragon screen. Anything made of gold or plated in gold is effective. Golden windchimes are especially auspicious since the sound of gold is considered most beneficial. I activate my Northwest with bells and singing bowls made from seven types of metals that include gold and silver to symbolize the energy of the sun and the moon.

41 The Southeast brings prosperity

An entrance in the southeast needs lucious plants to invite good chi.

The Southeast is the place of the *Sun* Trigram, whose element is **wood**. **It signifies money**. Not the kind of money referred to in terms of family estate and family net worth, but rather the kind of money associated with income levels. Earnings are a good way to describe the luck of *Sun*, which is also the *movement* trigram. *Sun* indicates activity, which in turns is said to generate income. If you wish to attract a higher level of regular income, this is the corner to energize. Since this is of the wood element, **use plants to create an indoor garden**. This will magnify growth chi for the home. Indoor gardens are very effective. Shown here is a simple but effective garden. In this context, I strongly encourage you to place fresh flowering plants in the Southeast corners of your indoor as well as of your gardens since this represents excellent feng shui. When the flowers have stopped blooming, you can get a fresh supply. In these days of instant gardens, you do not need green fingers to harness the *blossoming sheng chi* of plants. This will help all your plans come to fruition quickly.

The best way to activate for money luck is to construct a small waterfall and keep its waters moving with fish, tortoises, or water pumps to simulate activity. It should be well landscaped with healthy plants and flowers.

42 The power of water features

The best energizers for attracting prosperity luck, by activating the Southeast inside or outside the home, is to introduce water features. These need not be large nor elaborate, nor be stocked with expensive fish. In feng shui however, distinction is made between **YIN water**, which is quiet and still with neither fish nor plants inside them, and **YANG water**, which is moving and filled with life chi. Thus, yang water is usually oxygenated, has fish or has plants growing within.

To activate for **prosperity luck**, it is important you use only Yang water as energizers. This means that the water should be moving and there should be life within. In recent years, water features of every variety have been made available as more and more people become aware of the great benefits of feng shui. There are also a whole variety of ways to use water, which feature prominently in many of the compass formulas as well.

Left: Shown here are some water features from my home that are affordable and easy to install, to give you some ideas on how you can incorporate water into your home interiors and gardens.

Right: These bright red Chinese Goldfish are the best fish for bringing abundance. They look like carp but are completely red in colour. They are now less easy to find...

43 The Northeast for education luck

Facing one's good directions when studying is vital for education success.

I have lost count of the number of parents I have advised over the years by sharing with them the powerful Taoist feng shui secret of the **Northeast** direction. From a long time ago I have known about the powerful chi of the Northeast - how it can be activated to bring excellent examination results, scholastic honours and even scholarships to students.

I taught Jennifer how to activate her bedroom at school and at University to help her do well in her examinations. Thus in addition to the KUA formula which helped her select her most auspicious directions to study and to sit facing for her examinations, she also learnt to activate the Northeast of her rooms to attract scholastic luck. I am glad to say the feng shui helped her **stay very focused** as a result of which she had a very impressive academic record all through school and University. I am also happy to say that children of friends of mine who activated their Northeast corner also benefited hugely from this wonderful energizer.

CRYSTAL ENERGY FOR STUDY LUCK

The Northeast is an earth element corner. The ruling trigram here is the mountain trigram, so it suggests a time of preparation. The mountain trigram also suggests a time of training for the good things that will come later. So energizing this corner with earth energy can be especially potent. The most effective way to energize is to use crystals.

Crystals are the most powerful manifestation of earth energy. Crystals can be natural or man made, although natural quartz crystals are best. But the man made varieties which come from China carved into a globe are the most effective for harnessing *education* luck. Place a **crystal globe** like the one show here on a table in the Northeast corner of your child's bedroom. It will activate the chi of education and you should see improvements quite quickly. If for some reason you do not like this globe you can also use the triple fish or the **Dragon Carp** image – both of which are just as powerful. The Dragon Carp symbolizes the legend of the Dragon Gate, which is a famous Chinese metaphor. Crossing the dragon gate is likened to passing the Imperial examinations and the humble carp transforming into a dragon as it jumps over the dragon gate symbolizes this. Placing the dragon carp in the bedroom is said to manifest scholastic success.

A single-pointed crystal is an excellent energizer of study luck for children. Place in the Northeast.

In addition, it is also a good idea to invest in a **single-ended natural crystal** for your child. The crystal is said to be a most efficient way to store energy and knowledge. Let the crystal become a personal study companion amulet for your child. When you get it, first cleanse it of other people's energy by soaking it in a sea or rock salt solution for seven days and seven nights. Place it on a table in the Northeast when the child is studying. The crystal can be taken into the examination room to bring the luck of education. Keep the crystal wrapped in silk or velvet when not in use.

3

PERSONALISING YOUR FENG SHUI INTERIORS

Practising feng shui becomes very meaningful when you arrange rooms and furniture to facilitate the usage of the personalized directions of family members. This enables every person living in the home to benefit from their good directions and to avoid their bad directions while eating, sleeping and working. In the past years since I have introduced this method of feng shui to the world, it has helped many thousands enjoy a turnaround in their fortunes. The beauty of this system is that you can practise it equally effectively at elementary and at very advanced levels. It can also be used with equal effectiveness in a mansion or a small apartment. Personalize feng shui direction benefit you also at the office when you meet important people and when you sign important contracts.

This room has beautiful "earth" colors and they are perfect for this Northeast located living area. The lines are clean, the ceiling has no exposed beams and the red carpet enhances the earth element. Note the "sitting" direction of the sofas and chairs in your home so you know which ones are best for which members of your household.

44 Knowing your KUA number

Knowing the KUA formula of 8 Mansions feng shui is almost mandatory to practising personalized feng shui that brings the fullest benefit to every resident in the home. This is because the KUA formula is probably the fastest working and most user-friendly of all the formulas of feng shui. To use it, all you need to do is to work out your **personal KUA number, and from there, determine your lucky and unlucky directions**, as well as your lucky trigram, lucky number and lucky element. After that, it is a question of using this information to create the best feng shui possible from your interior space. So start by learning this formula and determining your directions, then follow through with the tips in this chapter and throughout this book, which show you different ways to use your directions. With practice, you should be able to incorporate this formula with other methods of feng shui to create powerfully balanced and harmonious chi energy for all your interiors.

The formula differs for men and women.

1. **Take your year of birth.** Convert it to the lunar year. This affects only those born in January and early February. Deduct a year from your year of birth if you need to convert. If you were born in the other months, the lunar calendar year is the same as the western calendar.
2. **Take the last two digits** of your year of birth and add them. Keep adding until the sum of the addition is a single digit (e.g. If you were born April 4th 1978, add 7+8 = 15 and then 1+ 5 = 6.) The next step depends on whether you are male or female.
3. **If you are male** deduct from10 so 10 – 6 = 4 and your KUA is 4. If you are calculating for a child born in or after the year 2000 deduct from 9 instead of 10.
4. **If you are female** then you add 5 so 5 + 6 = 11 and then 1+ 1 =2 and your KUA is 2. if you are calculating for a child born in or after the year 2000, add 6 instead of 5.

KUA CHART OF PERSONALIZED DIRECTIONS

	The Four Auspicious Directions				The Four Inauspicious Directions					
Kua	**Wealth**	**Health**	**Love**	**Growth**	**Bad Luck**	**5 Ghosts**	**6 Killings**	**Total Loss**	**Group**	**Self Element**
1	SE	E	S	N	W	NE	NW	SW	East	Water
2	NE	W	NW	SW	E	SE	S	N	West	Earth
3	S	N	SE	E	SW	NW	NE	W	East	Wood
4	N	S	E	SE	NW	SW	W	NE	East	Wood
*5									West	Earth
6	W	NE	SW	NW	SE	E	N	S	West	Metal
7	NW	SW	NE	W	N	S	SE	E	West	Metal
8	SW	NW	W	NE	S	N	E	SE	West	Earth
9	E	SE	N	S	NE	W	SW	NW	East	Fire

* For KUA 5, it becomes KUA 2 for males and KUA 8 for females.

Note your auspicious direction for wealth, for love and romance, for health and for personal development. From the unlucky directions, take note that the worst is the total loss direction. Also take note of your self-element. Your KUA number is your lucky number and your personal trigram is as follows: KUA 1 is Kan, KUA 2 is KUN, Kua 3 is SUN; KUA 4 is CHEN, KUA 6 is CHIEN, KUA 7 is TUI, KUA 8 is KEN, KUA 9 is LI.

45 East and West groups

According to the KUA formula everyone belongs to either the East or West group. These two groups are in conflict with each other and this means that West group people will suffer if they sit facing or are located in East group directions, and East group people are similarly affected if they face or locate in West group directions.

So the first thing to find out from your KUA number is whether you belong to the East or West group. You can look this up from the table in the previous page and in the sketch below. You will find that if your **KUA number is 1, 3, 4 or 9** you belong to the **East group** and all the East group directions North, South, East and Southeast are auspicious directions for you. These are marked in green in the Pa Kua graphic here.

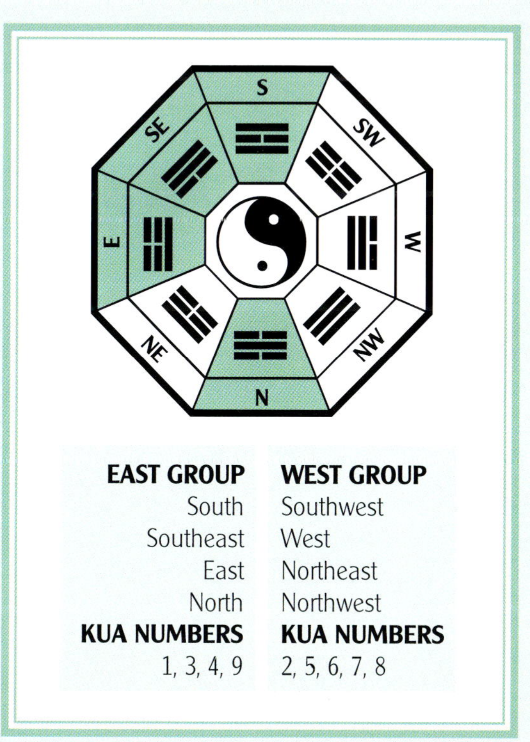

EAST GROUP	WEST GROUP
South	Southwest
Southeast	West
East	Northeast
North	Northwest
KUA NUMBERS	**KUA NUMBERS**
1, 3, 4, 9	2, 5, 6, 7, 8

The theory of Eight Mansions says that East and West group people get hurt by facing or locating in directions of the other group, so West group people are hurt by East group directions and vice versa. So the general rule to observe is to try and SIT facing one of your good directions, and to avoid facing one of your bad directions. Then you should likewise try to SLEEP with your head pointed to one of your good directions and avoid having your head pointed to one of your unlucky directions.

If your **KUA number is 2, 5, 6, 7, or 8** then you belong to the **West group** and all the West group directions West, Northwest, Northeast and Southwest are good for you. These are marked in white in the Pa Kua of directions above.

The above is the general rule – it is easy to understand and is only the start in your practice of personalized feng shui. In practice, of course, there will be many obstacles to you getting everything perfectly oriented to suit your directions. Invariably, tapping one's best direction is harder than we realize, simply because there are so many practical difficulties to overcome. **You should not get disheartened** if you cannot use your best directions all the time. And if you already have a room and you simply cannot change your sleeping direction then all you can do really is to file this information inside your head until you can use it the next time (e.g. when you move house) and in the meantime, try to use your personalized directions more often, at work, when you are out on a date or when at a job interview. And so forth. Just remember at all times what group person you are, and strenuously avoid your four bad luck directions.

46 Using Eight Mansions

There are many ways to use Eight Mansions KUA formula feng shui and it is particularly suitable for applications for home interiors. Before going into some examples of usage which will work like a tutorial for you to find applications in your own home situation, do take note of the difference between a ***facing direction*** and a ***sitting direction***. When you sit, the direction directly in front of you is your facing direction. The direction exactly opposite of that is your sitting direction. Now when you use the KUA formula, note that when we say "auspicious" direction, we are referring to both your sitting as well as your facing directions. So you must be very clear which direction you are "tapping" when you make any new arrangement to your sitting direction and location.

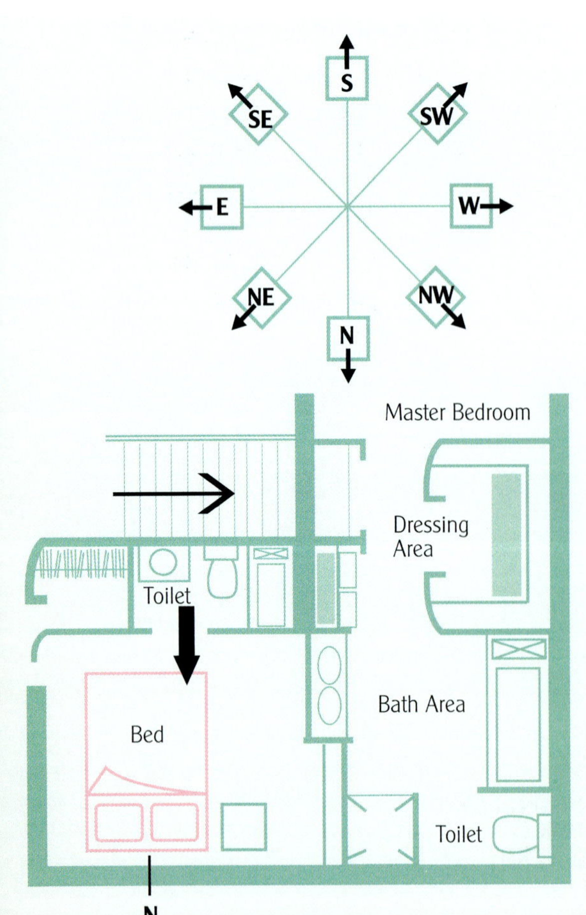

Sometimes, both your sitting and facing direction are good for you. For instance, if you sit South you are facing North, so both directions are good for you if you are an East group person. Likewise, if you sit Northeast and are facing Southwest, then both the sitting and facing are good for you if you are a West group person. In these two instances, there is no problem. Sometimes however, only one of the sitting/facing directions is good e.g. when you face West you will be sitting East. And when you face Northwest, you will be sitting Southeast. And these sitting/facing directions are in conflict, since they belong to different groups of directions. In such situations then, it is said that the **facing direction carries more weight**. So when faced with a dilemma, go with the facing direction.

The best usage of Eight Mansions KUA directions in the home is in the arrangement and placement of furniture. Thus dining table and sofa sets can be arranged to benefit residents. Dressing areas can also be designed so that you can be facing your best direction when you do your make up. Look at the diagram here showing a compass and the bedroom area of this home. If WEST is the good direction of the occupant, then the dressing area is most conducive, since she/he can sit facing West while dressing. The pink bed on the other hand is ideal for an East group person because it is pointed North. Alas, it is in the way of the toilet door, which sends harmful yin chi towards the bed. In such a case, it is better to rearrange the bed since good directions do not override Form School feng shui. This shows you that putting the Eight Mansions directions into practice may sometimes prove to be quite a challenge.

47 Using the KUA formula in the bedroom

Feng shui offers a great number of guidelines for the bedroom. There are also many taboos to be taken note of. These must be observed and taken into account, although a good sleeping direction contributes substantially to your good fortune. The ability to sleep with your head pointed to a direction from where good fortune comes is a great advantage. So if **financial success is** what you want, you would benefit from a bedroom in the house that corresponds to your wealth direction. And after that, to position your bed to enable you to tap your **wealth direction** while you sleep. This means the crown of your head points to your wealth direction. Then you will also have tapped the double goodness effect. The same analysis holds for those wanting romance, health and personal growth. In Eight Mansions, you select the kind of luck you want, then use the direction that corresponds to that kind of luck for you.

In reality, it is not always possible to achieve perfect feng shui. Consider this example below. You can see from the compass directions that the master bedroom is situated in the Northwest part of the house. In terms of location, this bedroom is beneficial for a West group person. If that person's KUA number is 6, then Northwest is his best direction for personal growth. So it is acceptable for the West group person, even though it is not the wealth direction. Since the bed direction is pointing West, it is his wealth direction. This bedroom and bed are excellent feng shui for a person with a KUA number 6. An extra bonus will be that if he is also the Patriarch of the family, then this Northwest part of the house is doubly good for him, since Northwest is simultaneously the direction of the patriarch. BUT this master bedroom is not good for an East group KUA person. The bed can be rearranged to let the head face North, which is an East group direction. So how much potential any house has for you depends how you use your KUA number.

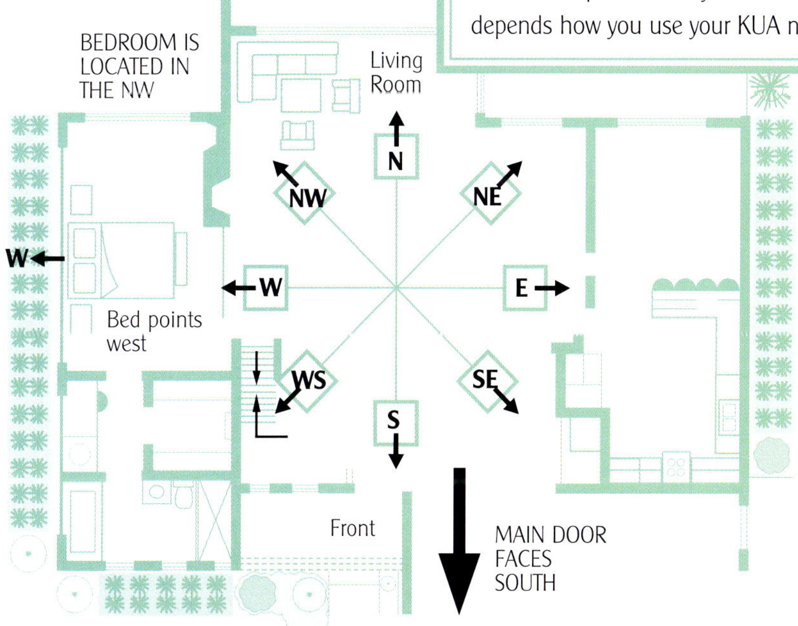

48 Sleeping direction

In attempting to benefit from the KUA formula's auspicious directions there are certain taboos associated with bedroom feng shui, which will override the direction. Thus please observe:

1. Do not let the bed "float" in the middle of the room. There MUST be a solid wall behind the bed. Otherwise you sleep is unbalanced. Please remember this.
2. Do not let your feet point directly at the door as this is the death position.
3. Do not let any mirror face the bed directly.
4. Do not have the bed share a wall with a toilet. This causes chi to be afflicted before entering your head.
5. Try not to sleep with a window behind you.

When we refer to the sleeping direction, we are always referring to the direction where the **top of the head points**. This is because chi enters a sleeping person through the crown chakra, which lies at the top of the head. So to benefit from the best direction, the top of the head must be pointing to the source of good fortune, and this is what the auspicious direction signifies. It is incorrect to use the feet's pointing direction.

Your correct **sleeping direction** represents very high priority in feng shui. Unless your sleeping direction is auspicious, or at least is one of the four of your auspicious Eight Mansions directions, it will be difficult for you to achieve success smoothly, unless of course under other systems of feng shui you are tapping another equally or more powerful formula. Generally speaking however, you would always have better feng shui if you succeed in positioning your bed to capture one of your four good directions.

WHAT IF YOU AND YOUR WIFE HAVE DIFFERENT KUA NUMBERS?

According to the feng shui classics, the sleeping direction should follow the direction, that benefits the man, since women had little relevance in the old days. I have always been uncomfortable with this. Since my husband and I belong to different groups, I solved the problem differently. I decided that we would BOTH be happier and more successful if we had different bedrooms, and I have to say my solution has worked really well. Despite our belonging to different group KUA numbers, and having separate bedrooms, we have been together now for 40 years, and we are very happy together.

49 KUA formula in the kitchen

Placement of kitchen appliances must consider the facing direction of its mouth.

Look at the cooker and oven in the kitchen pictured here. This is the cooking side of the kitchen. To follow Eight Mansions feng shui, both the stove and oven must have its "mouth" facing a good direction for the head of the household. The difficulty was to identify the **mouth of the stove**. Some feng shui masters interpret the *mouth* to mean the control knobs. Others say the mouth is the "source" of energy that brings power to the stove. I have been interpreting this to be the opening of the oven. In the case of the oven, since there is a door, it is easy, as this corresponds to the concept of the door of the home being the *mouth* of the home.

So I use the door of the oven to indicate the mouth. In my home, the oven door faces my best direction. I use my direction because I am still actively working, while my husband is retired. If your husband is the breadwinner of the family, then it is his direction that you should use.

In the case of the gas cooker, I use the direction of the gas coming into the cooker to be the operative direction. This is because there is simply no obvious oven mouth for me to use. As for the electric blender, I also make sure it is positioned for its incoming energy to come from my best energy direction.

So in applying 8 Mansions KUA formula in the kitchen, you have to use your judgment in positioning the stove and oven such that they successfully capture wealth based on personalized directions according to the KUA formula.

The "mouth" of this jug is the point where the electrical cord enters the jug.

50 Kitchen location based on KUA Number

The second guideline for the kitchen concerns its location. According to the KUA formula, for any kitchen to benefit the household, it should ideally be located in one of the **four bad directions** of the family patriarch. This is based on the premise that the powerful energy of the cooking fire in the kitchen is usually very strong. Often, it is so strong, it will press down on the luck of its location. Thus it is much better for the kitchen to press down on the bad locations rather than the good locations for the patriarch. In connection with the implementation of this tip, do note that even if the matriarch is the breadwinner of the family, the kitchen should press down on the **bad luck direction of the patriarch** rather than the matriarch. Also, remember that while the location of the kitchen should be in one of his four bad directions, the facing direction of the cooking stove or oven should be one of his best directions. Meanwhile, if you live alone, then it is your KUA directions that should be followed.

There are other guidelines regarding the kitchen. Take note that feng shui always warns against the **kitchen being located in the Northwest** corner or sector of the home. And the stove or cooker where you do the cooking should not be in the Northwest corner of the kitchen. This signifies *"fire at heaven's gate"*, something we must guard against.

If your kitchen IS located in the Northwest, it is a good idea to try to relocate the kitchen. I know this is something not easy to do and if you really cannot make this change, then try to alleviate the dangerous feng shui here by placing a **large urn of still yin water** in the kitchen. This overcomes the fire element energy created by the kitchen effectively, although of course it is really very unsightly having an urn of open water here. The urn of water should be at least 18 inches deep and 12 inches across to be effective.

AVOID HAVING KITCHEN IN YOUR GOOD DIRECTIONS

If the kitchen is located in your personal wealth **(sheng chi) direction**, the result is unpopularity, miscarriages and no livelihood. The kitchen will press down on your success luck.

If it is located in your **health (tien yi)** direction, you will often get sick and become easily exhausted and weak. The kitchen will absorb all your energy and vibrant chi.

If the kitchen is located in your **romance (nien yen)** direction, you will find it hard to get married, and if you are already married there will be quarrels and misunderstandings. The strong fire energy burns rather than nurtures all your relationships. It is a case here of excessive yang energy.

If the kitchen is located in your personal **growth (fu wei) direction**, you will be forever poor. You stagnate and live in a continuous state of fretful dissatisfaction. This is potentially the most harmful situation as it cuts directly into your sense of happiness and achievement.

KITCHEN IN YOUR "BAD" LOCATION IS AUSPICIOUS

On the other hand, if your kitchen is located in your **(cheuh ming) or total loss direction**, it will press down all your bad luck associated with this direction. You will have lots of sons, servants and good health. If the kitchen is in your six killings location, your family will enjoy steady luck. All bad luck dissipates easily and you escape misfortunes. If the kitchen is in the five ghosts direction you will successfully avoid getting sick and will have success. Kitchens located in the (ho hai) bad luck direction protect you from losing money and from being cheated by people. You will also have stronger resistance to illness.

51 Personalizing the door

One of the more powerful feng shui features to have in any house is a personalized main door whose location and facing direction is personally auspicious for the breadwinner of the house. This may be the man of the house or it can refer to the matriarch's good directions. The decision on whose KUA number shall determine the main door direction and location is up to you. But your decision will affect everyone in the house because it then defines the distribution of chi throughout the house. Please note this point carefully.

Why? Because according to all the formula methods of feng shui, once the **main door** is positioned in a house design, this usually also **defines the facing direction of the whole house**, and those of you familiar with Master level knowledge of Flying Star and Eight Mansions will know that the collective energy distribution in any house is always influenced in no small measure by its feng shui natal charts, which are determined by the facing direction of the house. In the case of apartments, these charts are determined by the facing direction of the whole apartment block.

What makes the practice of feng shui difficult is that there are always choices to be made regarding which direction to use, and then which chart to follow. There are always trade-offs involved when deciding on how best to use each of the formulas. This can boil down to simply having to decide which door to use and which room to allocate to which member of the family.

The ideal situation is to **personalize the main door**, i.e. have its facing direction be the facing direction of the house and then from this facing direction, design the rest of the house based on the natal chart created. This is the essence of good feng shui practice for interior spaces. If you really want to get the most out of feng shui interiors (layout and placement of furniture and objects in the rooms) you should have at least some knowledge of the different feng shui charts.

Generally, my advice is to **use a door into the house that faces a direction that represents one of your four good directions.** This will bring you good luck as you enter your house. It does not have to be the main door. Try not to use a door that faces one of your four bad directions, since this will cause you to bring bad luck with you as you enter the house. *Even if this means having to use a side door, or the back door, you should observe this advice.* In short, if the main door is not good for you according to the KUA formula, try to find a door that is. If you live in an apartment look for a way to get into the building using a door that brings you good fortune. Choose a good luck door.

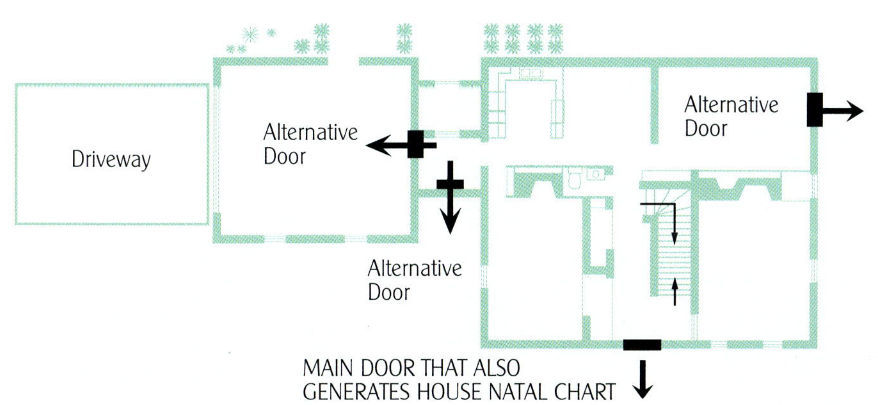

It is wonderful if the main door of the house corresponds to one of your good directions, but if it does not, you can use an alternative door to enter your house on a daily basis.

When tapping into your good direction, also remember some of the basic feng shui ground rules about the dining room. Here is a quick checklist for you to go through:

1. Try not to have the toilet opening off the dining room. If there is a toilet, keep the toilet door closed all the time. The foul energy coming out from there is harmful.
2. Have a wall mirror to reflect the food off the table, as this doubles your good fortune.
3. Do not eat directly under a toilet on upper floor above your table. Really bad luck!
4. Do not eat in the basement or lowest part of the home.
5. Have the dining room deeper into the home. If you eat too near the front door, your wealth tends to seep out.

52 Dining auspiciously

The KUA formula of auspicious directions can be applied in the dining room to benefit all members of the family. Use a compass to check the direction that each place setting will be facing, then allocate that place to one member of the family. There is greater flexibility of directions if you use an eight-sided table to cater for the eight directions of the compass that make up the KUA formula. This is how I arrange my seating arrangements for the members of my family and it is the reason why I use a Pa Kua table that only seats eight people. You can use any kind of dining table, although **round tables** are said to be very auspicious. **Square and rectangular tables** are also acceptable although of course, being four sided, such tables can sometimes prove to be awkward for tapping auspicious directions.

The direction you choose as your dining direction need not always be your wealth direction. I prefer to sit facing my family/ **romance direction** and I also place all members of my family in their respective family/romance direction. This augurs well for the harmony of the family, since this direction is also the nurturing matriarchal energy direction. When you eat together facing your respective *nien yen* directions, there will be less quarrels at the dinner table.

When all are facing their wealth/success direction, the amount of aggressive yang energy generated can sometimes cause heated arguments to arise. It is of course understood that you should not eat facing one of your four bad directions and especially, you should never eat facing your total loss (cheuh ming) direction. Doing so brings enormous bad luck.

53 Designing dining room feng shui

When building a new home, make an effort to design good feng shui in the dining room. In terms of layout, place the dining area at, or very near, to the center of the home, as this represents the heart of the home. The more spacious the dining room, the better will be the luck of the family. There should ideally be one solid wall in this room, which should be behind where either the father or mother sits. Dining rooms that are part of living rooms are excellent as this increases the feeling of space. This would be even better if the Flying Star charts indicate good "numbers" in this part of the home.

Try not to have toilets placed directly above the dining room area. Also try not to have toilets share any wall of the dining room. Kitchens placed next to the dining area should be level to or below the level of the dining area. Never let the dining room be in a sunken part of the home. If your house has a split-level, place the dining area on the higher level. But you should not designate a mezzanine floor as the dining room. Such half way floors are unlucky. **Mezzanine floors are suitable only as library areas**. Finally, try not to have *protruding corners or exposed overhead beams* in the dining area. Being hit by poison arrows as you eat is the surest way of contracting a serious illness.

Always disarm poison arrows emanating from exposed corners and square columns by blocking off the sharp edges with plants, furniture or other feng shui remedies.

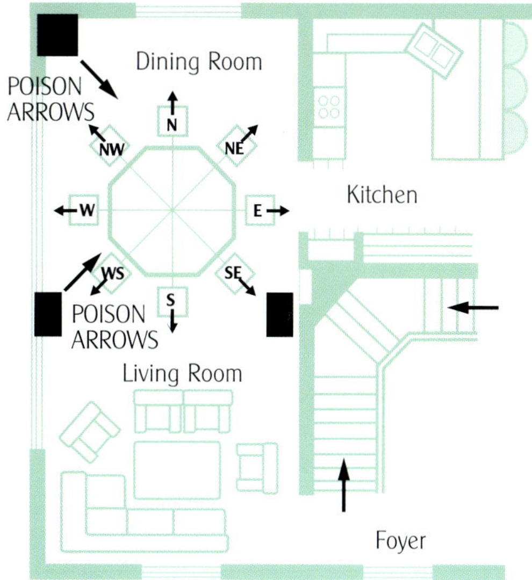

Avoid poison arrows that aim at you while you are seated at the dining table. If unavoidable, block with plants or hang faceted crystals to dissapate the shar chi.

Note the following if you do not disarm the poison arrows.

- Poison arrows from the **Southwest** cause problems with your womb and stomach areas. eg.indigestion or miscarriage.
- Poison arrows from the **North** affect your kidneys and ears.
- Poison arrows from the **East** bring illness associated with the lungs and the feet.
- Poison arrows from the **Northwest** give you headaches and severe migraine.
- Poison arrows from the **West** cause lung problems and danger to the head.
- Poison arrows from the **Northeast** cause back problems and vulnerability to accidents affecting the hands and fingers.
- Poison arrows from the **Southeast** cause illness associated with the thighs, buttocks and cause you to be easily susceptible to flus and colds.
- Poison arrows from the **South** cause problems with the heart and eyes.

54 Enhancing dining room feng shui

If your dining room is already built and you cannot afford to undertake any major changes to its placement, the next best thing is to try and improve its feng shui in order to benefit the family's luck. There are different ways to improve the feng shui of the dining room. Take a two-step approach:

First, correct all negative feng shui features with cures. Second, enhance the feng shui of the dining area with symbols of good fortune.

1. CORRECTING NEGATIVE FENG SHUI

- Place a potted plant in front of the sharp edges of any protruding corner or column.
- **Move the dining table** out from under exposed overhead beams.
- **Overcome the heavy energy** from exposed overhead beams by placing a pair of bamboo flutes in the shape of an A over the edge of the beam.
- **Close windows** of ugly views with curtains or blinds.
- Protect the dining area from excessive glare from the western sun.
- **Check the Flying Star** natal chart numbers of the dining area and use element therapy to overcome the effect of bad number combinations in the chart.

The Three Star Gods Fuk Luk Sau are extremely auspicious placed in the dining room.

2. ENHANCING THE FENG SHUI OF THE DINING AREA

- Place a set of the **FUK LUK SAU** or Star Gods in the dining room. Try and get the best you can afford. These images are very important in this part of the home. In many Hong Kong homes, I see fabulous versions made of jade, carved out of precious aventurine and some even engraved with real diamonds and gold. The Chinese believe that Fuk Luk Sau encompass all the aspirations of mankind and their image inside the home attracts a great deal of good fortune. In my home, I have them in my living, family and dining rooms.
- Place a **symbol of longevity** in the dining room area. Select one that appeals to you – a peach plant rendered in jadeite, an image of the God of Longevity, or perhaps an antique urn with images of cranes, bamboo or pine trees.
- **Hang a painting which can symbolize an abundance of food**, a harvesting of a successful crop or other suggestions of plenty. I snapped a picture of farmers harvesting rice in Bali as I read this scene as a very good omen. Never hang paintings of animals, abstract patterns or unhappy looking faces in the dining area. This should be a joyous room where family members interact happily with one another. Use the walls to create auspicious vibrations for your family.

This living area is heavily decorated with beautiful feng shui enhancers, all in the right places.

55 Living room feng shui

Your living room is the "face" you show the world. This is the part of the home most frequently visited by outsiders, so this is the public area of your home. It is beneficial to design the arrangements here to create the best feng shui for you according to your KUA directions. Do this by using colours, pictures, curtains and sofa seats that harmonize with the element indicated in your KUA number. You can also focus your attention on the placement of the sofas such that they face your good directions.

Sofa arrangements should enable you to sit facing your best direction while entertaining your guests. So if your sheng chi direction is East, then you should arrange your sofa set such that you can sit facing the East, or at least facing one of your four auspicious directions. Better still if you can sit in one of your lucky corners while at the same time face one of your lucky directions. This brings a double benefit.

This is my main living room. Note that I have placed two sofas here with a coffee table in between. Both the sofas face West group directions, which thus benefit me as I belong to the West group. I have another living room placed in the East and there the sofas are facing East group directions to benefit my husband and daughter who both belong to the East group of directions.

In the above picture, notice that I have placed a large Wu Lou made of brass on the coffee table, together with the Lin Zhi (lotus root). This picture was taken during a year when the annual number 2 star flew into the living room sector of my house, so as precaution, I made it a point to install these feng shui remedies well before the energies of the new year began to take effect. Living room feng shui can be spectacularly enhanced with some attention to detail and to the kinds of items you choose to put on display there.

56 Applying the concept of elements

When selecting sofas and curtains for the living room, you can give your creativity a free rein. But it is also a good idea to consider the distribution of the chi in this room according to the five elements. To know which colour is best for each of the corners and walls of the room, you must know the compass orientations of the room.

Stand in the center of the room and using a good compass, take note of the directions indicated for each of the walls and corners. The directions will indicate the element of each corner. **East** and **Southeast** are wood (green). **South** is fire (red). **West** and **Northwest** is metal (white). **Southwest** and **Northeast** are earth (yellow). **North** is water (blue or black). Applying elements and colours will help you create wonderful feng shui.

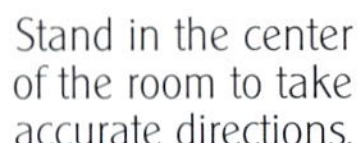

Stand in the center of the room to take accurate directions.

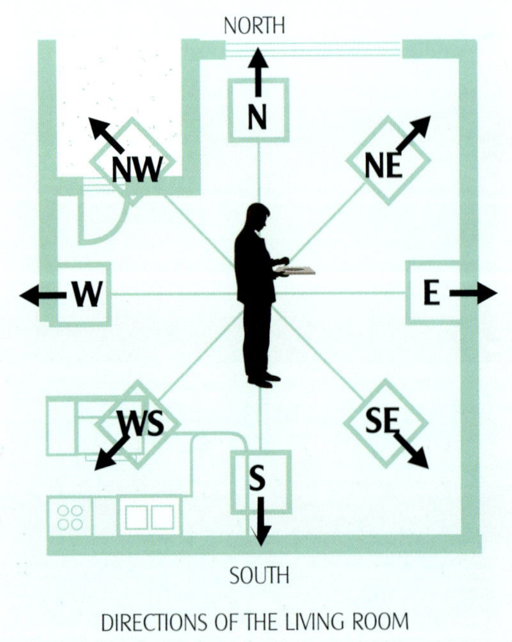

DIRECTIONS OF THE LIVING ROOM

This living room shown here is located in the East of the house so you will notice a preponderance of wood. This is because the East and Southeast are wood corners according to the Pa Kua so placing predominantly wood furniture here will create great harmony in this room.

The colour green will also be beneficial and you should always have a display of flowers in this part of the home since flowers in bloom in the East indicate the successful fruition of projects and enterprises. Wood corners also benefit from things that suggest the water element, so using blue curtains or a blue carpet will be very beneficial as well. In the room here, black scatter cushions are very beneficial.

57 Sofa and curtain colours

Red curtains and flowers activate the south of this room.

If the living room is located in the South part of the house, then a preponderance of red will be most beneficial. This does not mean you need to have so much red here that it overwhelms. But it does mean that the colour red should dominate the colour scheme of the room. The pictures here give you an idea.

In this South located living room, red curtains and red scatter cushions activate the fire element and anyone spending time here will benefit from this tapping of recognition luck. Those belonging to the East group (i.e. with KUA numbers 1,3,4 and 9) will enjoy a double benefit when they spend time in this room.

Red sofas benefit living rooms located in the Southwest of the house, which makes them earth element rooms. Here, note that the background curtain has a cream, earthy colour, which signifies the earth element.

Cushion covers are conduits of excellent chi when they come in bright colours and have auspicious symbols.

The red sofa represents the fire element and since fire produces earth in the cycle of elements, this selection of colours has positive feng shui benefits. This colour scheme is less beneficial in a metal element direction (West and Northwest) or in a wood element direction (East and Southeast).

58 Enhancing the living room

The use of black leather furniture is part of the design aspect of the interior design and has no feng shui significance. But the curtains reflect the earth element. The room is also very well lit as it faces the main door. The single largest feng shui item in this room is the painting of the **Eight Immortals**, who are revered as Taoist saints. The Chinese believe that images of the Immortals in any home bring in the eight types of luck. Most paintings also contain the symbols of good fortune carried by each Immortal, symbols such as the **crane, the red bats, the pine tree, the peach, the fan, the ru yi, the wu lou and the fly whisk**. In the center of the coffee table is the Pi Yao, a celestial creature said to have the power to appease the Grand Duke Jupiter (also known as the God of the Year). Every house benefits from having at least one **Pi Yao** to guard against any ill effect of inadvertently being affected by the Grand Duke, which changes location each year.

The living room is probably the best room in the home to decorate with auspicious objects since this is the first room you see as you enter the home. Thus you will notice that the tribute horse being pulled in by the God of Wealth is placed on a small side table. There is also a large sailing ship filled with gold ingots sailing in from my most auspicious direction placed on the floor just out of the picture and a red calligraphy scroll with the good luck character "fook" written in a hundred different ways. A small bowl of growing auspicious Kuan Yin bamboo is placed on a glass table by the window. This is the "wealth corner" of the room being diagonal to the door.

This is a living room located in the Southwest of the house. Note the feng shui aspects of this room. The most powerful energiser in this room is the painting of the 8 Immortals that dominates the room. Very auspicious for the period of 8.

59 Bringing the garden indoors

This is a picture of a simulated "Green Dragon" which is best in the East side of your garden. Here, this small garden "dragon" created with plants and bushes is very effective and also adds to the lushness ambiance of the house.

Many people have written in to ask me if feng shui can be used in the garden to enhance their overall luck, and my answer has been a resounding yes. Although we do not have much control over our external environment, our garden space is within our control and there is much we can do to ensure that it adds to the feng shui of the home. I have written a detailed book on "FENG SHUI FOR GARDENERS" and you can refer to this book for many different suggestions if you are an enthusiastic gardener.

If you live in the city and your garden is very small, look on it as an extension of your home. Use the compass to identify the directions of the different corners of the garden, apply the five-element theory in the choice of flowers, the use of different materials and in the placement of water features to enhance prosperity luck. A garden that is well cared for where plants grow lush and abundant indicates a very lucky home. Gardens that are cluttered and dirty, with **overgrown grass and rotting dry leaves attract foul energy**. Clogged drains are bad news. Gardens that look good from inside the home bring in good sheng chi (growth chi) representing a continuous supply of fresh energy. Plants, trees and flowers in feng shui come under the wood element and are particularly auspicious in the East and Southeast. The East is the direction that signifies the eldest son. It is the side of the Dragon. So the East side of your house benefits from a garden with lots of lush growing plants.

4

USING EAST/WEST FENG SHUI

One of the more powerful and easy to use feng shui formulas that is based on the directions of the compass is popularly known as the EIGHT MANSIONS FORMULA which defines houses accodring to their sitting and facing directions. Thus all homes are either East or West homes. Likewise, all of us are either East or West group people and when the house vibrates seamlessly with your East or West energy, you will enjoy much better and more coordinated feng shui.

It is a good idea to determine if yours is an East or a West house and then check your own KUA number to see if your feng shui direction aligns auspiciously with your house.

60 Eight Mansions & Nine Palaces

Feng shui for interior spaces takes on exciting possibilities when we start to use formula based compass charts. These represent the compass technology of feng shui – referred to as Eight Mansions & Nine Palaces. These charts are invaluable for addressing different dimensions of feng shui that take account of the dynamics of changing luck patterns over time. In this and the following chapters, I will be introducing the use of **feng shui charts** which will give your practice of feng shui a quantum leap. This book is thus an elementary introduction to the scientific aspects of feng shui. It is a little harder to learn but very much easier to practice. When we use charts, remember that we are taking a more scientific approach to feng shui. There is less subjectivity to the practice. What is required for success is accuracy in taking **directions with a proper compass**. Accurate directions are required to create the charts. The subjectivity comes in when we have to choose between different options based on what the different charts are telling us. We have to decide how much weight to place on each of the different formulas and different methods.

I hope this will convince those who insist on looking at feng shui as a spiritual esoteric practice. It is not. Remember there is the western approach to science and there is the Chinese approach. There is some mystery to the Chinese view of the Universe in that it focuses on an *intangible* concept – that of energy, the dragon's cosmic chi – so we should be forgiven if we are tempted to think there are spiritual overtones to feng shui practice. In introducing you to different feng shui charts, I am sharing with you some powerful ways to read the intangible chi of your home space based on very tangible information (i.e. compass directions, dates of construction and so forth.) It is these tangible facts that enable the feng shui practitioner to draw up the natal chart of any house or building.

These charts reveal information about the chi of the different parts of the building, which are expressed as different compass corners. They are excellent for improving the feng shui of your interior spaces. They have the potential to effect BIG changes in your luck.

In this chapter we look at **Eight Mansion charts** and Trigram Zuan Kong charts. Eight Mansions charts use the **facing direction** of the house and Trigram charts use the house **sitting direction**. Analyzing the two charts together highlights East group and West group houses. For apartments, the charts refer to the whole apartment building.

EIGHT MANSIONS CHART OF A LI HOUSE

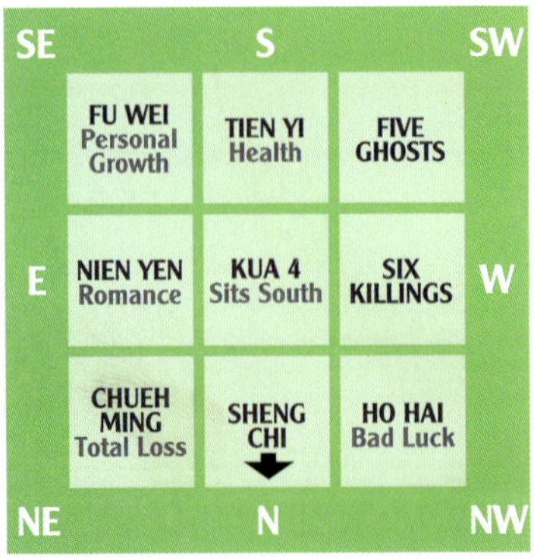

SE	S	SW
FU WEI Personal Growth	TIEN YI Health	FIVE GHOSTS
NIEN YEN Romance (E)	KUA 4 Sits South	SIX KILLINGS (W)
CHUEH MING Total Loss	SHENG CHI ↓	HO HAI Bad Luck
NE	N	NW

TRIGRAM CHART OF A LI HOUSE

SE	S	SW
8	4	6
E 7	9	2 W
3	5 ↓	1
NE	N	NW

Here is the trigram chart of a **LI house** and its equivalent Eight Mansions chart. In compass feng shui, the two charts can be analyzed to give a full reading of the luck sectors and how each resident's luck is affected according to where his/her room is located, and also based on his/her KUA number. When you look at the meanings of the numbers, note that often, these numbers exert a greater impact on your luck than indicated by the 8 Mansions chart. Judgement is required.

61 "Eight Mansions" charts

The Eight Mansion charts are simply a visually efficient way of showing you how eight types of luck (4 good and 4 bad) are distributed in your house. It is called Eight Mansions because there are eight types of mansions with different distributions of chi. The Trigram and Flying Star charts use all nine grids so there are said to be nine palaces. The information contained in Trigram and Flying Star charts are expressed as numbers, while Eight Mansions use descriptions to reveal the type of chi present. All charts are based on house orientations, facing and sitting. Presented here are the 8 Eight Mansion charts. See which chart applies to your house. Use a compass to check your house facing direction and find the chart that corresponds to your *house facing direction*. Then use the charts to analyze your home.

SE		S		SW
	SHENG CHI	NIEN YEN Romance	CHUEH MING Total Loss	
E	TIEN YI Health	KUA 1 Sits NW	HO HAI Bad Luck	W
	FIVE GHOSTS	FU WEI Personal Growth	SIX KILLINGS	
NE		N		NW

SE		S		SW
	NIEN YEN Romance	SHENG CHI	HO HAI Bad Luck	
E	FU WEI Personal Growth	KUA 3 Sits North	CHUEH MING Total Loss	W
	SIX KILLINGS	TIEN YI Health	FIVE GHOSTS	
NE		N		NW

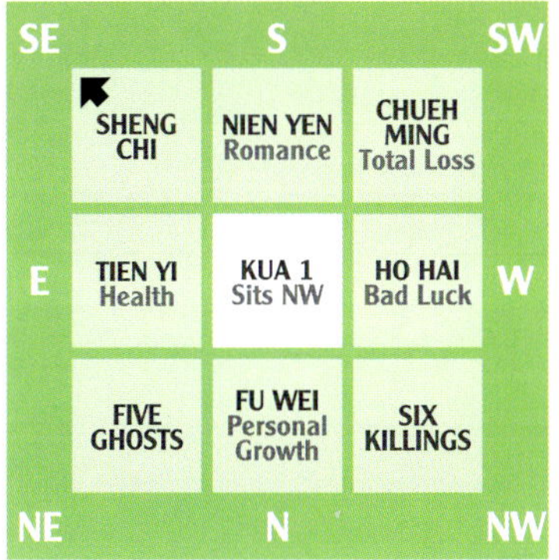

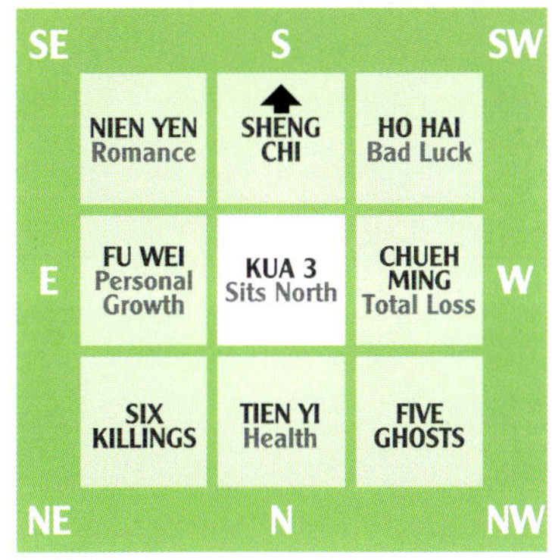

SE		S		SW
	CHUEH MING Total Loss	HO HAI Bad Luck	SHENG CHI	
E	SIX KILLINGS	KUA 5/8 Sits NE	NIEN YEN Romance	W
	FU WEI Personal Growth	FIVE GHOSTS	TIEN YI Health	
NE		N		NW

SE		S		SW
	TIEN YI Health	FU WEI Personal Growth	SIX KILLINGS	
E	SHENG CHI	KUA 9 Sits West	FIVE GHOSTS	W
	HO HAI Bad Luck	NIEN YEN Romance	CHUEH MING Total Loss	
NE		N		NW

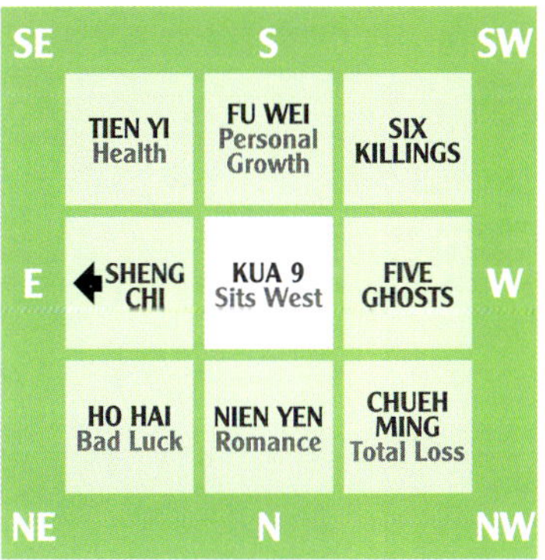

The arrows in the charts indicate the house facing direction. Note the four good directions (sheng chi, health, romance and personal growth) and the four unlucky directions (ho hai, five ghosts, six killings, and total loss). Identify your lucky & unlucky rooms.

SE		S		SW
	HO HAI Bad Luck	CHUEH MING Total Loss	NIEN YEN Romance	
E	FIVE GHOSTS	KUA 6 Sits East	SHENG CHI	W
	TIEN YI Health	SIX KILLINGS	FU WEI Personal Growth	
NE		N		NW

SE		S		SW
	FIVE GHOSTS	SIX KILLINGS	FU WEI Personal Growth	
E	HO HAI Bad Luck	KUA 2 Sits SW	TIEN YI Health	W
	SHENG CHI	CHUEH MING Total Loss	NIEN YEN Romance	
NE		N		NW

SE		S		SW
	FU WEI Personal Growth	TIEN YI Health	FIVE GHOSTS	
E	NIEN YEN Romance	KUA 4 Sits South	SIX KILLINGS	W
	CHUEH MING Total Loss	SHENG CHI	HO HAI Bad Luck	
NE		N		NW

SE		S		SW
	SIX KILLINGS	FIVE GHOSTS	TIEN YI Health	
E	CHUEH MING Total Loss	KUA 7 Sits SE	FU WEI Personal Growth	W
	NIEN YEN Romance	HO HAI Bad Luck	SHENG CHI	
NE		N		NW

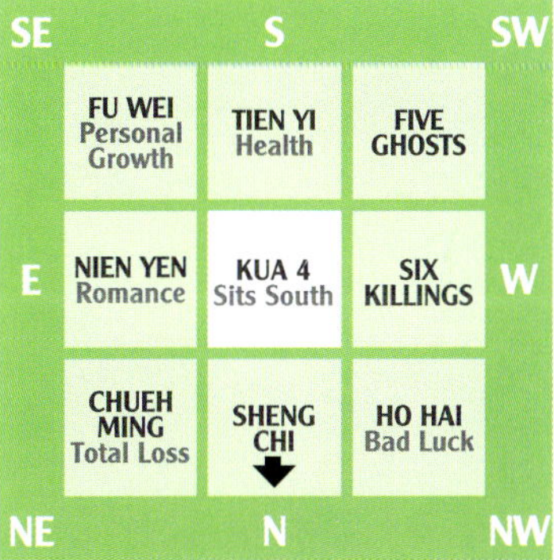

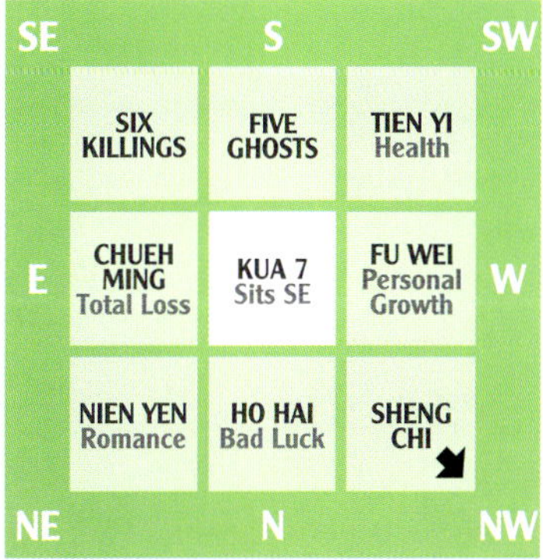

62 Compatibility of house & individual

The Eight Mansions charts show the luck distribution of a building. These charts are based on the facing direction of the building. Note that the facing direction of the house does NOT necessarily have to mean the facing direction of its door, although in most cases it does. In some cases, the house may be facing one direction while the door faces another. Generally, you have to decide the **facing direction of the house** by looking at it and selecting from several possible criteria. Thus the facing direction of the house can be:

- The direction where the main road is. This is the source of maximum yang energy
- The direction with the most unencumbered view where there is a big glass window
- The direction facing lower ground where there might be a patio looking out
- The direction facing the driveway into the house.

Once you have determined the facing direction, select the Eight Mansions chart that applies to your house. There are only eight charts (thus eight mansions) and the directions are based on four primary and the four secondary directions. So the facing direction is read as angles of directions, with 45 degrees per angle of direction.

The Eight Mansions chart describes the distribution of luck in exactly the same way as Eight Mansions works for individuals. If your KUA number corresponds to the eight mansions chart then you and the house are said to be compatible and the house is lucky for you. Always try to stay in a house that is compatible with your KUA number.

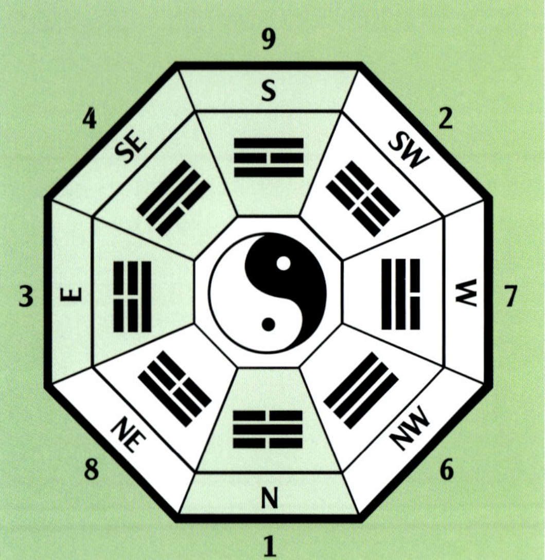

Example: If your KUA number is 1, then your sheng chi direction is Southeast. So a house facing Southeast would be best for you, since then, the distribution of luck in the house will correspond exactly to what is good for you. Note that East group people living in a house that faces an East group direction would find the house compatible, since the good and bad luck directions would be the same for the house as for the individual. Note that East group directions are East, Southeast, North and South.

It is the same if you are a West group person. The houses that are compatible with you will face a West group direction i.e. West, Northwest, Southwest and Northeast.

The Pa Kua here summarizes the **East and West group KUA numbers** and the facing directions. The directions shaded green are the east group directions and these are North, South, Southeast and East. Those with KUA numbers 3, 4, 9 and 1 belong to the East group.

The directions shaded white are the **West group directions** and these are Southwest, West, Northwest and Northeast. Those with KUA numbers 2, 7, 6 and 8 belong to the West group.

63 Eight types of luck explained

The Eight Mansions formula categorizes houses into eight sectors and each sector stands for one type of luck. There are four sectors of good luck and four sectors of bad luck. You can use Eight Mansions to examine whether your bedroom has good or bad luck, and whether it has the type of luck you want.

West group KUA people living in East group KUA houses will find that the distribution of luck in the house will directly clash with their personal good and bad luck directions. According to master practitioners of Eight Mansions, if you are either the father or the mother of the house, the room you occupy should bring you good luck under both the house chart and under your personal KUA number. If you are one of the children or relatives, it is advisable to use your personal KUA number to select the rooms that are best for you and to thus ignore the house Eight Mansions chart.

In every house the GOOD LUCK locations are:

Sheng Chi

This signifies the place of wealth and prosperity luck. This is always the entrance into the building and corresponds to the facing palace in Flying Star feng shui. So do note that this part of any house is always the part that brings prosperity to the household and its residents. Always keep this part of the house well activated. No clutter, no poison arrows and always a lot of light, space and enhancers.

Nien Yen

This signifies the place for marriage and romantic luck and for descendants luck. This place will be different depending on the facing direction of the house. The charts will reveal the room that has this type of luck.

Tien Yi

This pinpoints the room with the best health luck. Members of the family more prone to falling sick should be given rooms with tien yi luck.

Fu Wei

This signifies the space with personal development luck. School going children would benefit from this part of the house.

The BAD LUCK locations are:

Ho Hai

This signifies a place of mild bad luck. If you stay in a Ho Hai room, you will find minor irritations annoying you. Projects take longer to come to fruition. There are setbacks and disappointments.

Five Ghosts

This signifies relationship problems and bad luck associated with troublemakers and being a victim of gossip and scandal mongering. Five Ghosts bad luck can sometimes get transformed into immense good luck by the auspicious feng shui charts under other systems and formulas such as Flying Star.

Six Killings

This signifies six types of misfortunes. The bad luck here can be described as quite severe and comes in battalions. Illness, loss, death, loss of good name, loss of wealth, loss of descendants – misfortune in many different manifestations occur.

Chueh Ming

This signifies a state of total loss and usually this can mean bankruptcy or even a whole family being wiped out altogether. In any home, it is a good idea never to stay in a room afflicted by Cheuh Ming UNLESS the Flying Star chart indicates a change of luck there.

64 The trigram of houses

We can determine the Trigram of a house as follows. Look at the eight trigrams of the Pa Kua based on the Later Heaven Arrangement. In this Pa Kua (shown above), each trigram is allotted a direction according to the sequence of trigram arrangement shown in the yang Pa Kua. Note the names of the trigrams, as well as the Lo Shu number of the trigrams as follows. Then note:

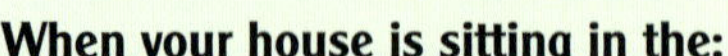

When your house is sitting in the:

North – it is a KAN house (1)
South – it is a LI house (9)
East – it is a CHEN house (3)
West – it is a TUI house (7)
Southeast – it is a SUN house (4)
Southwest – it is a KUN house (2)
Northeast – it is a KEN house (8)
Northwest – it is a CHIEN house (6)

TRIGRAM HOUSES ARE BASED ON SITTING DIRECTION

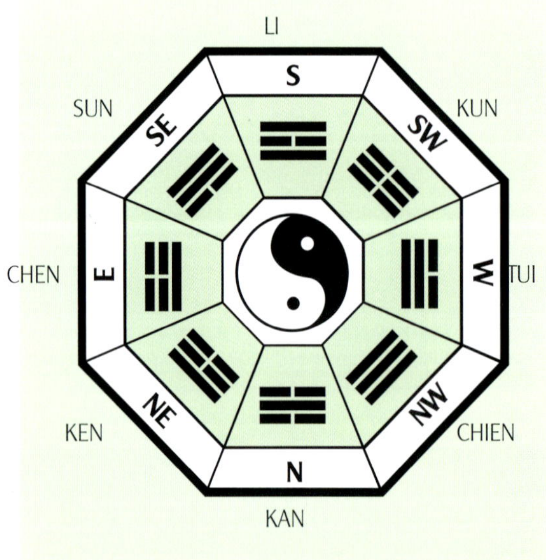

When taking directions, stand at the main door-inside facing out to get the facing direction. The opposite to that is your "sitting direction", used to find the Trigram chart of your house.

TAKING COMPASS READINGS

To determine what kind of trigram house yours is, you must learn to use a compass to take directions. Invest in a good compass. Try to obtain a reliable and accurate one, which has the degrees marked out clearly. Make sure to take accurate readings. In fact, for feng shui purposes, it is a good idea to take at least three readings for accuracy.

Please note that readings should always be taken at the main door, standing inside and facing squarely outwards. This direction is known as the facing direction of the house. **Once you know the facing direction of your house, you can determine its sitting direction.** This is the direct opposite direction of the *facing direction*. So when the house faces North, it is sitting South, and it will be a LI house. When a house faces East, it is sitting West, and is a TUI house and so forth.

Each trigram house has its own reigning Lo Shu number and from this number, the feng shui chart of the house can be generated based on the flight sequence of the star numbers according to the original Lo Shu Square.

65 The trigram charts

These charts are based on the SITTING DIRECTION of the house. In the texts, they are referred to as Trigram Zuan Kong charts. Under this system, all houses are differentiated according to the ruling trigram and these charts are read by first analyzing the meanings of the single numbers in the different sectors (as superimposed on the house). After that, the annual Flying Star chart numbers are added into each of the grids, so creating two numbers in each grid. The two numbers are combined to promise good luck or offer warnings of misfortunes during the year in question. "Combined numbers" charts are on the next page.

CHART OF A SUN HOUSE

CHART OF A LI HOUSE

CHART OF A KUN HOUSE

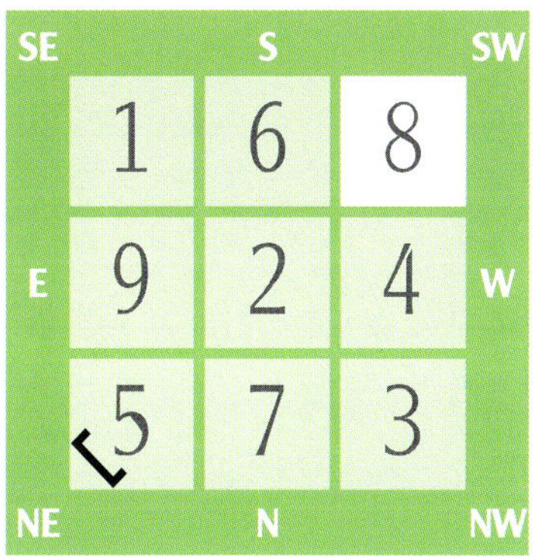

CHART OF A CHEN HOUSE

SE	S	SW
2	7	9
E 1	3	5 W
6	8	4
NE	N	NW

The trigrams correspond to the sitting direction of the house or building. The center numbers are derived from this direction. The rest of the numbers are based on the flight sequence of the original Lo Shu magic square.

CHART OF A TUI HOUSE

SE	S	SW
6	2	4
E 5	7	9 W
1	3	8
NE	N	NW

CHART OF A KEN HOUSE

CHART OF A KAN HOUSE

CHART OF A CHIEN HOUSE

66 Combined trigram and annual energy charts

The charts on this page show how each trigram chart can be combined with the numbers of the annual flying star charts for 2011 and for 2012. Using these charts and the meanings of the number combinations that are organized in the following pages will open up countless opportunities to improve your feng shui, and also to remedy the afflictions of the feng shui of your rooms from year to year. The charts in this illustration cover 2011 and 2012. As you learn to **combine the numbers**, you will eventually develop the expertise needed to combine with 2012 numbers and beyond. Honestly it is that simple!

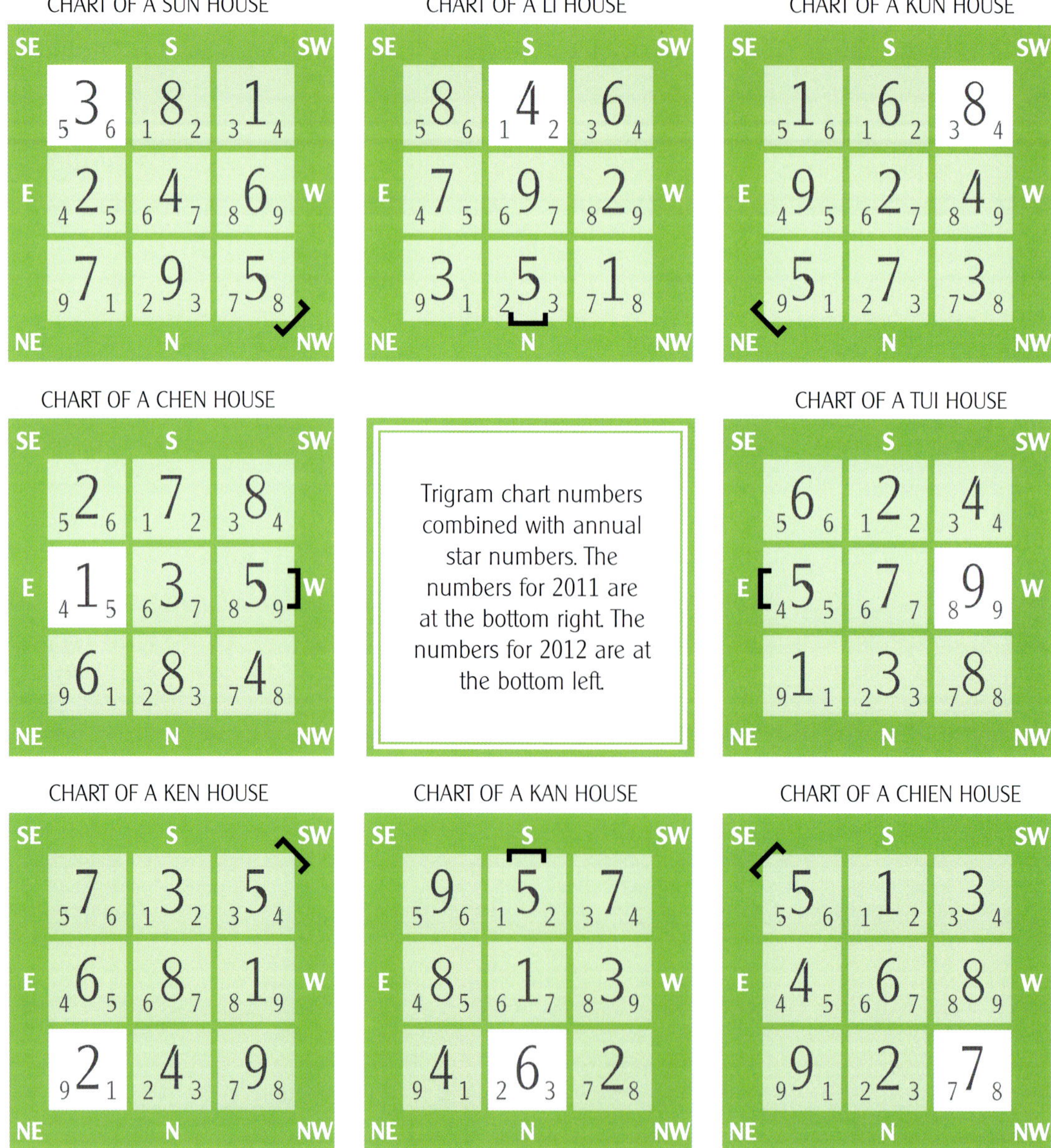

Trigram chart numbers combined with annual star numbers. The numbers for 2011 are at the bottom right. The numbers for 2012 are at the bottom left.

67 Reading the trigram chart

The trigram chart is the base chart of numbers, and to analyze the luck of houses or buildings from year to year, a second set of numbers representing the year in question are added to the trigram chart numbers. There will therefore be two sets of numbers in each of the nine grids that make up the chart.

Meanwhile, the little numbers by the side of the center black numbers are the annual numbers for the year 2009. You will see that **every sector has its own annual number**, and to undertake the analysis, you first have to determine what type of house yours is and then by adding the annual number, you will have a chart to show the two numbers in each square. This will reveal the map luck of the house for the year. With this chart, you are able to identify which sector of the house has good or bad luck during any particular year.

To interpret the meanings of the number combinations, you will need to know about the **element interactions of the numbers** as well as the meanings of the numbers themselves. Knowing how to read this chart thus reveals important information for residents staying in the different sectors of the house. This requires you to superimpose the chart over the floor plan of your house. It is not difficult to learn this system of feng shui. What is needed is a basic knowledge of the Lo Shu square, the flight sequence of its numbers and the numbers that are associated with each of the eight directions.

This is just one of the formulas taught in my **Master Practitioners Course (MPC)** organized few times a year for feng shui enthusiasts who want to learn practical feng shui. The MPC does not pretend to be an academic course – it goes into deeper detail in analyzing the charts, but it is also very practical, fun and effective. To date, we have had students come from the United States, Russia, Australia, UK, Germany, New Zealand, Canada, Switzerland, France, Africa, Mexico, India, Slovenia, South America, Singapore and other countries. Some come to learn to become Professional Practitioners. Others to get a solid grounding in compass formula work to incorporate feng shui into their own homes. They find this to be far more efficient and cost effective than hiring a Feng Shui consultant. Many also enjoy learning alongside students from different parts of the world.

FACING WEST

A CHEN HOUSE IN 2011
FACING WEST SITTING EAST

Look at the example chart shown here. This is a CHEN house because it is sitting EAST and facing WEST. Since the number of east is 3, this becomes the center number of the chart. With the center number in place the rest of the numbers can be filled in according to the flight sequence of the numbers found in the Lo Shu chart.

To read the luck of the different sectors of the house, you need to combine the numbers of the **annual chart with the trigram chart** of the house. The luck of each sector is then read in accordance with the meanings associated with the combination of the two numbers. To enable the reader to undertake the analysis of each of the eight houses in years 2011 and 2012 given in the illustration on the previous page, the following pages give tables that set out the meanings of the combinations of the trigram with the annual numbers. These tables are very valuable as they summarize the key meanings of the numbers. Which help bring you success in doing the feng shui of your interior rooms.

68 Understanding trigram charts - 1

COMBINATIONS OF TRIGRAM NUMBER 1 & ANNUAL NUMBERS

The number 1 is a white number and is regarded as one of the three luckiest numbers in this method of feng shui analysis. If your bedroom is located in a sector of the house that has the number 1, it is a lucky indication. When combined with 1, 6 or 8, the luck is further magnified.

TRIGRAM NUMBER	ANNUAL NUMBER	MEANINGS	ENHANCERS / REMEDIES
1	1	Excellent for academic studies, research and creative work. Good money luck. If afflicted by month star 5 or 2, there could be kidney related illness. Accidents can also happen, caused by excessive drinking and alcoholic problems as this signifies excessive water. A double 1 is however a very good indication.	To enhance and also to control affliction, use a 6 rod all metal windchime. Watch out for when the 5 or 2 flies in during specific months. To be safe hang metal windchimes here.
1	2	There could be marriage problems and also a danger of losing a child through miscarriage. Beware of car accidents. The number 2 is not a good number to combine with 1 – it makes it afflicted.	Use plants to exhaust the water number 1 and strengthen earth element.
1	3	Brings heartache caused by gossip and slandering. There could be lawsuits and legal entanglements brought by the 3.	Use water to enhance and water plants to transform the hostility of 3.
1	4	Political luck. Media and publicity luck. Romance luck especially for women. Good writing luck for authors. This is a very good combination for literary work.	Use slow moving water but not too much. Too much water can bring problems associated with sex.
1	5	Health problems. Sicknesses, food poisoning. Injury caused by accidents. The 5 is always to be feared.	Use 6 rod metal windchime to exhaust the 5. This also strengthens the 1 of water.
1	6	Excellent career luck. Promotion. Good money luck. Headaches especially when month 5 or 2 enters.	Enhance with still metal like coins, ingots and gold art.
1	7	An indication that there will be cut throat competition.	Enhance with crystals or a gem tree. Look for citrines as these interact well with 1.
1	8	Excellent wealth luck. There could be misunderstandings between loved ones, siblings and good friends. Business partners have problems.	Enhance with white crystals, and also with moving water to attract wealth luck.
1	9	Good for both career and money luck, but can turn bad when 5 flies in. Eye problems.	No need to enhance. Go easy with reds.

69 Understanding trigram charts - 2

COMBINATIONS OF TRIGRAM NUMBER 2 & ANNUAL NUMBERS

The number 2 is the illness number and is regarded as one of the danger numbers in this method of feng shui analysis. If your bedroom is located in a sector of the house that has the number 2, you should install windchime remedies immediately, especially when the annual 2 and monthly 2 flies in to strengthen the illness luck.

TRIGRAM NUMBER	ANNUAL NUMBER	MEANINGS	ENHANCERS / REMEDIES
2	1	Stress develops in the marriage if this combination is in the bedroom. There is danger of miscarriage, and other accidents - and loss of loved one.	Use metal wind chimes to control and exhaust the bad star 2. It is also a good idea to move to another room.
2	2	Not a good indication. Magnifies strong negative feelings. Illness and accidents possible. The double 2 is to be feared.	6 rod wind chimes, coins and bells. What is needed is strong metallic sounds.
2	3	Arguments and misunderstandings of the most severe kind. There is hostility, back stabbing, hatred and legal disputes. If your room is afflicted with the 2/3 combination, it can be a stressful time.	Use still YIN water to cool tempers. Do not disturb the energy here with chimes, music or noise. Keep the room very quiet.
2	4	Wives and mothers in law quarrel and fight. Family disharmony is in the air. Good indications for writers and those in the journalism field. Good for those at school, but the luck can be short-lived.	Use YIN water in an urn to create some harmony. Also try using smooth crystal balls. This can be quite effective to overcome in law problems with mother.
2	5	Extremely inauspicious. Total loss and catastrophe. This is one of the most dangerous combinations in Flying Star technology, and when the 5 flies in, anyone staying here can suddenly develop terminal illness.	Use strong windchime (plenty). Beware do NOT have fire or there could be a death. Whenever the 2 and the 5 occur together it is necessary to be careful.
2	6	Very easy life of ease and leisure, power and authority. This auspicious combination is spoilt if a 5 rod windchime is placed here. The trinity (tien ti ren) gets activated in a negative way.	Do not use windchimes. If there is sickness related to stomach place red amulet here. Placing crystal gem tree here would be excellent.
2	7	There is money during the period of 7 BUT luck of children will not be good. Problems conceiving children. Unscrupulous people at work will tend to politic against you.	Use metal (bells) and metal windchimes. Also hang sword of coins to overcome work aggravations. Also use a porcelain rooster.
2	8	Richness and wealth but there is ill health, although this can be remedied.	Use water to overcome bad health star. Place a wu lou.
2	9	Extremely bad luck. Nothing succeeds unless remedied. Not a good indication for children.	Use water plants. Also use coins or windchime

70 Understanding trigram charts - 3

COMBINATIONS OF TRIGRAM NUMBER 3 & ANNUAL NUMBERS

The number 3 is the quarrelsome number. If this number afflicts your room, you will have to endure hostility and quarrelsome luck unless you install the necessary remedies.

TRIGRAM NUMBER	ANNUAL NUMBER	MEANINGS	ENHANCERS / REMEDIES
3	1	Heartache caused by gossip and slandering. There could be lawsuits and legal entanglements.	Use water to enhance and water plants. If already engaged in a lawsuit move out of the room temporarily and move to another less afflicted room. An obelisk natural crystal will help.
3	2	Dangerous for those in politics; Lawsuits, even jail. Gossip, slander. Bad luck for women - obesity.	Some Masters recommend gold and fire. I also like using paintings that feature goldfish in gold and red.
3	3	Gossip and slander. Quarrels. Get robbed. A very dangerous indication which can get out of hand very easily. You must make every effort not to have too much noise in the part of the house afflicted by the double 3. In flying star feng shui the double 3 brings hostility and aggravations.	Use sword of coins –metal is needed but not the sounds. Still water is always helpful, so blue carpets and curtains can help to soften the situation. Use dark rather than light blue.
3	4	Heartache caused by sexual scandal. This manifests in the presence of third parties into your family life.	Use bright lights to dissipate scandalous chi – also place amethyst crystal under the bed where the feet are.
3	5	You can over come this with crystal under the bed. Loss of wealth. Severe cash flow problems. If bedroom is here, financial loss is severe. If kitchen is here sickness is inevitable. Do not stay here.	Exhaust the 5 with copper mountain painting. Yin metal is very effective to overcome affliction.
3	6	Time of slow growth. Leg injuries. Bad for young males.	Use still water.
3	7	You will get robbed or burgled. Violence. Possibility of injury from knives or guns. Blood.	Use still water. This will exhaust the ferocity of 7 in this combination.
3	8	Not good for children under 12 years. Danger to limbs.	Use bright lights to cure.
3	9	Robbery encounter. Lawsuits. Fights.	Use yin (still) water.

71 Understanding trigram charts - 4

COMBINATIONS OF TRIGRAM NUMBER 4 & ANNUAL NUMBERS

The number 4 is considered an auspicious number as it brings academic luck. It is also regarded as the romance number although this can turn scandalous when it meets up with excessive water energy.

TRIGRAM NUMBER	ANNUAL NUMBER	MEANINGS	ENHANCERS / REMEDIES
4	1	Very good romance luck but too much water leads to sex scandals. Affairs lead to unhappiness and breakup of family. Must guard against being carried away. But excellent creative and writing luck.	Kuan Yin statue or image of laughing Buddha for some divine help might enhance the luck further and also save you from going overboard.
4	2	Illness of internal organs - Husband has extramarital affair, or at least could be lured into a situation of some risk – could lead to scandals.	Use amethyst crystal under the bed. Do this as a precaution – make certain the amethyst used is big enough.
4	3	Emotional stress due to relationship and sexual and emotional problems.	Use a strong red to overcome – perhaps cinnamon red cushions, curtains ... wall hangings.
4	4	Excellent for writing and creative luck. Very attractive to opposite sex. Romance will flourish.	Fresh flowers to enhance growth of romance. Be wary of having too much water, but activate with the double happiness and other symbols of romance.
4	5	Sexually transmitted skin diseases. Breast cancer. The illness risk is great.	Use painting of water & mountain as cure. Also use windchime to control the 5.
4	6	Money luck but creativity dries up. Bad luck indicated fro women especially pregnant women. If pregnant women should move to another room.	Strengthen earth element with crystals. Also place wu lou by the bedside.
4	7	Bad luck in love. Will get cheated by opposite sex. Sickness of the thighs and lower abdomen. If in bedroom the affliction is severe. If the front door is here place pair of chi lin here.	Use water to control. There are several water cures you can consider for this but if in the bedroom use blue or black.
4	8	Excellent career luck for writers. Bad for very young children. Injury to limbs indicated.	Use lights to combat threat to children. Enhance the 8 luck with round solid natural crystals – larger the better.
4	9	A time for preparation. Good for students. Need to be careful of fire breaking out.	Use wood or plants. But make certain fire element does not get too strong.

72 Understanding trigram charts - 5

TRIGRAM NUMBER 5 & ANNUAL NUMBERS

The number 5 is a very unlucky and dangerous number in this system of feng shui. Each time it flies into your bedroom, or afflicts the main door, it brings illness, accidents and severe financial loss in its wake. Fortunately, it is not too difficult to control.

TRIGRAM NUMBER	ANNUAL NUMBER	MEANINGS	ENHANCERS / REMEDIES
5	1	Hearing problems and also sex related illness could break out The 5 combined with 1 is bad news.	Use 6 rod all metal hollow wind chimes. This exhausts the 5 and strengthens the 1.
5	2	Misfortunes and extreme bad luck. Illness may be fatal – it is a good idea to move out of the afflicted room. These two numbers together are to be feared. Illness is certain but losses can also result.	Use plenty of 6 rod wind chimes, gold coins and metal energy because the combination of 2 with 5 is self sustaining and the effect is very severe.
5	3	Money troubles. Disputes. Bad business luck – could lead to law suits that trigger extreme stress to the residents.	Use 6 coins stuck onto walls and placed above door way.
5	4	Creativity dries up. Sickness. Skin problems could become severe.	Use water/mountain. Place plants with large leaves to absorb the bad energy and to enhance the 4. Do not use plants with thin spiky leaves.
5	5	A very critical combination. Extreme danger indicated by the double 5 – mishaps take place with great ferocity. Serious illness & accidents that can be fatal. Take care.	Use metal 6-rod wind chimes to overcome. Paint the room white and also have 6 gold coins under the carpet and over the doorway.
5	6	Bad luck for financials. Loss. Diseases related to the head region. Danger also to the man.	Place six coins under the carpet in the room to help strengthen the metal energy.
5	7	Arguments abound. Mouth related illness.	Coins and bells are a good remedy here – also wind chimes will be a great help. In period 8 this combination becomes dangerous.
5	8	Problems related to the limbs, joints and bones of the body. It is necessary to be careful of rough sports.	Use water to pacify.
5	9	Bad luck all round. Do not speculate or gamble as you are sure to lose. Eye problems. Danger of fire.	Use water and also red and gold painting. Windchimes are also effective against the 5/9 combination.

73 Understanding trigram charts - 6

COMBINATIONS OF TRIGRAM NUMBER 6 & ANNUAL NUMBERS

The number 6 is another lucky white number and is regarded as one of the three luckiest numbers in Flying Star and Trigram feng shui analysis. If your bedroom is located in a sector of the house that has the number 6, it indicates extremely good fortune.

TRIGRAM NUMBER	ANNUAL NUMBER	MEANINGS	ENHANCERS / REMEDIES
6	1	Financial luck and high achievers in the family manifest joyousness. It is an excellent indication of good fortune. Headaches through excessive stress.	Enhance with metal energy as metal creates water and also enhances the 6. Use a bowl of metal gold ingots.
6	2	Great affluence and everything successful. Stomach problems. Patriarch could have sickness.	No need to enhance. But control with bells. The idea is to strengthen the 6 while suppressing the 2. so place metallic energy.
6	3	Unexpected windfall. Speculative luck. Leg injury. (Protect against this with strong plant energy and removing metal).	Enhance with gemstones - or a "bowl of diamonds". This is simply the best enhancer of wealth luck.
6	4	Unexpected windfall for women of the family. Lower body injury. Pregnant women must be careful.	Enhance with smooth and round crystal balls. Do not enhance with metal energy as this could become dangerous.
6	5	Money luck blocked. Sickness could prevail.	Use bells and brass mirrors to overcome the 5 annual.
6	6	Excellent money luck from heaven. But too much metal can be dangerous. So do not enhance with metal.	No need to enhance - better not to.
6	7	Competitive squabbling over money. Arguments. Hostility could break out into something ugly. Also success breeds jealousy. Must tread carefully.	Use water to curb and control the arising of gossip and envy.
6	8	Wealth, popularity, prosperity. Great richness. Probably the best combination in flying star technique. Those in love are in for a lonely period.	Enhance with water and make sure you have an entrance or window in that sector. This is a very auspicious combination - use crystal diamonds.
6	9	Money luck. Frustration between generations leading to arguments between young and old.	Water to reduce the daily friction. Also use a brass mirror to absorb bad chi and reduce the possibility of misunderstandings escalating into something more serious.

74 Understanding trigram charts - 7

COMBINATIONS OF TRIGRAM NUMBER 7 & ANNUAL NUMBERS

The number 7 is an unlucky number that brings burglary, accidents and even violence. If your bedroom is located in a sector of the house with the 7, safeguards should be put in place to correct the malevolent energy created.

TRIGRAM NUMBER	ANNUAL NUMBER	MEANINGS	ENHANCERS / REMEDIES
7	1	Extremely good prosperity luck. But competition is deadly and can turn ugly. Tread carefully with partners and business associates.	Use water feature to strengthen the 1 as this will bring good chi into the combination.
7	2	Money luck dissipates. Children luck is dimmed. Young children should be careful.	Use windchimes.
7	3	Grave danger of injury to limbs. Be careful. Do not strengthen the metal energy as it will turn dangerous.	Use water to overcome and exhaust the metal energy. The water must be in an urn that is at least 18 inches deep.
7	4	Taken for a ride by someone of the opposite sex. (use an amulet to guard against losing your money here). Pregnant women should also take care.	Use water. If the home belongs to older people it is necessary to remove flowers from the bedroom.
7	5	Problems caused by excessive gossiping. Danger of poisoning or anything to do with the mouth.	Use metal coins, bells or wind chimes. Also red energy might help in this combination.
7	6	Sword fighting killing breath although in certain circumstances the 6 can prevail.	Use water to exhaust the 7.
7	7	Prevail over the competition. Money luck. Sex life gets a boost for young people. Beware over indulgence.	Use water to curb excesses. The 7 must be kept under control at all times.
7	8	Same as above but better because of the 8 energy. Here good luck is stronger than the bad luck.	Use water and also lots of crystal energy. This will boost the energy of the 8 bringing good fortune and lots of luck.
7	9	All troubles are caused through vulnerability to sexual advances. There is danger of fire hazards.	Use earth (big boulders) to press down bad luck. The 7 must be kept under control here. Use water chi – bleus, blacks and water motifs.

75 Understanding trigram charts - 8

COMBINATIONS OF TRIGRAM NUMBER 8 & ANNUAL NUMBERS

The number 8 is the third white number and is regarded as the luckiest number in Flying Star and Trigram feng shui. The most important thing about 8 is that it is the number of the current period. This means that whenever 8 is present, it brings very powerful and strong good fortune energy. This is because it is intrinsically a lucky number and because it is also the current reigning number of the period, its presence is sure to bring prosperity.

TRIGRAM NUMBER	ANNUAL NUMBER	MEANINGS	ENHANCERS / REMEDIES
8	1	Excellent and auspicious prosperity luck. Career advancement. Money luck. But sibling rivalry prevails.	Enhance with water and with crystals. Place ships with sailing boats and filled with diamonds as a powerful enhancer of wealth.
8	2	Wealth creation possible. Properties and asset accumulation. But there is the danger of illness. generally however the 8 is a string lucky number and will prevail.	Use mountain principle. Boulder with red thread. Overcome the 2 with metal energy and enhance the 8 with earth energy.
8	3	Move children away from this sector. Limbs injury. Some hostility and misunderstanding arising from envy.	Use red, yellow.
8	4	Overpowering matriarch. Love life of younger generation suffers from mother and potential mother in law problems. Limbs injury. (protect with amulet).	Use fire, or red to overcome. Red is especially powerful s this appeases the matriarchal energy.
8	5	Problems related to the limbs, joints and bones of the body. It is necessary to be careful of rough sports, climbing mountains, skiing and other activity using the limbs.	Use water to pacify. Also overcome the threat and danger of accidents by placing a brass mirror in the room.
8	6	Wealth, popularity, prosperity. Great richness. One of the best combinations in flying star system. Love life goes through a rough patch but will be smooth in the end.	Enhance with crystals make sure there is an entrance or window in that sector to bring in the good luck.
8	7	Prevail over the competition. Money luck. Sex life gets a boost for young people. Beware over indulgence.	Use water to curb excesses.
		Excellent wealth creation luck. Very favourable.	No need to enhance.
8	8	Excellent for money and celebration. But misunderstandings between the young and older generation can turn nasty.	Use water to calm the fire.
8	9		

76 Understanding trigram charts - 9

COMBINATIONS OF TRIGRAM NUMBER 9 & ANNUAL NUMBERS

The number 9 is the ultimate magnifying number – combining the fullness of heaven and earth. It can be excellent when triggered by an auspicious annual number, but it can also be deadly when combined with a 5 or a 2. The main thing about 9 is its strong fire energy. When under control, it is excellent, but when out of control, the 9 can bring disasters.

TRIGRAM NUMBER	ANNUAL NUMBER	MEANINGS	ENHANCERS / REMEDIES
9	1	Good for both career and money luck, but can turn bad when 5 flies in. Danger of eye problems.	Do not enhance.
9	2	Extremely bad luck. Nothing succeeds unless remedied. Not a good indication for children. Here the 9 magnifies the bad star number 2.	Use water plants. Also use coins or windchime, Do not use bright lights here.
9	3	Robbery encounter. Lawsuits. Fights. Fire hazard.	Use yin (still) water.
9	4	A time for preparation. Good for students. Be careful of fire – as a combination 9/4 possesses hidden dangers so it is a good idea to be very careful.	Use wood or plants but do not over do the energizing of fire energy. It is better to have young wood than old wood energy so young plants here will be good.
9	5	Bad luck all round. Do not speculate or gamble as you are sure to lose. Eye problems. Danger of fire.	Use wind chimes to overcome this potentially deadly combination.
9	6	Money luck. Frustration between generations – leading to arguments between young and old. Usually manifest as problems between daughter and father.	Water will reduce the frictions but a better remedy is for any young girl staying in such a room to move to another room.
9	7	Troubles caused through vulnerability to sexual advances. There is also danger of fire hazards.	Use earth (big boulders) to press down bad luck. Also keep an amulet to ward off danger of being sexually assaulted.
9	8	Excellent for money and celebration. But misunderstandings between the young and older generation can turn nasty. There is also danger of envy and insecurities clashing badly.	Use water to calm the fire. Place a large urn of still water. Fire energy must be pressed down, especially if this occurs in the South.
9	9	Good or bad depending on other indications. Generally a double 9 can be neutral and depends on monthly star numbers flying in. When incoming month stars are good the luck gets magnified. When incoming month star is 5 or 2, misfortunes are more severe.	Do not enhance.

77 Interpreting a trigram chart

When you use trigram charts to complement your feng shui analysis, the way to do it is to superimpose the chart onto the floor plan such that the compass locations of the number combinations are placed on the plan. In the example here, we have a trigram CHEN house, which is **sitting East and facing West**. Since the number of East is 3, notice that the big center number in the chart is 3 and from this number the whole trigram chart is created.

Next, we look at the numbers 2011 and for the year 2012 to read the luck of the main rooms of this house in the coming two years. The most important parts of the home are its main entrance area and bedrooms. First, we look at the master bedroom, and here we see that residents have better luck in 2011 than 2012. **In 2010**, number 8 coming to this part of the house brings good luck. The other bedrooms enjoys good luck in both 2011 and 2012. In the entrance area note that 9 combines with the base number 5 in 2011 but in 2012 the 8 flies in. So this house has difficult luck in 2011 and better luck in 2012.

In addition to analyzing the numbers per se, we can also undertake an elements analysis of the numbers. Learn the corresponding elements of numbers and directions, and then analyze how the element of annual numbers interacts with the element of the sector it occupies.

ANALYSIS FOR 2011 NUMBERS

Example: In the master bedroom, the annual 2011 number 8 is earth. It flies into this Northwest corner of the house, a metal corner. Since earth produces metal, the number 8 is excellent for this corner based on element analysis.

Example: Look at back door numbers. Here 5 is earth element. It flies into the East – a wood direction. In the cycle of elements wood overcomes earth. So here the 5 is controlled by the sector it occupies. So the danger of the 5 is not as severe here as elsewhere.

Example: Once again above, the bedroom in the Northeast has the number 1 (water) flying into the Northeast (earth). Earth defeats the good water star 1, thus weakening it.

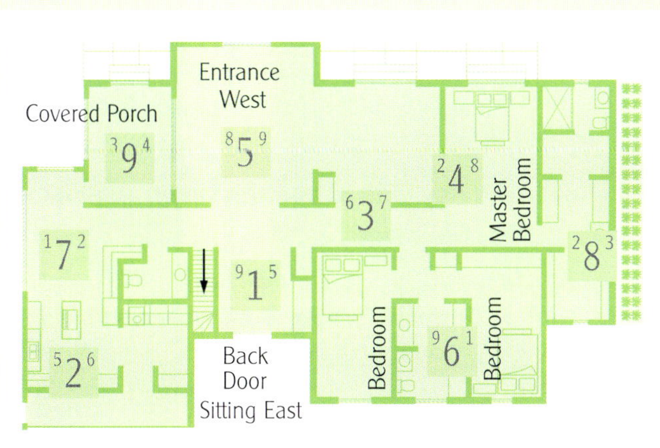

SW	W	NW	
9 (3, 4)	5 (8, 9)	4 (7, 8)	
S: 7 (1, 2)	3 (6, 7)	8 (2, 3)	N
2 (5, 6)	1 (4, 5)	6 (9, 1)	
SE	E	NE	

Lower right number is for 2011.
Lower left is for 2012.

78 Time influences on feng shui

Feng shui has a time dimension that can be investigated using Flying Star annual and monthly charts. The method of investigating the luck of your house or apartment and its different rooms from year to year and from month to month is what gives feng shui practice its **time aspects**. In Hong Kong, feng shui masters are usually kept on a retainer basis by the tycoons so that before the start of each lunar New Year, the feng shui of all their work and residential premises is "updated". In the past, this vital aspect of feng shui practice was seldom referred to and books on feng shui rarely talked about the impact of time on one's feng shui. In recent years however, with feng shui becoming a global household word with demand for its many "secrets" growing, a great deal of feng shui knowledge is being revealed to the general public, including information about the **annual and monthly charts** that can be drawn up to investigate the luck of different houses. This is truly a breakthrough!

SE	S	SW
6	2	4
E: TAI SUI 5 5 YELLOW	7 RABBIT 2011	9 :W
1	3	8
NE	N	NW

SE	S	SW
TAI SUI 5 5 YELLOW	1	3
E: 4	6 DRAGON 2012	8 :W
9	2	7
NE	N	NW

Shown here are the annual Lo Shu charts for 2011 and 2012, with auspicious and afflicted locations.

USING ANNUAL & MONTHLY CHARTS

In the preceding few tips I have referred to the annual star charts for 2011 and 2012 and explained how to read the numbers in conjunction with the trigram charts of houses. These annual charts are presented in the same format as the Lo Shu nine palaces grid. So what an annual chart is, is simply a chart that shows which of the nine numbers rule each of the eight direction sectors in any year or month. By looking at the numbers and knowing their meanings, we will know whether they bring good or bad luck to the sector. Using element analysis we can go deeper in our investigations. It is exactly the same with monthly charts. They look the same as the annual charts. The difference lies only in the placement of the different numbers.

The way the annual and monthly charts are created is based on the ruling Lo Shu number of the year or the month. There are also Lo Shu numbers for the day and hour for those who want to go into greater detail. Ruling Lo Shu numbers for the year, month, day and hour are part of the Chinese Almanac. From this number, charts are created. How? Simply by placing the ruling number in the center of the square and from there, using the flight pattern of the original Lo Shu square, we can fill in all the numbers of the other sectors. **So the key is to obtain the center number of the year or month**. To obtain this crucial number, we can refer to the thousand years HSIA calendar or to the Almanac. **At www.wofs.com**, the annual and monthly charts are written up each month to update readers on the luck of compass sectors in each month – much like a feng shui horoscope.

79 The feng shui horoscope

For those of you who want to know how to cast your own annual and monthly charts, and use these to regularly update the feng shui of your premises, below is the table based on the **HSIA calendar** which should enable you to cast your own feng shui horoscope charts. You can then use the tables of meanings given on pages 65 to 73. These charts give the meanings of all the annual chart numbers combined with the trigram chart numbers. These combinations also apply to monthly chart numbers of each of the sectors. This way you will know the luck of your own home/shop/office in any month. Try it out. **You will be surprised at how accurate it is**. For instance, when the monthly and annual 8 converges in the sector where you have your front door of your shop, you will find sales shooting up. When the 5's converge on the other hand, sales are sure to take a drop. Unless you put remedies into place! Herein lies the great benefit of knowing time dimension feng shui.

SE	S	SW
6	2	4
5	7	9
1	3	8
NE	N	NW

(E on the left, W on the right.)

Example: In Year 2011 the reigning number is 7, so the Lo shu square created for that year is based on 7 being the center number. The other numbers are placed into the different grids using the original Lo shu square, which has 5 in the center as a guide. Try to work out how the 2011 chart is made. See how the next number 8 is placed in the Northwest and then the next number 9 is in the West and so on... this sequence of the numbers being placed from one direction to the next is exactly the same as in the original Lo Shu square above.

YEAR	REIGNING NUMBER
2011	7
2012	6
2013	5
2014	4
2015	3
2016	2
2017	1
2018	9
2019	8
2020	7

YEAR	REIGNING NUMBER
2021	6
2022	5
2023	4
2024	3
2025	2
2026	1
2027	9
2028	8
2029	7
2030	6

The Lo Shu numbers for different years from 2011 to 2030.

80 Monthly feng shui horoscope

Once you have mastered the annual star numbers and learnt how to get the charts for each year, you are ready to move on to the monthly charts. Once again, here you use the reigning Lo Shu numbers to create the charts. These will be the reigning numbers for the different months. Note that we are using the **HSIA** calendar, which is different from the Lunar calendar. So you will see that each year the first month starts on **February 4th**, which is described as the **Lap Chun** – the first day of Spring. Sometimes it starts February 5th but the dates indicating the start of each of the Hsia calendar months are fairly accurate. Using this precious table below enables anyone to create the monthly chart for any month at all for the next thousand years! So I hope you appreciate the value of this chart here.

Once you know the monthly numbers of each sector of the grid chart that represents your home, you will be able to do pretty advanced feng shui work on your interiors. If you find it hard to understand all this at first, **please do persevere**. This is not difficult but you do need to concentrate. This is part of the theory of feng shui science using the compass and the Luo Pan. It is a very powerful formula for fine tuning the feng shui of your home, office and shop and you can use it to find out why you had such good luck in some months and why in certain months so many things seemed to go all wrong.

The vital thing to do is to **apply remedies to overcome the bad numbers** when they fly into each of the sectors. It is in this context that feng shui symbols and cures are so important.

MONTH	START OF MONTH	LO SHU NUMBER IN YEAR OF RAT, RABBIT, HORSE & ROOSTER	LO SHU NUMBER IN YEAR OF DOG, SHEEP DRAGON & OX	LO SHU NUMBER IN YEAR OF TIGER, SNAKE, BOAR, & MONKEY
1	Feb 4th	8	5	2
2	March 6th	7	4	1
3	April 5th	6	3	9
4	May 6th	5	2	8
5	June 6th	4	1	7
6	July 7th	3	9	6
7	August 8th	2	8	5
8	September 8th	1	7	4
9	October 8th	9	6	3
10	November 7th	8	5	2
11	December 7th	7	4	1
12	January 6th	6	3	9

Note: The dates may have a variation of plus or minus one day. The above is the summary of the 10,000 year calendar which should be consulted for more accurate analysis of the luck according to months and years.

81 Overcoming the illness star 2

Looking at your charts, note that the illness star can be quite bad and when they come together in any sector of the house with the numbers 5, they can be deadly. Of these two numbers, 2 brings illness while 5 brings loss, accidents and misfortune. **The deadly 5** is a number to be most feared in time dimension feng shui. It is important at the start of each HSIA calendar year to check where the annual 5 is. In feng shui terminology, this is referred to as the 5 Yellow or "Wu Wang."

In 2010 the 5 Yellow is in the Southwest and in 2011, it flies to the East. This means that these parts of the house will be afflicted with the five yellow star number in 2010 and 2011 respectively. If your front door is located there, you can protect against the five yellow by hanging a 6-rod all-metal windchime. The sound of metal on metal is a very powerful cure. The **windchime** becomes even more powerful when it has 6 rods because 6 is the number of big metal. A 5-rod windchime is also very effective. Also take note that usually, hollow rods are better than solid ones. This enables the chi to move up through the rods, transforming bad energy into good.

Metal windchimes are also excellent for controlling the illness star 2, because 2 is an earth element number. The metal windchime will exhaust the earth energy of the 2. If your bedroom is occupied by the number 2 (the 2 is in the South sector in 2011 and the North sector in 2012) you can also place six metal I-Ching coins near your bed, preferably by the side of the bed.

Windchimes should be hung along the side of the room. They should never be directly above the bed or directly above the doorway, since we do not want to be sleeping under a windchime. Another excellent cure for the 5 Yellow is the **5 Element Pagoda**. Some say this is even more powerful than the windchime as a cure.

Use a windchime that is all-metal, has a coin in the center, 6 hollow rods and a hanging longevity symbol. If used for ovecoming the #2 star, a Wu Lou can be incorporated into the design.

THE 5 YELLOW

This is an even more dangerous star than the illness star and the cure for this can also be the all metal 5 element pagoda. For 2010 and 2011, it is especially beneficial to have the Tree of Life etched on to the pagoda, turning into a good fortune activator as well as a feng shui cure.

82 Subduing the quarrelling star

In time dimension feng shui, the number 3 is said to create aggressive energy. This is the quarrelling star that can lead to misunderstandings, hostility and in extreme cases, court battles. When the **number 3** is doubled in any sector (in that it occurs in the trigram chart and also the annual chart) the afflicted sector will see a surplus of this hostile energy. This is usually the cause behind marital strife and arguments between siblings and members of any household. **When the 3 combines with the 2**, the effect of quarrelling becomes worse and can lead to separations.

To subdue the 3 star, the best is to use silent cures that exhaust the element essence of the number without destroying the growth energy of its intrinsic wood element. Thus **the colour red** used in small quantities can be most effective. Bright lights would be too strong. One of the best cures for the 3/2 are Happiness Buddha images.

Candles floating on water are an ideal cure for subduing the number 3's aggressive nature. Place this on tabletops in sectors, afflicted with the number 3 star numbers. Another excellent cure would be a **painting of red goldfish** done with some metallic paint. This is especially good for countering a 3/2 combination as it uses fire and metal energy to subdue the aggressive nature of this combination. **Do not place moving objects** such as fans, stereo systems and windchimes in sectors of the home afflicted by the # 3 star.

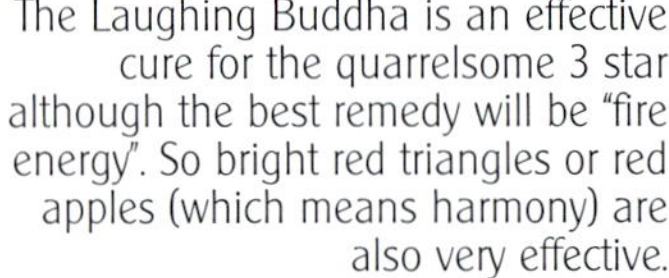

The Laughing Buddha is an effective cure for the quarrelsome 3 star although the best remedy will be "fire energy". So bright red triangles or red apples (which means harmony) are also very effective.

83 Cures for harmful combinations

There are some combinations of numbers (of the trigram number with the annual or monthly number) which can be very harmful. Residents hit by combinations of these numbers will feel the negative effect in the particular month and year when the combination appears. Below are some particularly bad number combinations and what you can do to remedy their ill effects.

Place the suggested cures within the sectors affected by these numbers. Use the grid method to demarcate the sectors of the home that are affected. Usually if these negative energy numbers are near the entrance door or in the bedroom, family room or dining room, their ill effect will be felt more strongly. If they are in toilets & storerooms, they are in effect "imprisoned' so cannot cause so much harm. If they are in the kitchen, the 5/2s, 5/9s and 2/9s will get magnified by the fire energy in the kitchen. In such cases, placing an urn of still water in the kitchen should overcome the ill effects.

2/5 and 5/2: Use windchimes to overcome this very deadly combination. You might need to hang at least six windchimes or use 6 large coins here. Do not have fire energy here (i.e. avoid bright spotlights OR the colour red OR open fire).

5/3 and 3/5: These combinations cause loss in one's finances, leading to severe cash flow problems. It is important to exhaust the 5 with metal energy, but the metal must be silent, so windchimes are unsuitable. Instead, use a painting of a copper mountain. Yin metal is an excellent remedy.

2/7 and 7/2: These combinations are especially harmful to children. An excellent cure is a white porcelain rooster. A sword of coins is also said to be a powerful remedy.

2/3 and 3/2: These are the quarrelsome combinations. They cause backstabbing and legal disputes to flare up. Use still water to cool tempers. A silent red flame will also work.

3/9 and 9/3: Legal disputes take a turn for the worse. The best cure for this is yin water.

5/9 and 9/5: These combinations are to be feared because the 9 magnifies the deadly effects of the 5. So there will be bad luck all round, with danger posed to the eyes and limbs. The best remedy against this combination is using metal windchimes to silence the 5. A gold and red painting can also be effective.

5/5 and 2/2: These are two very critical combinations and extreme danger is always indicated by the double 5, while fatal illness is indicated by the double 2. 6-rod windchimes are a powerful cure. Painting the afflicted room white is another good way to exhaust the harmful star numbers. You can also use metallic bells and 7-metal singing bowls. I have found that a daily dose of the singing bowl's magical harmonics does wonders in overcoming the deadly effects of the 5/5 and 2/2.

5/3 and 3/5: These combinations cause loss in one's finances, leading to severe cash flow problems. It is important to exhaust the 5 with metal energy, but the metal must be silent, so windchimes are unsuitable here. Instead, use a painting of a copper mountain. Yin metal is an excellent remedy.

2/4 and 4/2: These combinations indicate problems involving the in-laws. Use water in an urn to reduce its ill effects.

84 Enhancing with symbols

The Pi Yao is an excellent remedy and enhancer as it pacifies the Grand Duke Jupiter and attracts wealth and good fortune too.

In the same way that negative stars can be remedied and their ill effects diffused, feng shui also recommends the use of symbolic enhancers that can activate the good effects of the good star numbers.

When I first learnt Flying Star and **time dimension feng shui**, I was thrilled by how easy its practice was, despite so many feng shui masters trying to tell me how difficult it was. I discovered that they considered it difficult simply because in the old days, the classical method of explaining Flying Star was made complicated almost on purpose. This was due to the usage of special terms in Chinese when referring to the number combinations, as well as the directions and the years. All the different directions and all the different years had special names, so that unless one learnt these names by heart, it was really confusing to follow the explanations given in the texts.

But once I realized this and broke the secret code of names, so to speak, it really became so easy. This is because the principles of feng shui are so logical and so scientific.

1/1 numbers

Use water features to enhance corners or rooms with this combination. I love those wonderful water turning crystal balls that come in so many different designs. They are simply so auspicious. I have them in the water corners of all my public areas and also during months when the 1/1 appears as month and annual star numbers. The exception is bedrooms. Never put water inside bedrooms.

6/6 numbers

Use metal enhancers such as a gold plated sailing ship, a silver vase or anything else made of metal. 6 is a powerful number that does not really require enhancing but if you are anything like me, you will create a whole harbour of gold ships. This brings many sources of income!

8/8 numbers

The number 8 is a super auspicious number that does not need enhancing, but I have discovered that placing eight crystal balls where the 8 appears brings really great good fortune. It brings harmony and peace. The whole house will be enormously peaceful indeed. Or place eight crystal obelisks to attract power.

I am constantly amazed at **how powerful these symbols** are in enhancing good luck. For me it is like discovering magic. No wonder the whole of China practises symbolic feng shui. If you have visited China, you will find that in every city, town and village, you see symbols like Fu Dogs, Pi Yaos, flowers, motifs and the placement of wealth deities everywhere. In the beginning I was very skeptical indeed, but over the past twenty over years, I have seen it work so many times that I am now persuaded symbols have enormous credence and power. Perhaps it has to do with the energy vibrations that surround these symbols. Maybe when **placed strategically** according to the distribution of luck in the different sectors of the home, they become more effective. You can try placing the symbols in different corners of your living rooms and bedrooms to activate the good numbers and see if your luck improves. Test it out. Don't just take my word for it.

The sailing ship shown here is excellent for bringing in wealth from "the winds and waters". This is an especially good symbol for those in trading businesses. But you should put some "cargo" in your wealth ship in the form of golden coins, ingots or crystals that look like diamonds. You can even roll up real money for your ship to carry in for you!

5

FLYING STAR FENG SHUI

Flying Star is a branch of compass formula feng shui. It uses the facing direction of buildings to determine natal charts that map out the distribution of relationship and wealth luck from one cycle of time to the next. These natal charts reveal the map luck of buildings over twenty year time periods. Like the trigram chart, these highly detailed charts can also incorporate the **month and year numbers** to expand the investigation, thereby offering clues on how to improve the feng shui of your interiors from year to year, and from month to month. But more than the trigram charts, these charts offer a map for capturing the wealth, relationship and health luck by working on the rooms inside the house to directly benefit residents. This is done by identifying, then activating the auspicious mountain and water stars of the chart wherever they occur.

All buildings should visually look "new" to attract the good energy of the current period of 8. Better still they should be renovated to re-energise their "spirit" and "energy" to benefit residents.

85 Flying star natal charts

Flying star charts are sometimes referred to as nine palaces charts. These charts map out the "luck" of yang buildings – revealing lucky and unlucky areas via the numbers that get placed in each of the nine grids. These are known as the **nine palaces** of the home. The numbers themselves are known as stars, so flying stars mean flying numbers. And because these numbers move in accordance with compass directions and time periods, they are known as flying stars. Hence, the name of this system is Flying Star feng shui.

Take the **facing direction** standing at the main door entrance and using a compass. Here it is clear that the house facing direction is the same as as the main door facing direction. So there is no confusion. When the two directions are not the same, then it is the house facing direction that will determine the natal chart of the house. Please remember this fine point when determining your chart. Also note that the facing direction is often the direction that faces the road, an open field or has the most spectacular view.

This method is more complex, more detailed and more comprehensive than the Trigram method explained in the previous chapter. Flying Star feng shui divides time into 20-year periods and each period has a designated period number. We are currently in the **Period of 8**, which started **Feb 4th 2004 and ends Feb 4th 2024**. All houses and buildings built, completed or renovated inside this twenty year period are referred to as Period of 8 houses and Period of 8 natal charts represent maps of luck sectors of such houses.

It is likely that even if your house or apartment was built before 2004 and thus could be a Period 6 or 7 building, if some sort of renovation or repainting was done to your apartment building, this could have transformed it into a Period 8 building. At the same time, although Period 8 comes to an end on Feb 4th 2024, for purposes of analysis, the natal chart of your home continues to be the Period 8 chart **UNLESS you do major renovations**. However the meanings of some of the numbers change when the period changes.

Flying Star natal charts used throughout this book as examples in the analyses of home interiors are Period 8 charts. To identify the chart that applies to your house or apartment building, use a compass, stand directly in front of your house and read its facing direction. This tells you which of the 16 possible charts applies to your house.

APARTMENT DWELLERS TAKE NOTE:
Those living in apartments should determine the facing direction of their whole building and then use the relevant natal chart to analyze their apartment. Always use a good compass to identify the directions and sectors.

86 The age of buildings

FLYING STAR natal charts are created according to the **facing direction** and the **age** of the building under investigation. These charts reveal the luck maps of the building based on their respective flying star numbers. In any period there are 16 different natal charts. In every chart there are nine grids inside each of which are at least three numbers. The chart is often referred to as the **nine palaces** chart because it demarcates space into nine sectors exactly like the Lo Shu square. Then, based on the numbers in each little grid, one can read the luck of the corresponding sector of the building, and also the wealth and relationship luck indications of the different sectors of the house over a twenty year period.

Formula feng shui is based on the premise that the luck of the interior spaces of buildings is never static but instead waxes and wanes in accordance with the passage of time. Thus Flying Star feng shui takes account of the age of buildings and the changing energy over periods of time. A full era of time takes 180 years, and this comprises three cycles lasting 60 years each – the **Lower, Middle and Upper cycle**. Each of these cycles is further divided into 20-year periods and each Period is ruled by a dominant number known as the reigning number of that period. We are presently living through the Period of 8.

While this book does not teach you Flying Star in an academic way, you will find there is more than enough information here to enable you to design excellent feng shui for your interiors, the kind of feng shui that will enable you to **directly activate good fortune in the wealth and relationship sectors** of your home using the principles of Flying Star feng shui. With the Flying Star chart, anyone can identify the luckiest part of the home, and even extend this to identifying the luckiest part of each room!

Learning Flying Star requires basic knowledge of the Lo Shu square and its sequence of numbers. But this may not be sufficient to draw up the charts. There are **controversial issues in Flying Star** feng shui, and not all professional practitioners are in consensus on these issues. Usually, unless you have undergone a proper course of study in Flying Star feng shui, it is possible you will feel some confusion and frustration when trying to use these charts. Professional consultants tend to be rather dogmatic (secretive) in their approach to feng shui, so it is useful for readers to be aware of the differences in approach adopted by different practitioners. Thus do note that:

- Not all experts are in agreement as to what constitutes the **Period of a building**. Some say it is when a building is completely built. Others say it is when the building is renovated. They also cannot agree on the precise definition of the word renovation. Other practitioners stubbornly maintain it is when the last residents moved in. The house period is a vital issue, since this is the basis of the natal chart.
- Not all experts are in agreement on how one should determine the **facing direction**. Some say it is where the house faces the road – the place of maximum chi, others where it faces the most unencumbered view and still others, where the main door faces. This matter requires judgement and on-site investigation.
- Not all experts agree on the **prescribed cures for** flying star afflictions. A small minority stubbornly maintain that there are simply no cures other than to move out of afflicted spaces. Many others use the powerful practice of symbolic feng shui and 5 element theory to prescribe cures for flying star afflictions with great success.

87 Identifying your flying star chart

How do you go about determining your own flying star chart? In this book, I am presenting the complete set of flying star charts that apply to Period 8 houses, buildings and apartments.

To be able to analyze the feng shui luck map of your home, you will need to know how to select the chart that applies to your house. To do this, you will need to determine the following two things about your house or building.

AGE OF YOUR BUILDING:

When was your house or building built? When was it last renovated? This determines the Period of the building. Since Period 7 started in 1984, I am assuming most readers homes will belong to this period, as I am assuming many people will have renovated their home at least once in the last eighteen years. If these charts do not apply to your home, you will need to get my FLYING STAR FENG SHUI book to learn how to construct your own natal chart. By and large, however, I am confident that the majority of home dwellers are living in Period 7 homes.

FACING DIRECTION OF YOUR BUILDING:

How do you determine this? First invest in a good compass that contains the three sub directions of each of the eight main directions. (you can invest in such a compass from the world of feng shui store at Midvalley, KL Plaza or Subang Parade in Kuala Lumpur, Malaysia or via the **www.wofs.com** website. Next, consider the facing direction by determining where the building is facing, as a whole. Look at the building from all directions.

MAIN ROAD - PLACE OF MOST YANG ENERGY

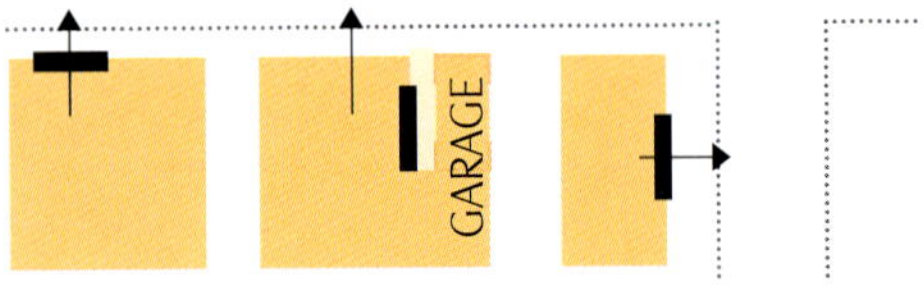

GARAGE

Consider the source of the most "yang" energy. **This is usually the main road**. Consider most importantly where the main door is facing and use this as the orientation UNLESS the main door is facing a garage or a wall completely away from the main road. The center house in the mini sketches shown below has a door which faces the garage, but the orientation of this house is taken to be where the arrow is pointing, and this is considered the facing direction of the house.

Usually for **link houses**, it is not a problem getting the facing direction of the house, but for apartment buildings and complex modular bungalows, where there is more than one entrance, it can be tricky. Look for the direction that faces the road or the view and use this as the facing direction of the building or of your house. If in doubt, analyze a couple of charts to see which one best describes the present luck of your house. Remember that for apartments, you need to get the facing direction of the whole building to determine the chart that applies to your apartment. It is the same with office buildings.

Once you have determined the facing direction of your house, you may find that this is not the same as the facing direction of your main entrance into the house. This is where a certain amount of judgement will have to come in, since you must be the one to judge which direction you should use as the facing direction.

A good quality compass is essential in getting your feng shui right.

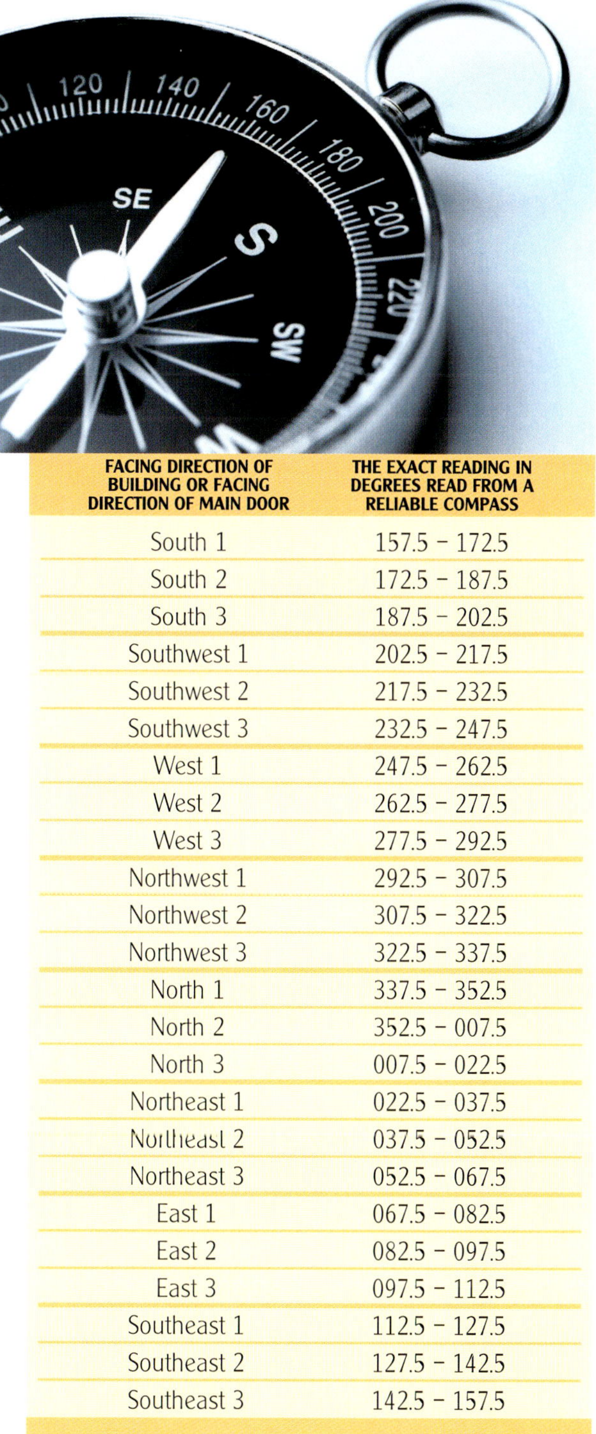

FACING DIRECTION OF BUILDING OR FACING DIRECTION OF MAIN DOOR	THE EXACT READING IN DEGREES READ FROM A RELIABLE COMPASS
South 1	157.5 - 172.5
South 2	172.5 - 187.5
South 3	187.5 - 202.5
Southwest 1	202.5 - 217.5
Southwest 2	217.5 - 232.5
Southwest 3	232.5 - 247.5
West 1	247.5 - 262.5
West 2	262.5 - 277.5
West 3	277.5 - 292.5
Northwest 1	292.5 - 307.5
Northwest 2	307.5 - 322.5
Northwest 3	322.5 - 337.5
North 1	337.5 - 352.5
North 2	352.5 - 007.5
North 3	007.5 - 022.5
Northeast 1	022.5 - 037.5
Northeast 2	037.5 - 052.5
Northeast 3	052.5 - 067.5
East 1	067.5 - 082.5
East 2	082.5 - 097.5
East 3	097.5 - 112.5
Southeast 1	112.5 - 127.5
Southeast 2	127.5 - 142.5
Southeast 3	142.5 - 157.5

88 The 24 mountains of directions

The 24 Mountains is the name given to the 24 directions used to describe directions in Flying Star feng shui. Each of the 8 main directions is subdivided into three sub-directions. So what we have are 3 times 8 directions, making 24 sub-directions in all. Thus South is South 1, South 2 and South 3. And West is West 1, West 2 and West 3 and so on. **Each sub-direction occupies 15 degrees of the compass**. To help you determine your facing direction and find the chart that applies to your house, refer to the table of 24 directions. Look for the direction that corresponds to the facing direction of your house. If yours is a Period 8 building, the Flying Star chart that maps out the luck of your house can be found in this chapter, and you can use your house chart to analyze the feng shui of your home, then design your interiors to benefit from maximum wealth and relationship luck.

If you live in an apartment, you should consider the facing direction of the whole apartment building and use this to identify the relevant natal chart. Do not forget to check when the building was built or last renovated.

Then using the same natal chart, superimpose onto your apartment unit layout plan to undertake the analysis of your apartment. You can also identify where your apartment is located in the buildings' Lo Shu chart. This gives you a general idea of the luck of your apartment, since you can see instantly if the numbers in that grid are auspicious or not. This is one sure way of identifying the lucky apartments in any apartment block building.

89 Getting the most from the charts

What you want to get from these charts is How To Use Flying Star To Improve Your Own Feng Shui. So what you really want to know is,

i) which stars stand for wealth and which ones stand for relationship luck.

ii) what are the lucky and unlucky numbers.

iii) how they can be enhanced or remedied. So first you will need to familiarize yourself with a typical chart.

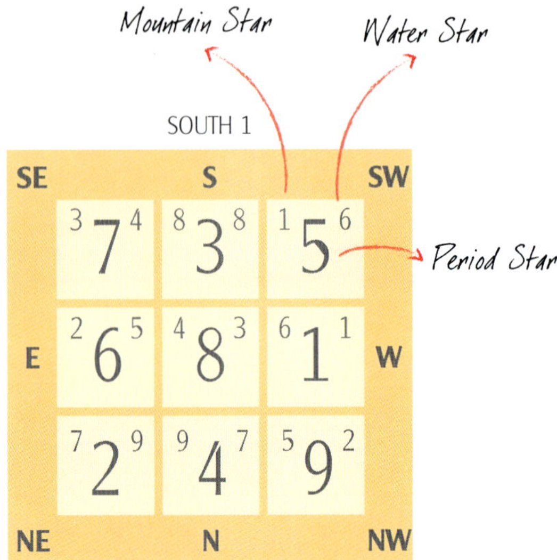

Take note as follows:

1. The **combinations of all the numbers** inside each grid are important. The little numbers on the left and right of the big central number are the mountain stars (on the left) and the water stars (on the right). These numbers indicate relationship and wealth luck respectively. These are the important star numbers to take note of, so look out for them.

2. The interpretation of charts also takes account of how annual numbers impact on the numbers of the **water star and mountain star**, and on the **period star.** The period star is the big number in the center.

3. **Good water star** numbers are activated by the **presence of water**. If wealth is what you want, look for where the water star 8 is and then build or buy a beautiful water feature to place there. Invest in one of those really beautiful water features that allow you to have fish, moving water and plants. This is because what you want is *yang water*.

4. **Good mountain star** numbers are activated with **earth element objects**. If romance is what you want or if you wish to strengthen your marriage OR if your husband is in politics and you want to ensure continued support for him, then look for the mountain star 8 in your home and in that corner or room, place a large natural crystal. Or invest in a large porcelain figurine or stone sculpture OR hang a painting or picture of a mountain range. This will vastly improve your relationship luck as well as your health. The best energizers are large natural crystals in their original state.

5. Never forget to assess the impact of the **month and year star numbers**. These exert their influence on the sectors, and when there is a concentration of BAD numbers on a particular month, any negative effect is considerably empowered. Use the feng shui horoscope to factor in the time effects of the month and year numbers on the map luck of your house.

6. Finally, note that when **bad stars or good stars combine**, they usually require a catalyst - an external feature or structure - to trigger an effect. Like karma ripening at a particular moment in time. Thus external forms and structures combine with flying star to speed up good and bad effects. Symbolic decorative pieces have a vital triggering effect on your luck. When a bad annual star flies into a sector with unlucky natal chart numbers, bad luck gets triggered much faster if a poison arrow is also hurting the sector.

90 Interpreting flying star charts

Flying Star feng shui charts are easy to understand once you know the meanings of the lucky and unlucky numbers. Furthermore, by studying the numbers of the *water and mountain* stars in the particular chart that applies to your house or apartment, you will be able to practise awesomely potent feng shui. For instance, you can determine which rooms have wealth luck and which have loss luck. You can then energize or suppress accordingly using the cures and energizers recommended. Flying Star charts reveal good and bad sectors. The auspicious numbers in any Flying Star chart are the white numbers 1, 6 and 8, with 8 being the most auspicious. In simple flying star feng shui, what you need is to take note of are the good and bad numbers in the charts.

MEANINGS OF THE NUMBERS

i) The danger numbers to fear are **5 and 2** because these two numbers are described as the sickness numbers. Wherever they appear in any chart, residents who stay or sleep in those sectors will suffer ill luck, get sick or suffer misfortune.

ii) The **number 3** is a hostile number and it brings misunderstandings quarrels, and fighting. If the 3 hits your room, you could be slammed with a law suit.

iii) The **number 4** is lucky for romance and brings literary luck in Period 7 but will turn unlucky in Period 8. It must not be too near water as this can lead to sex scandals.

iv) The **number 9** is a magnifying number and has the power to magnify the ill effects of 5 and 2. It is to be feared when it occurs with these two numbers. But on its own it is a very good number encompassing the completeness of heaven & earth.

v) The **number 7** is lucky in this period but turns dangerous and bloody in the next period, bringing burglary, robbery and fatal accidents.

vi) The **numbers 1, 6 and 8** are the most auspicious numbers but it is the number 8 that is truly auspicious. The energy of 6 is weak and needs to be activated.

MOUNTAIN AND WATER STARS

You must differentiate between the mountain star and the water star. The water star is the facing star and the mountain star is the sitting star. These two stars are the vital luck indicators of the Flying Star chart. Their numbers are very indicative of the luck of the sectors they occupy.

WATER STAR: The water star is placed on the right side of the Period number. This little number in each of the nine little grids of the chart will indicate if the space in that grid has WEALTH chi. If the number is 8 it indicates maximum wealth luck. If it is 5 or 2, it indicates bad luck with money. So looking for the 8 water star is the key to wealth. When you find your water star 8, activate it with a gurgling water feature – it is as simple as that!

MOUNTAIN STAR: The mountain star is usually placed on the left side of the period number. This little number here indicates relationship and health luck. If the number is 8, it suggests excellent relationship luck, which gets activated if there is mountain nearby. Inside the house, this means placing a large natural crystal a feature wall or special boulder where the mountain star 8 occurs.

91 Overcoming afflictions

Flying Star charts are excellent for highlighting afflicted energy in the different corners of your apartment or house. So it is the **BEST method for preventing bad luck**. Afflictions manifest as illness, loss, failure and the breakup of relationships. These are based on the intangible forces of time and they cause health as well as material, physical and financial problems. Feng shui involves identifying these afflictions and protecting against their occurrence. Remedies require use of the five-element theory. Thus special symbols that symbolize water, fire, wood, earth and metal can be used with great potency to disarm the 5/2s, 5/9s and 3/2s of negative Flying Star number combinations. These symbols include objects such as windchimes, longevity symbols, brass mirrors, crystals, candles, plants, water, protector images, cranes, tortoises and so forth.

FIVE ELEMENT PAGODA WITH TREE OF LIFE

This special cure has been designed to control the number 5 or 2 star which has flown into Wood sectors such as the Southeast or the East. The Tree of Life on the five element pagoda corrects the balance needed when metal is placed as a cure in these two wood sectors.

EXAMPLE:

The illustrations on the page overleaf shows a Flying Star Chart superimposed onto the layout plan of this two level townhouse. This is a **Period of 8 house** facing **North 2/3**. This chart reveals six afflicted sectors (shaded areas) and the chart repeats itself on both levels.

Let's start by analysing the chart of the lower level. Here the main door is located in the North, which suffers from the 7/9 combination. The number 7 Mountain star suggests **cheating in relationships** which can manifest in the form of third party affairs for either husband or wife. It could also indicate theft from a business associate if the family is involved in business. Since this is the main door, it is vital that the 7 be controlled. The Number 7 star is a metal star, and is thus exhausted by the element of water. If a pond were to be built here by the entrance, it will activate the future prosperity of the Water 9 star and effectively drown the number 7 star.

Upstairs, the master bedroom is also equally afflicted by the 5/2 combination. These two stars are considered the most deadly of all the flying star combinations for it spells loss and illness. The 5 Mountain star brings **loss in relationships** and the 2 Water Star brings illness that cause **financial misfortune**. Both the 5 and 2 are earth stars, and it is very lucky that these two stars are located in the East which is ruled by the wood element, and hence the potential for these stars to cause problems are weakened to some degree. To effectively control these two stars, the element of metal (which exhausts earth) can be used. Here I would advise placing the **5 Element Pagoda** and a **metal windchime** in the East sector to suppress both these stars.

PLAN OF TOWNHOUSE FACING N 2/3

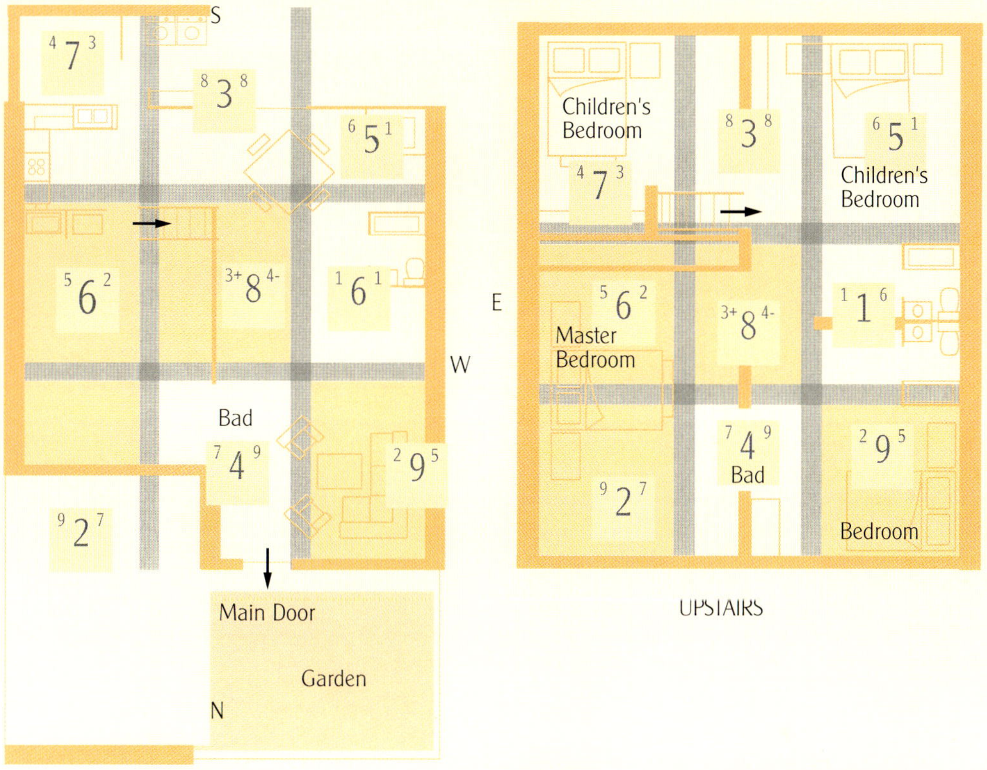

DOWNSTAIRS

UPSTAIRS

The "afflicted" sectors are shown shaded a darker shade. These parts of the home have troublesome stars which need to be remedied so that its ill effects do not affect the residents of the home.

AFFLICTED AREAS ARE SHOWN SHADED

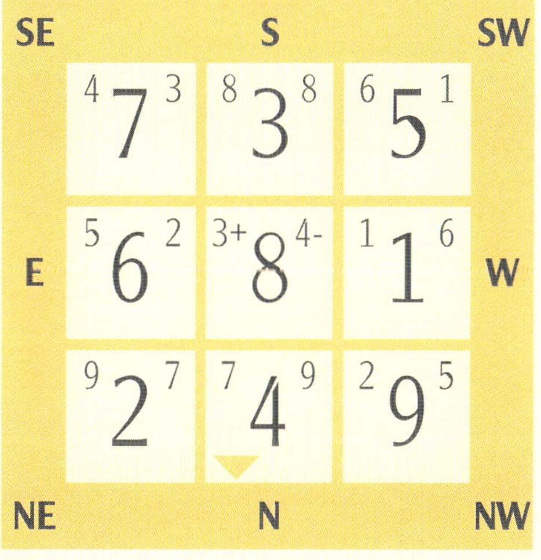

FLYING STAR CHART OF A N2/3 HOME

92 Mapping the luck of an apartment

When you use Flying Star feng shui to analyse the luck sectors of apartments, note that the chart to use is the one that coincides with the **facing direction of the whole building**, and NOT the entrance to the apartment. Once you have determined the chart that applies to your building, you then superimpose it onto the apartment layout plan according to the compass directions. This uses the application of small tai chi.

Shown overleaf is an apartment building which faces West-1. Hence the chart for West-1 is used and superimposed onto the layout of the apartment. Notice that this apartment has **three auspicious areas** – the master bedroom, the centre of the apartment and the main door foyer. These three sectors enjoy favourable stars, which are the 1, 6 and 8 stars.

The main door of the apartment faces North, and this sector has the 1/6 combination. 1/6 brings excellent relationship and financial luck! The number 6 star is metal star and is activated with the presence of moving metal. Thus this sector benefits from **metal windchimes**. The 1/6 combination also brings peach blossom luck – which brings many suitors to young residents who are seeking marriage.

The centre of this apartment has all **three white stars – 681**. This is exceptionally fortunate and sets the tone for the overall energy of this apartment. Residents enjoy good financial gains from the Water star 1and the Mountain star 6 brings divine luck for in relationships in the family and with others. Unfortunately, there is also a small little toilet in the centre of the apartment, and hence this toilet should be kept closed at all times. A small water feature can be installed here to activate the Water 1 star.

SIX TIER WATERFALL WITH BIRDS

This water feature is an excellent choice for activating water stars 1 and 8 whenever they are located in Earth sectors such as the Centre, Southwest or Northeast of a home. In the element cycle, both water and earth clash, and hence it is important to incorporate the presence of Earth in these water features so that balance is achieved. Here, this waterfall simulates the presence of a mountain (big earth), and hence, earth and water work harmoniously together to create wealth.

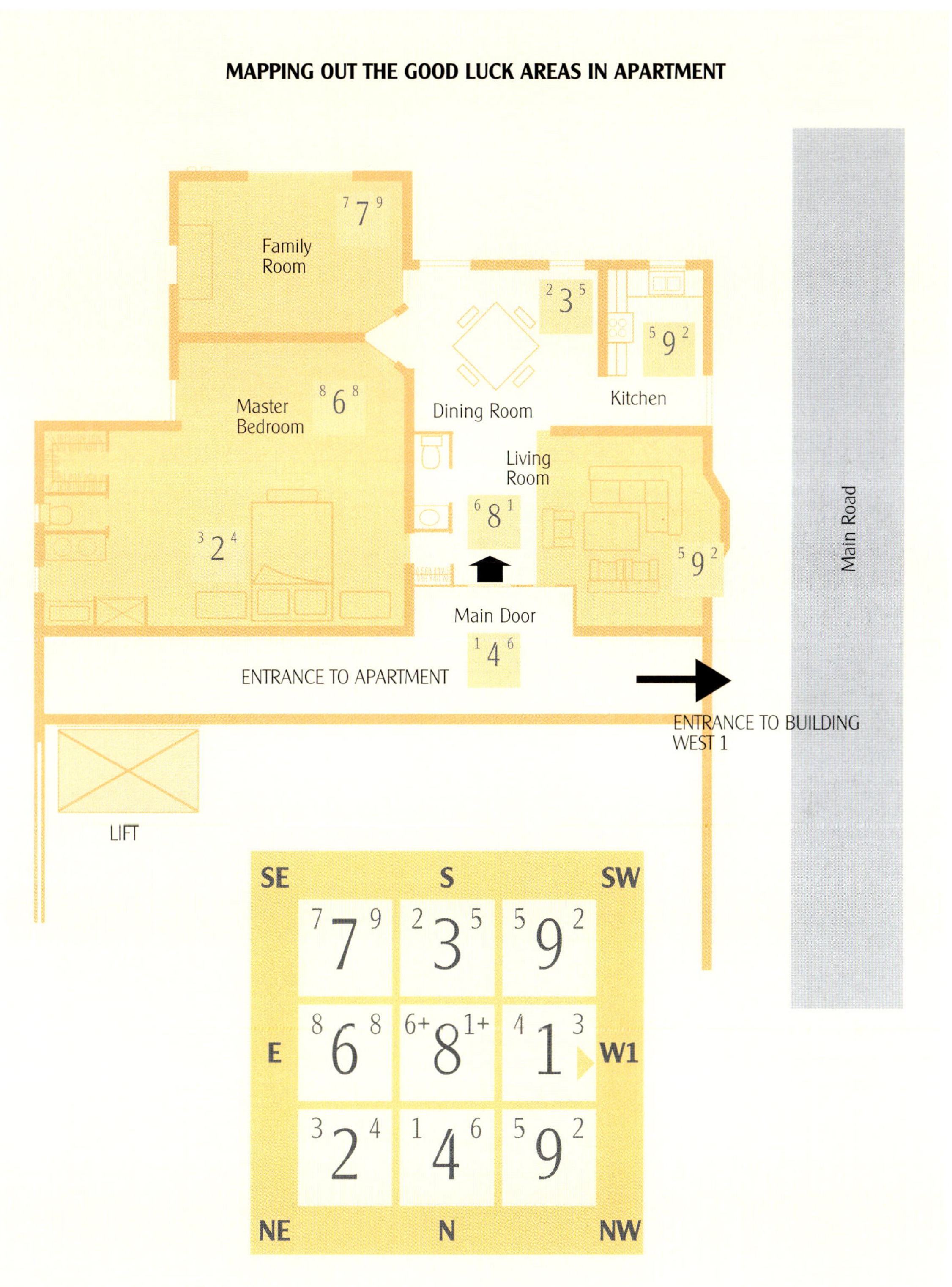
MAPPING OUT THE GOOD LUCK AREAS IN APARTMENT
7 7 9
Family Room
2 3 5
5 9 2
Kitchen
Dining Room
8 6 8
Master Bedroom
Living Room
6 8 1
3 2 4
5 9 2
Main Door
1 4 6
ENTRANCE TO APARTMENT
ENTRANCE TO BUILDING WEST 1
Main Road
LIFT
SE
S
SW
7 7 9
2 3 5
5 9 2
E
8 6 8
6+ 8 1+
4 1 3
W1
3 2 4
1 4 6
5 9 2
NE
N
NW

93 Mountain & Water Star Combinations

MOUNTAIN STAR	WATER STAR	INDICATED OUTCOMES	ENHANCERS TO TRIGGER GOOD LUCK OR SUPPRESS BAD LUCK COMBINATIONS
1	2	Marriage problems caused by dominating women. A water number as mountain star is a sign of danger similar to *mountain falling into water* - a bad sign indeed.	Use plants to exhaust the bad water star and fire energy to strengthen the earth element of the good mountain star. Here the need is to strengthen relationships & guard against losses.
2	1	The matriarch is too strong leading to marital problems.	Use metal to exhaust the earth. Windchimes. Place water feature here.
1	3	Wealth and fame luck are indicated, but law suits and gossip causes aggravation.	Use water plants to enhance and yin water to diffuse misunderstandings caused by afflicted water star.
3	1	Prosperity luck is so good, but if you don't have the karma/luck to live here, you will change residence.	Plant a bamboo grove in front of the house to strengthen your luck. Also place water to activate the water star.
1	4	Political luck. Media and publicity luck. Romance luck for women.	Use slow moving water but not too much. Plants are also good.
4	1	Romance luck, but too much water leads to sex scandals. Affairs leading to unhappiness and breakup of family. Literary success.	Use plants to strengthen wood element of mountain star and small amount of water to activate the water star for prosperity.
1	5	Health problems dealing with the womb and kidney. Food poisoning.	Use windchime to overcome the 5 and exhaust the 1 mountain star.
5	1	Hearing problems and sex related illness.	Use windchime to overcome these afflictions.
1	6	Auspicious for second son. Scholastic success. Intelligence with great commercial skills.	Enhance with metal, which can be windchimes, coins, bells, and auspicious symbols.
6	1	Peach blossom luck. Financial luck and high achievers in the family.	Enhance with metal, which can be windchimes, coins, bells, and auspicious symbols.
1	7	Good money luck in period of 7 only, in period of 8 this combination means loss of wealth.	Enhance with crystals or gem tree. The best enhancer would be citrines or crystals and lights.
7	1	Danger of burglary.	Use water feature.
1	8	Excellent wealth and prosperity luck.	Enhance with water feature to activate water star 8.
8	1	Excellent and auspicious luck. Money and family luck.	Enhance with boulder and crystals to enhance relationship luck.
1	9	Good combination but can turn bad when 5 flies in.	Do not enhance. When 5 flies in, use windchimes.
9	1	Some good luck but danger of heart problems and sex diseases. Constant changing of jobs.	Do not disturb, but when 5 flies in as annual star, use windchimes.
2	3	Arguments and misunderstandings of the most severe kind. Back stabbing, hatred, legal disputes.	Use yin water to cool tempers. Use red and gold to control. ie. Golden Red Dragon.

94 Mountain & Water Star Combinations

MOUNTAIN STAR	WATER STAR	INDICATED OUTCOMES	ENHANCERS TO TRIGGER GOOD LUCK OR SUPPRESS BAD LUCK COMBINATIONS
3	2	Dangerous for those in politics; Problems with matriarch. Females afflicted. Best to avoid this room.	Some Masters recommend gold and fire. Also still water. Ksitigarbha Fireball or Red Mandara.
2	4	Wives and mothers-in-law quarrel and fight. Disharmony in love.	Use water to overcome mountain star 2 and plants to enhance 4.
4	2	Illness of internal organs. Husband has affairs. Mother-in-law problems.	Use water to reduce stress.
2	5	Extremely dangerous to health. A situation of total loss financially. A catastrophe. A most dangerous combination and when annual 5 flies in, anyone staying here will suddenly have accident or develop terminal illness.	Use windchime (plenty) or any moving metallic object like clocks, fans, and coins. Metal sound is powerful to overcome this combination. Beware do NOT have fire or bright spotlights as this can lead to bankruptcy and even death.
5	2	Misfortunes and extreme bad luck. Illness may be fatal. Be very wary.	Use windchime etc as above. Better to move out of this room.
2	6	Very easy life of ease and leisure. This auspicious combination is spoilt if a 5-rod windchime is placed here. The trinity (tien ti ren) gets activated in a negative way.	Do not spoil the luck here with windchimes. Said to attract earth spirits! Activate the water star with water, which also suppresses the 2 mountain star.
6	2	Great affluence and everything successful.	Place a boulder to strengthen the mountain star.
2	7	Luck of children is bad. Problems conceiving children.	Use water. When 9 enters as annual star, place a large urn of water or there could be a fire. Blue Elephant is an exellent cure.
7	2	Money luck dissipates. Children luck is dimmed.	Use windchimes to exhaust and water to suppress the 7 mountain star. Blue Rhinocerous is an excellent cure.
2	8	Richness and wealth but there is ill health. This can be remedied. Excellent water star.	Use water to overcome bad health star and simultaneously activate the 8 water star.
8	2	Mountain star 8 brings relationship luck. But water star 2 brings loss.	Use mountain principle, so strengthen mountain and weaken water.
2	9	Peach blossom luck for women. Romance does not last. Nothing succeeds unless remedied.	Use water plants to disarm bad mountain star and balance effect of 9 water star.
9	2	Problems with children, but good relationship luck.	Better to do nothing. Use metal to control the 2 water star.
3	4	Danger of mental instability. Mature women get stressed. Theft.	Use bright lights to exhaust the wood element. Be wary of excesses.
4	3	Emotional stress due to relationship problems. Stress.	Use red to overcome stress but not naked flames.

95 Mountain & Water Star Combinations

MOUNTAIN STAR	WATER STAR	INDICATED OUTCOMES OF THE COMBINATION IN PERIODS 7 AND 8	ENHANCERS TO TRIGGER GOOD LUCK OR SUPPRESS BAD LUCK COMBINATIONS
3	5	Loss of wealth. Severe cash flow problems. If bedroom is here, financial loss is severe. If kitchen is here, sickness is inevitable.	Exhaust the 5 with metal. but not with windchimes or bells. Use copper mountain painting. Better not to stay in this part of the house.
5	3	Money troubles. Disputes. Bad business luck. Bad for sons.	Use yin water to disarm the mountain star 5 and control the 3 water star.
3	6	Period of slow growth. Limbs have problems. Danger of accidents.	Use yin water.
6	3	Unexpected friendships. Danger of betrayal. Danger of car accidents.	Balance with real crystal gemstones.
3	7	You will get robbed or burgled. Violence.	Use yin water to overcome the effect of this dangerous combination. Place Laughing Buddha here to disarm.
7	3	Grave danger of injury to limbs. Be careful. Also car accidents and theft.	Use yin water. Place Laughing Buddha here to disarm.
3	8	Not good for children under 12 years. Homosexuality.	Use bright lights to cure the 3, but activate water star 8 with water.
8	3	Move children under 12 away from this sector or accidents happen.	Activate mountain star 8 with big crystal or wall or boulder.
4	5	Prone to sexually transmitted diseases. Breast cancer. Bad skin.	Control the 5 with windchimes and other metal. Combination is bad.
5	4	Skin diseases and severe illness.	Use water/mountain and windchimes.
4	6	Bad luck for women who will bear heavy burden.	Strengthen earth element. Use water to activate water star.
6	4	Unexpected windfall for women of the family and excellent romance.	Enhance with windchime and crystals. Activate with dragon image.
4	7	Bad luck in love. Will get cheated by opposite sex. Miscarriage.	Use yang water as remedy for this combination. Paint walls blue.
7	4	Taken for a ride by someone of the opposite sex. Cheated as well.	Use yang water. Install lights to remedy danger of being cheated.
4	8	Bad for very young children, but water star 8 here brings prosperity.	Use lights to combat effect on children and activate water star with water.
8	4	Overpowering matriarch. Love life of younger generation will suffer from the wiles of the mother.	Use fire, or red to overcome. Also activate mountain star 8 with boulder or crystal. Activate with dragon image.
4	9	A time for preparation. Good for sons who excel at school. Bad for daughters. Danger of fire.	Use plants. Also goldfish. Activate with crystal globe and dragon image.
9	4	Good luck for those starting new business.	Use water to enhance. Add goldfish and image of dragon.
5	7	Problems caused by excessive gossiping. Danger of poisoning or anything to do with the mouth.	Use water.
7	5	Mouth related problems. Arguments leading to emotional stress	Use water. Also use plants to combat the 5 water star.

96 Mountain & Water Star Combinations

MOUNTAIN STAR	WATER STAR	INDICATED OUTCOMES OF THE COMBINATION IN PERIODS 7 AND 8	ENHANCERS TO TRIGGER GOOD LUCK OR SUPPRESS BAD LUCK COMBINATIONS
5	8	Problems related to the limbs, joints and bones of the body. Danger of paralysis. It is necessary to be careful of rough sports. Emotional problems. But water star 8 is here.	Use yin water to pacify. The water star here is auspicious and must be activated. So water is the best feature here.
8	5	There is danger of paralysis and illness of a serious nature. But the mountain star 8 here is auspicious.	Strengthen the mountain star 8 with large natural crystal but also hang windchime here to fight the 5 yellow.
5	9	Bad luck and tempers. Excessive mental disorder or stress - there is unhappiness and dissatisfaction.	Use windchime here to combat the strengthening of the 5 yellow by the 9. Water/mountain theory.
9	5	Very bad indications of health and also for loss of wealth through gambling. Possible problems with eyes and stubborn people.	Use windchimes, as this is the best cure for this combination of numbers. Always beware of the 5/9 and 9/5 combinations.
6	7	Sword fighting killing breath. A case of double metal clashing – daughter and father fight. Daughter causes loss of face and honour.	Use yin water to control. Important to disarm the water star with fire energy. Bright lights are a good idea here.
7	6	Jealousy and constant arguments. Father and daughter have serious arguments.	Use yin water to control. Important to disarm the water star with fire energy. Bright lights are a good idea here.
6	8	Wealth, popularity, prosperity. Great richness. Probably the best combination in flying star technique. Water star 8 is most auspicious.	Enhance with water and make sure you have an entrance or window in that sector to invite in the prosperity.
8	6	A great combination, which holds the promise of good relationship luck, popularity and recognition.	Enhance the mountains star with a large boulder or sculpture. Very auspicious indeed.
6	9	Fire at heaven's gate. Arguments and danger of fire. Must not have kitchen here or there will be fire.	Look for a wide mouth container and fill with water - to reduce danger of fire causing wealth loss.
9	6	Same as above. Danger to family Patriarch who must not stay here.	Same cure to reduce danger of spoilt reputation and loss of popularity.
7	9	Extreme problems during period of 8. All troubles caused through excessive vulnerability to sexual advances. Danger of fire hazards.	Use water or earth (big boulders) to press down on the bad luck. A very dangerous combination.
9	7	Problems arise from extreme flirtatious tendency. Fire is a danger.	Use yin water to control both the 7 and 9.
8	9	Joyous and happy. Good indication for marriage to those who stay here.	No need to activate any more, but if you want marriage, display a double happiness image.
9	8	Excellent indication of happiness occasion. Excellent for marital bliss.	No need to activate further.

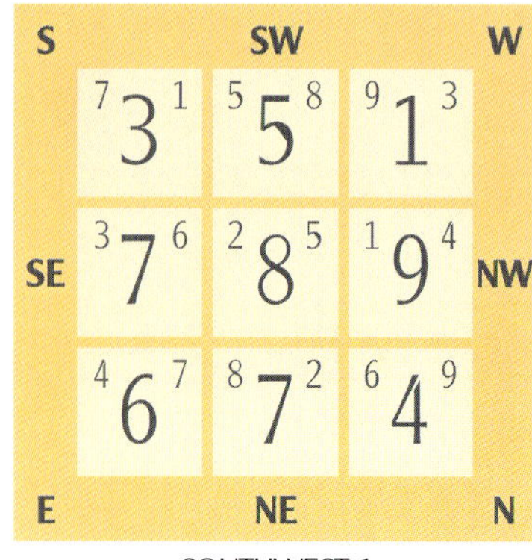

SOUTHWEST 1

97 Period of 8 house facing Southwest

Houses that face **Southwest** 1, 2 or 3 have excellent sectors. You will discover that the difference between the two charts facing Southwest is that in varying the facing direction by just 15 degrees, you can transform your house from a Southwest 1 to a Southwest 2/3 house and vice versa. This has the effect of flipping the lucky stars from front to back and back to front! In this case, both the front and back sectors have either the Mountain or Water 8 stars making both sectors very auspicious.

Let's analyse this floor plan with these both charts and see which chart provides the best energy distribution for this house. This house faces Southwest-1. The **water 8 star** is at the main entrance, bringing excellent financial luck to the residents here. But the **mountain 5 star** brings loss, so to kill off the evil influence of this star, a pond can be dug by the entrance and this effectively "drowns" the number 5 star. The living room in the Southeast has the 3/6 combination. The water 6 star is auspicious but relationships can suffer due to the quarrelsome wood 3 mountain star. Hence, **metal windchimes** here is a good solution to activate the 6 and reduce the power of the 3. In the Master bedroom, the 6/9 combination causes the "fire at heaven's gate" formation and is cured using **yin water**. Water is never a good solution for the bedroom; hence **an urn of still water** can be placed in the North sector of the garden just outside the bedroom instead.

Let's see if the energy distribution improves should the facing direction of the house be tilted slightly to face Southwest 2/3. The main entrance now enjoys the auspicious mountain 8 star. The master bedroom then has the 7/1 combination. Here in the master bedroom, the water 1 star is excellent and brings prosperity to the occupants. The 7 Mountain star however, brings domestic violence; this can easily be remedied with the use of a symbolic cure. A **Blue Elephant** or **Blue Rhinoceros** in the North can be placed to counter the 7 star in the bedroom. Outside the bedroom in the garden, a pond can be dug to activate the number 1 water star and drown the 7 star. Just by doing this, this master bedroom enjoys excellent prosperity luck for the period of 8.

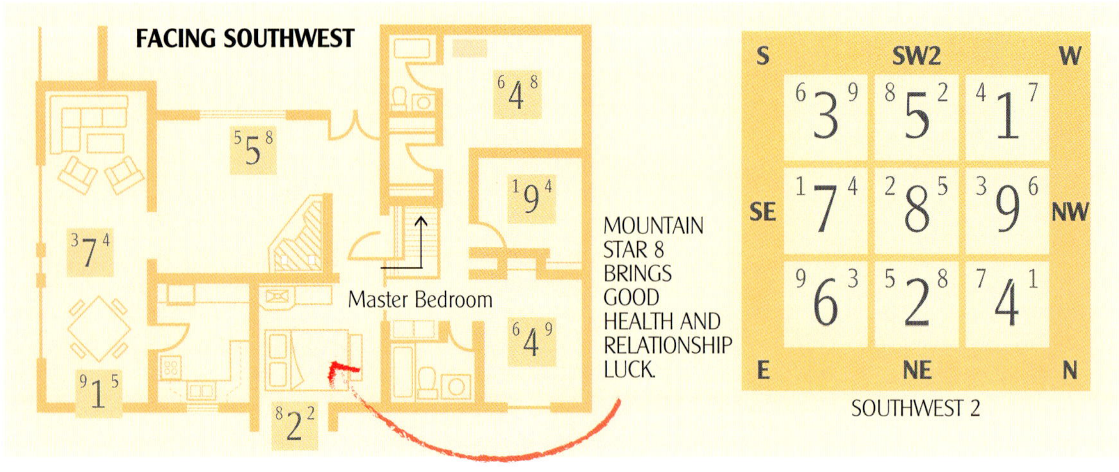

SOUTHWEST 2

98 Link house facing North

Here is an example of a link house facing **North** that was built in 2007, If you live in a house that was built between 2004 to 2024, and your home faces North, then one of the charts here will be the correct Flying Star chart for your house. To decide which of the charts is the correct one, you must use a good compass to take the facing direction of your house. In this example here, this house faces North-1. To make the analysis easier, I have "turned the chart" so that NORTH is facing the same direction as he floor plan illustrated.

Look at the numbers inside the little grids, then superimpose them onto the floor plan. This will clue you in on which part of the house is lucky and unlucky. Refer to the table in pags 126-127 to get the meanings for the numbers of the water stars and mountain stars. In this example, you can see that the **entrance door is very lucky** as it has the double 8 stars! The main entrance will benefit tremendously if a **waterfall feature** is installed just in front of the entrance. It is important to note that this water feature must have a **"mountain" feature** as we want to activate both the mountain and the water stars 8. **A pond or a hole in the ground** would be unsuitable as this would surely destroy the auspicious mountain 8 star, and thus destroy luck for the marriage and family unit.

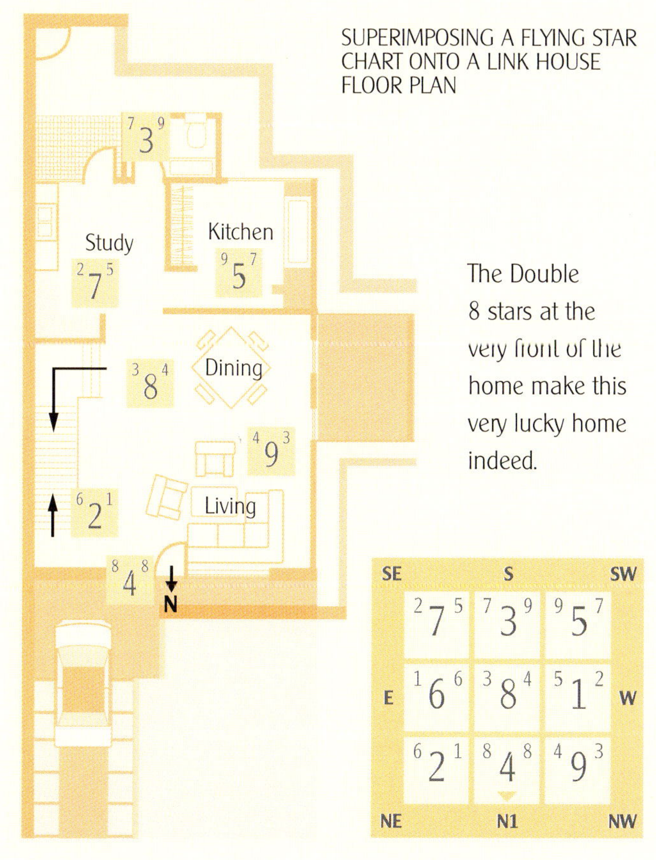

NORTH 2/3

SE	S	SW
4 7 3	8 3 8	6 5 1
5 6 2 (E)	3 8 4	1 1 6 (W)
9 2 7	7 4 9	2 9 5
NE	N	NW

99 An apartment facing East

To get you familiar with Flying Star feng shui, here is another example. This time we use an apartment to show how the chart is superimposed for analysis. Here the apartment building faces EAST 1 and the apartment also faces EAST 1, so we use the EAST 1 chart. Once again, we turn the chart to make analysis easier. Remember, you must invest in a good compass with the 24 mountains indicated. Then it will be very easy to identify the Flying Star chart of your home. Do remember that for apartments, you MUST use the facing direction of the BUILDING to identify your chart. Then you superimpose that chart onto your layout plan according to the compass directions.

Once the numbers are placed inside the layout plan, it is easy to start "reading" the meanings of the numbers. Here we see that the centre of the house has the auspicious 1/6 combination. This is excellent and one can activate the mountain 1 star with a large crystal. However both the bedrooms in the Southeast and Northeast have afflicted stars that are in need of remedy. Bedroom 1 suffers from the 9/7 which brings burglary and theft; hence a **Blue Rhinoceros** in the Southeast will alleviate this problem. Bedroom 2 has the quarrelsome 4/3 combinations. This can easily be dissolved with the fire element; placing the **Red Ksittigharba Ball** in the Northeast will suppress the harmful effects of the 4/3.

EAST 1 NATAL CHART

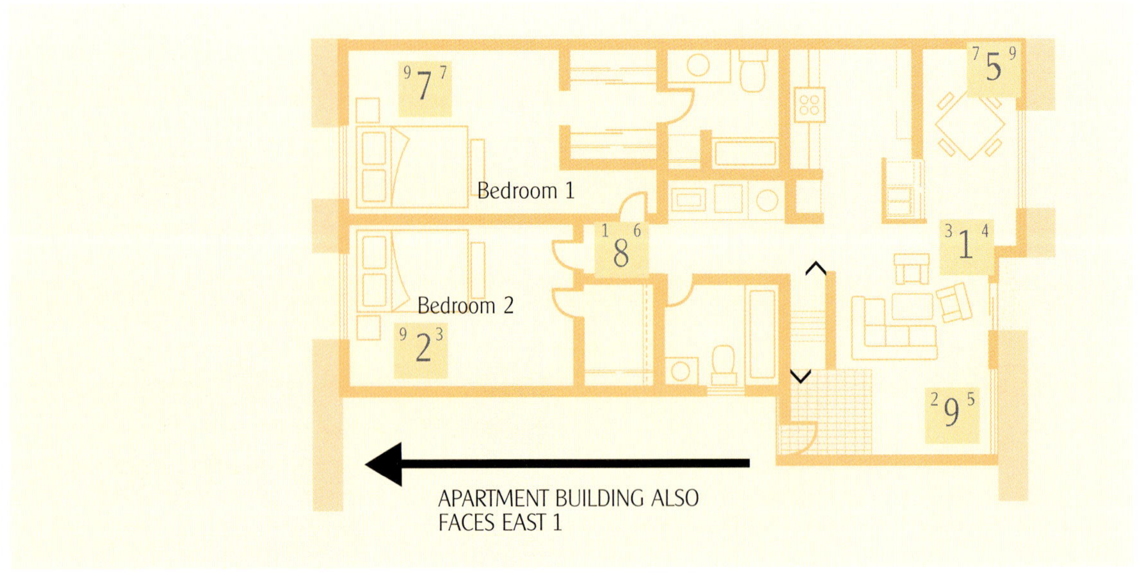

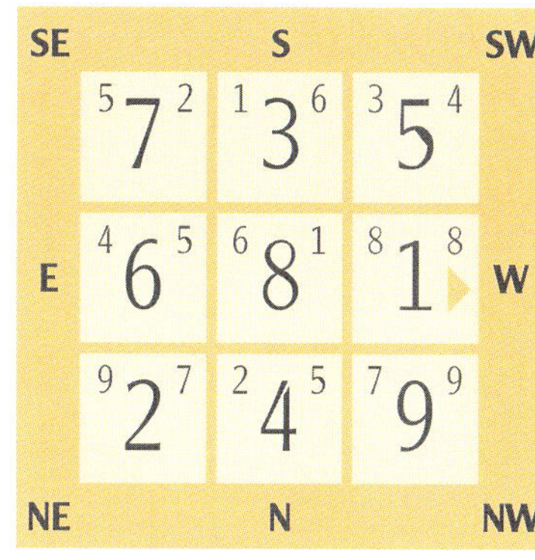

SE
S
SW
5 7 2
1 3 6
3 5 4
E
4 6 5
6 8 1
8 1 8
W
9 2 7
2 4 5
7 9 9
NE
N
NW
WEST 2/3 NATAL CHART

100 A West facing apartment building

Below is an apartment located in a building that faces the West 2 direction, so even though the entrance into the apartment is facing North and is located in the Northeast sector, we use the West 2 chart to analyze the Flying Star distribution of luck. See if you can analyze the effect of the Flying Star numbers here, paying attention to the numbers in the bedrooms and in the main door area. Note that the chart has been "turned" for easier analysis.

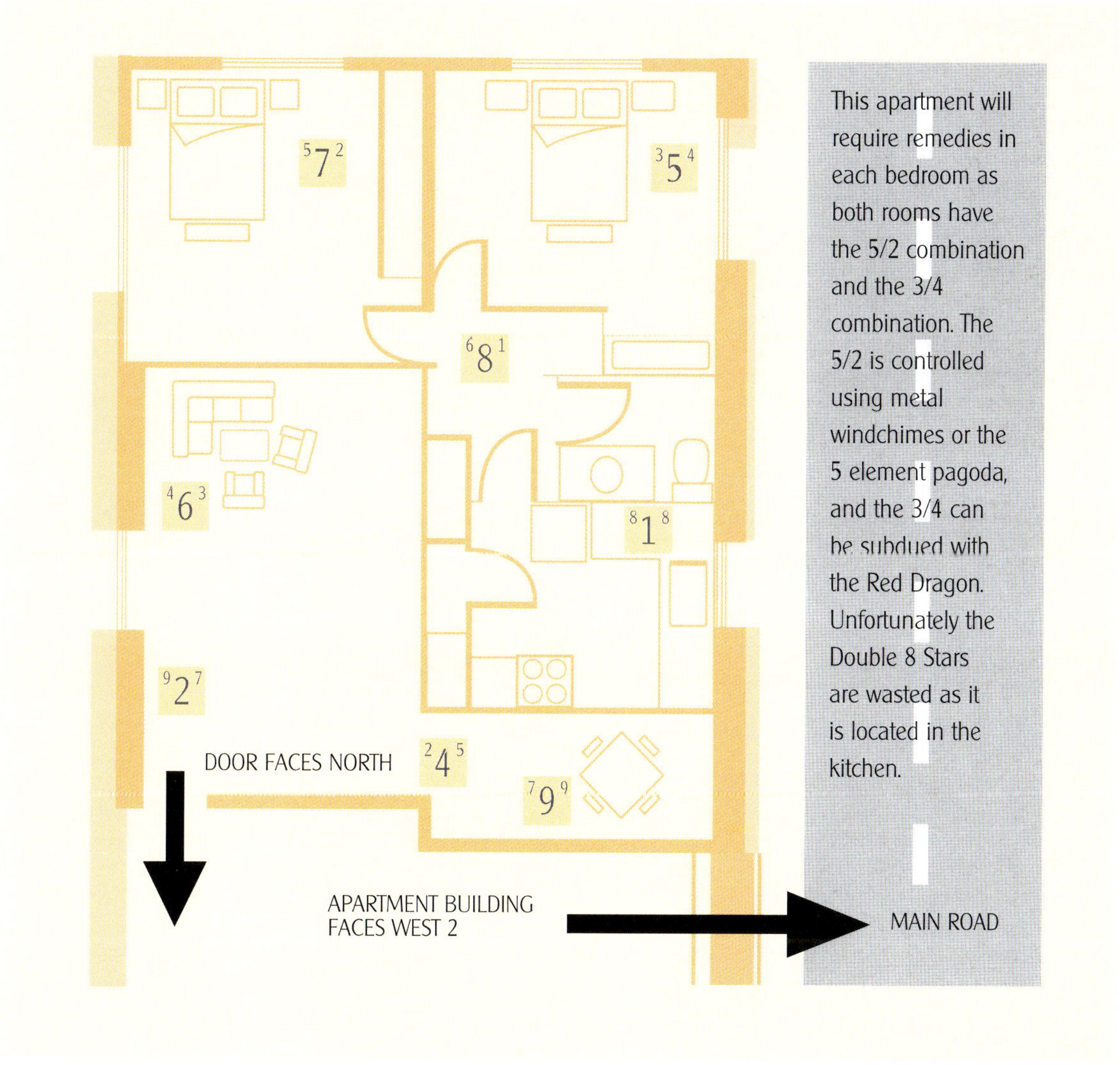
5 7 2
3 5 4
6 8 1
4 6 3
8 1 8
9 2 7
2 4 5
7 9 9
DOOR FACES NORTH
APARTMENT BUILDING
FACES WEST 2
MAIN ROAD
This apartment will require remedies in each bedroom as both rooms have the 5/2 combination and the 3/4 combination. The 5/2 is controlled using metal windchimes or the 5 element pagoda, and the 3/4 can be subdued with the Red Dragon. Unfortunately the Double 8 Stars are wasted as it is located in the kitchen.

101 A mansion facing Northeast

Here is an L-shaped mansion that faces NE1. However, because it is L-shaped, there is a missing corner, which occupies two grids. When you have a situation like this, the numbers that fall OUTSIDE the house do not affect the interiors. So here, we actually have two auspicious sets of numbers, one of which is almost outside the house. The facing direction is Northeast 1 and therefore the entrance enjoys the water 8 star. A **pond** type of water feature is most suitable as it will activate the water 8 and drown the mountain 2 star which brings illness. At the back of the house in the kitchen and family room is where the Mountain 8 star is located; hence the family will excellent family happiness if they spend time here. **Bedroom 1 in the East** has troublesome 7/4 combination.

NORTHEAST 1

This has to be subdued or a couple living there will see a third party entering into their marriage. Here a Blue Rhinoceros and Elephant should be displayed in the East of the room, and bright lights turned on outside to subdue both the 7 and the 4. Luckily the 9/6 stars in in the North are outside and hence cannot exert its harmful influence.

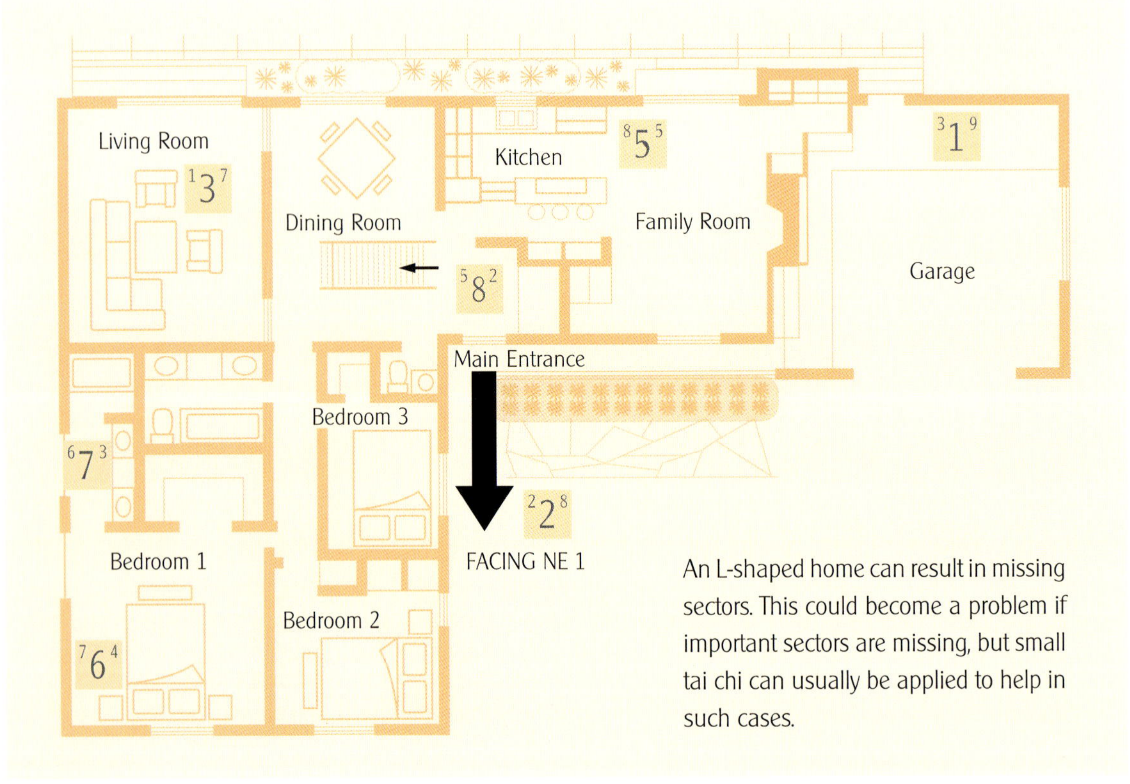

An L-shaped home can result in missing sectors. This could become a problem if important sectors are missing, but small tai chi can usually be applied to help in such cases.

102 A Southeast facing condominium

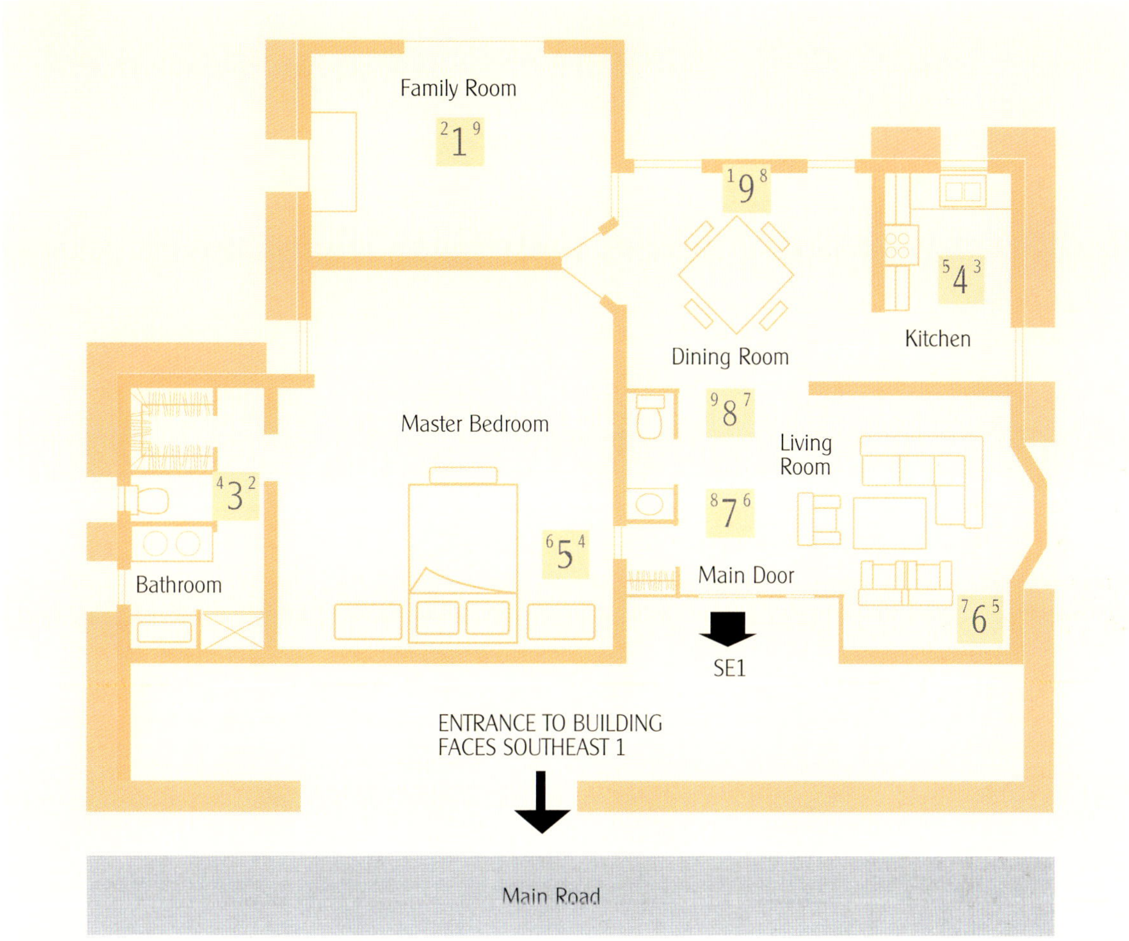
Family Room
2 1 9
1 9 8
5 4 3
Kitchen
Dining Room
9 8 7
Master Bedroom
Living Room
4 3 2
8 7 6
6 5 4
Bathroom
Main Door
7 6 5
SE1
ENTRANCE TO BUILDING
FACES SOUTHEAST 1
Main Road

This is a ground floor condominium unit in a building that faces Southeast 1, so the Southeast 1 chart applies. I have superimposed the relevant numbers onto the layout plan for you to practice reading the numbers. In all the previous examples, I have only undertaken a very simple analysis. If you use the table of meanings and read deeper about Flying Star, you will realize that the numbers offer a wealth of information that is breathtakingly valuable for doing interior feng shui. Try further analysis to get a "feel" for this powerful use of Flying Star.

W
NW
N
2 1 9
1 9 8
5 4 3
SW
6 5 4
9 8 7
3 2 1
NE
4 3 2
8 7 6
7 6 5
S
SE1
E

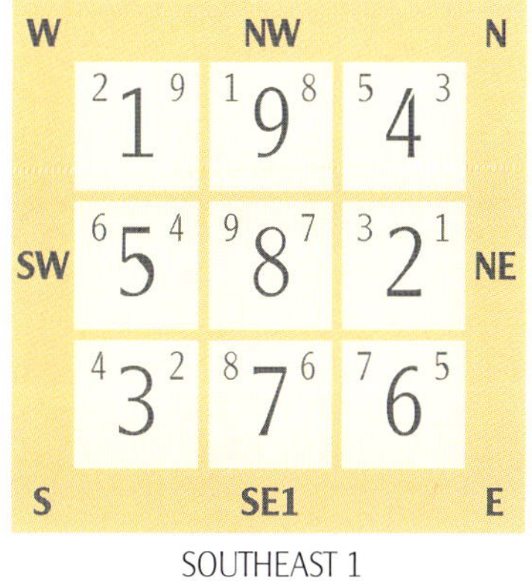

SOUTHEAST 1

NORTHWEST 1

103 A Northwest facing house

Here is a house that faces the direction NW1. I have provided a chart, which has been 'turned' to aid you. Follow how **I superimpose the numbers** onto the floor plan. The next stage after doing that is to try and interpret the numbers. Refer to the table of meanings for the mountain and water star combinations in pages 124-127.

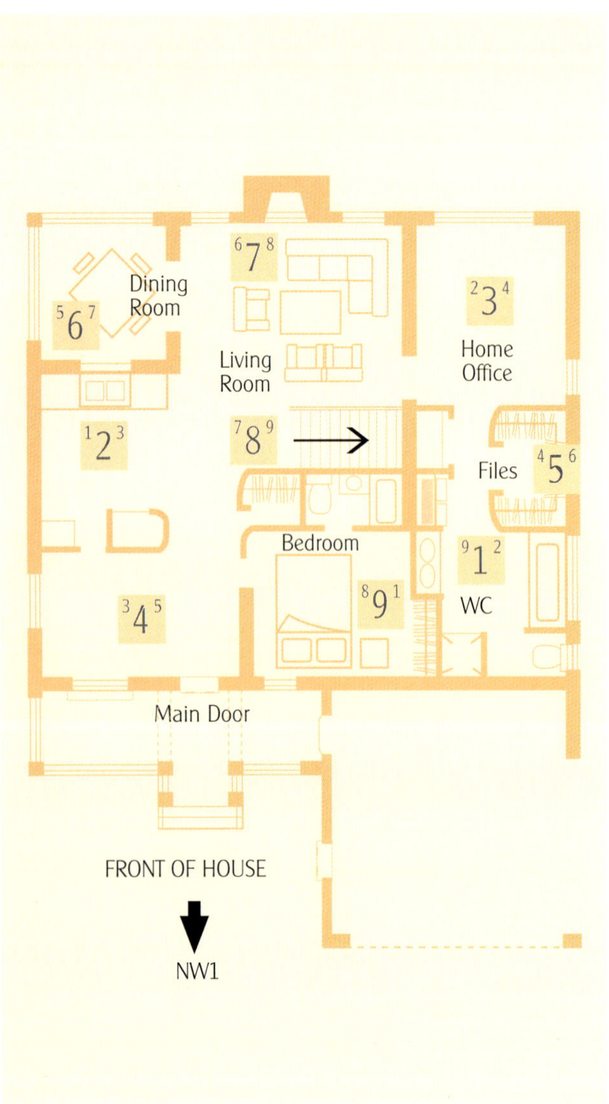

The steps involved in using Flying Star charts are thus:

- Identify the **correct chart** that applies to your house.
- **Superimpose** all the numbers onto your floor plan correctly.
- Refer to the **table of meanings** to read the meanings of numbers.
- Place **suitable cures** where necessary to overcome bad star numbers.
- Try to **activate** the good star numbers, for instance, the number 8 water and mountain stars, wherever possible. Soon, you will also be able to factor in the **annual and monthly Flying Star** charts which enable you to update your feng shui effectively and powerfully. If you are having difficulty following this method, study the preceding examples again. This is part of what I teach my students in my Master Practitioner's Course (MPC).

104 A Northeast facing house

Period of 8 houses and buildings that face any one of the three Northeast 1 or, 2/3 directions benefit from extremely auspicious charts as both natal charts enjoy "specials" that only occur in 6 out of 16 possible home natal charts in the entire flying star system of feng shui for the Period of 8.

Northeast-1 houses enjoy the **Parent String Special** – where all the numbers in every square have the combinations of 147, 258 or 369. Houses with this special are said to bring excellent money and relationship luck if the house is of a regular shape like a square or rectangle, and no single sector is missing.

Northeast 2/3 houses enjoy another "special" known as the **Sum-of-Ten Special.** The Sum of Ten Special occurs when two stars in each sector (mountain and water, water and period, or period and mountain star) consistently add up to 10 in every sector. Study the Northeast 2/3 chart and you will see that in every square, the water star and the period star adds up to 10! This special is said to bring money and prosperity luck to the occupants for 20 years! Again, this "special" is activated if the shape of the house is square or rectangle, and no directional sectors are missing.

When you examine both the charts that are possible for Northeast-facing houses, notice that the Water and Mountain stars appear in opposite locations in both charts. For example, the combination of 2-8 in the Northeast-1 chart appears in the Northeast; whereas in the Northeast 2-3 charts, they appear in the opposite location – in the Southwest. This is also the case with all the other charts and when you understand this you will be able to make adjustments to the luck distribution of your house simply by moving the facing direction of your door a few degrees to tap a different natal chart. Do not however attempt to do this without a full understanding of the charts. My suggestion is that if you are building your own house, it is really a good investment to learn the complete professional flying star system in a course. This will enable you to design and fine-tune your feng shui exactly the way you want it.

NORTHEAST 1

NORTHEAST 2/3

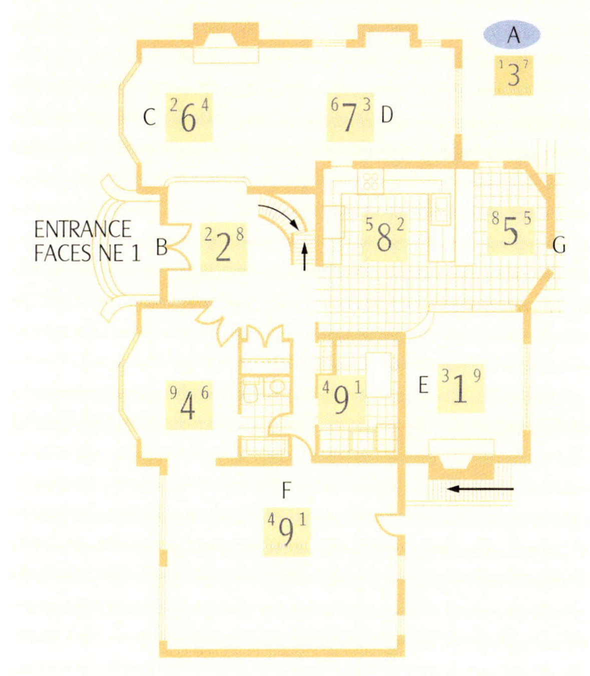

This house faces Northeast-1. The entrance **(B)** enjoys the auspicious water 8 star and can be activated with a pond just in front of the entrance. The 1-7 star in the South **(A)** brings burglary but since that sector is missing, this energy does not affect the occupants. The mountain star is located at the back of the house **(G)** - this can be activated with a painting of a mountain and a solid brick wall built just outside the window.

6

THE DESIGN FACTOR

There are many feng shui options available to anyone wanting to enhance the luck of their home interiors, and these can be addressed room by room using a mix of feng shui methods. Just using the **yin and yang** principles to ensure there is sufficient yang energy in your home and applying the five elements principles to ensure there is balance will generate many good ideas. Practising feng shui is **never a static chore**. Instead, feng shui is a wonderfully dynamic practice that involves keeping the flow of chi moving. You can use the five element principles to choose **colours, shapes and the art** you hang on your walls. You can use these principles to choose between metal, wood or stone materials. You can select auspicious decorative objects that symbolize different types of luck and you can use Flying Star feng shui to tap into very potent and intangible forces of chi. Bringing feng shui into the design of your interiors is feng shui that is within your control.

Good Feng Shui transcends tradition, culture and even religion. You can arrange your home to reflect your personal tastes & preferences and as long as they follow basic feng shui guidelines, you will enjoy auspicious health, wealth and happiness.

105 A good flow of chi

The first principle to bear in mind when designing your home interiors is to keep an eye on the way invisible energy moves inside the home. This is the famous flow of chi concept that generally determines whether your home feels balanced and harmonious, or not. It is how you subconsciously direct the way **human traffic** moves within the home. It has to do with the way furniture is placed so they do not block the flow of chi, and how natural passageways are created that direct people from one part of the home to another and from room to room.

9 TIPS TO GOOD CHI

1. Go for a **meandering flow** rather than a straight line flow.
2. Don't have doors in a **straight line** as this causes a poisonous straight flow.
3. Try to make your conduits of chi **spacious** rather than cramped.
4. Let the chi from the outdoors flow freely in. **Open your windows**.
5. **Block off unsightly views** from your flow of chi – throw out dying plants.
6. **Don't let energy stagnate** at corners, store rooms, and closets.
7. Try to let the energy move **diagonally** across rooms.
8. Let **all the spaces** inside the home get activated occasionally.
9. Lastly, let **external breezes** and sunlight bathe the home in fresh chi.

The flow of chi in the apartment illustrated below is auspicious. Although it is a straight line going into the **master bedroom (A)** the foyer area is large enough for the chi to slow down. Hanging a painting or mirror on the side wall will enhance the flow of chi here. Going into the family room, the **chi here at (B)** can easily slow down with clever placement of furniture here. Traffic moves naturally into the dining area and into the kitchen. Moving to the upper level where the rest of the bedrooms are located, there is a narrow **corridor at (C)**. As long as this corridor is well lit the chi will move in a benevolent fashion. In narrow spaces like these, do not place cupboards as these can cause potential blockages to the flow of chi. If the owner of this flat wants to improve the flow of chi, the entrance into the bedroom can be changed and the present door closed up. But the advantage gained is marginal.

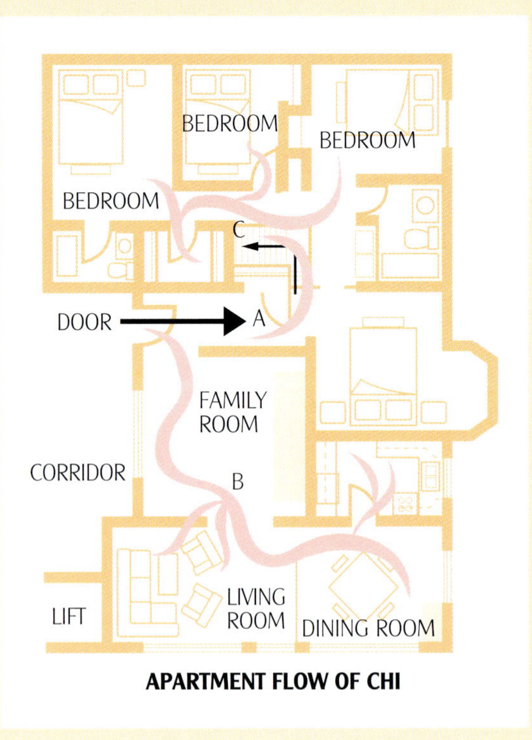

APARTMENT FLOW OF CHI

106 Auspicious room layout

There are different feng shui methods you can follow when designing room layout in your home – where to place the rooms and how big to make these rooms and so forth. Here is where knowing all your options can make such a difference to eventually having an auspicious house. For instance, you can decide as follows:

1. You can use the **Eight Mansions KUA** formula method to personalize sleeping and sitting directions for different members of the family.
2. Or you may want to select the most auspicious part of the house according to **Flying Star feng shui** so that you can be sure that your master bedroom is located in the part of the house with the best star numbers.
3. Or you may wish to arrange house layout according to the **Pa Kua eight aspirations** method focusing on the kind of luck you want for your bedroom.
4. Or you may even want to select the rooms according to the Pa Kua's allocation of spaces according to different **members of the family** e.g. the father in the Northwest, sons in the East and so forth.

For example if you do not want to have your bedroom at the back of the house as recommended by a Feng Shui Consultant, you will know how to have your way and move the bedroom in front without spoiling your feng shui.

Knowing Flying Star feng shui enables you to change the energy of the home based on the orientation of the home. There is really a great deal of common sense in feng shui. It is for this reason that I am the loudest advocate of knowing how to do one's own feng shui. I really believe that many of the different methods of feng shui are valid and have something to offer – even those that have been adapted for modern living. There is no need to be dogmatic about ancient feng shui knowledge. I have met many western **New Age practitioners** and many of them demonstrate genuinely wonderful insights into the practice of feng shui which even seasoned masters with many years of experience failed to pick up. In discussing feng shui with them, I feel I have expanded my knowledge so much.

Please note that all the different methods of feng shui work, and some work very well. The advantage in personally knowing different methods of feng shui is that **you** are the person who will decide from between several options. It is not an indifferent consultant who will design the way your bedroom is arranged. It should be you. Also, by knowing feng shui, you can discuss more intelligently with your architect and interior decorator on what exactly you want.

A solid wall at the head of the bed provides excellent feng shui support.

107 Choosing furniture correctly

Selecting auspicious furniture plays an important role in improving your feng shui. The principle to take note of is that your furniture should always **give you support**. For this reason, armchairs, sofas and other chairs in the home should always have high enough backrests to support you. It is also important for the **patriarch** of the family to sit in chairs with armrests. This ensures that he is never lacking in support. Furniture should never block the flow of chi, so there should not be so much furniture as to create a feeling of tightness and constriction. But being **too minimalist** with grey and black tones that suggest a ZEN like atmosphere is also much too yin. In a yang dwelling, there must always be a large source of yang energy. So although you may be keen on the minimalist look that suggests a spiritual environment, also **introduce yang** features to create balance. This means sound and light sources should also be present.

BEDROOM FURNITURE

There must be support so a bed head is important. There should never be shelves behind or above you. The bed you sleep on must never be too small or too short for you. This constricts growth and is especially **harmful for growing children**. You must make certain that the bed is at least long enough for growing boys if you do not want to physically and symbolically constrict their growth. Never put **two single beds** together to become a double bed. This will create an invisible line of separation between the couple. Do not have two mattresses on one bed frame for the same reason. Any kind of invisible or unconscious separation of the bed is always bad. Better to sleep on two separate large beds.

DINING FURNITURE

Comfort is an important consideration at the dining table. **Uncomfortable chairs** here suggest difficulty in sustaining your present life style. Chairs that are too small for you limit your growth and upward mobility. It is always better to have chairs that are larger than smaller. **Dining tables** are best when they are round and regular in shape. Dining tables that are too small or too narrow suggest your success and good fortune is short lived and cannot be sustained. Pa Kua shaped tables are regarded as auspicious, but round tables are best.

LIVING ROOM

Sofa sets must have backing and even if you like the modern Italian designer look like I do, you really must also display at least one sofa set that has **back rests**. I keep mine in the room where I meet guests. This ensures I have a chair to sit on that gives me support when meeting guests. Because most of my living room furniture has little back support and is basically for display and not designed to encourage lounging around, I do not spend much time in my living rooms. In my family TV room, the sofa is **lush and very supportive**. This ensures good support for family members.

108 In the bedroom

Canopy beds are excellent as they suggest a protective shield for your sleeping hours. **A full canopy is better than a half canopy**. Beds should also have headboards and whatever the design, they should be solid looking enough to give you good sleeping support. I find that having the wonderful longevity symbol carved onto beds is excellent for health.

NEVER place beds floating in the middle of the room. I have discovered this to be harmful causing imbalance and uncertainty. I tried this at the advice of a Feng Shui master who was an expert in eight mansions. His view was to tap the personal sheng chi direction at all costs and I discovered that despite sleeping in my sheng chi direction, if the bed does not have a solid wall or at least a window (which must be closed with curtain at nights) the effect was really not good at all. So, better to sleep with head facing a less auspicious direction but have support behind your head.

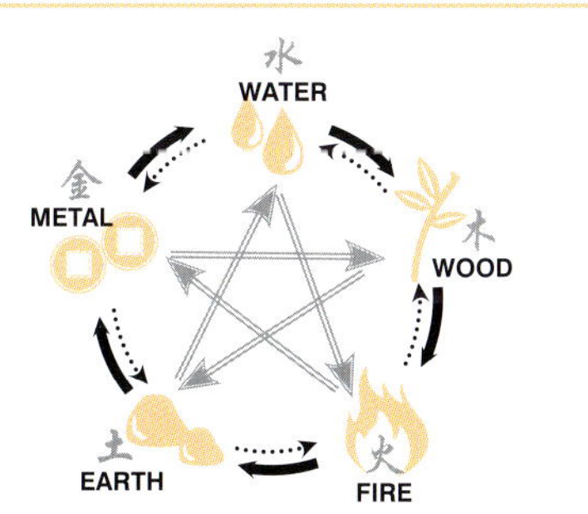

Use the production cycle to obtain the most auspicious type of bed. Wooden beds are excellent for fire people. Water beds are destabilizing so wood element people can use blue sheets and duvet covers. Water element signs benefit from brass beds while anything red benefits earth element signs. Metal signs should always sleep with white sheets.

SLEEPING ON THE FLOOR

Beds should never be too low. Sleeping on the floor can be harmful when element energies clash. For instance, if you sleep on a cement floor, Earth energy permeates your body and if you are a Fire person (e.g. born in the years of the Snake or Horse which are Fire elements) you will be **exhausted** instead of being rested each morning when you wake up. This is because earth saps the energy of fire. Snake and Horse people should also never sleep on waterbeds.

COMPATIBILITY WITH YOUR ZODIAC SIGN

Zodiac signs of the Dog, Dragon, Ox and Sheep belong to Earth element. Their chi is exhausted if they sleep on wooden floors. Such people should also **avoid brass beds**. Boar and Rat people are Water and should avoid too much wooden furniture. Tiger and Rabbit people are Wood element and should avoid Fire energy (i.e. red sheets will sap their energy). Monkey and Roosters are Metal, so **waterbeds** would be harmful.

109 Auspicious bedroom

The positioning of the bed here is good with the window on the left and a solid wall behind. This is a very bright bedroom filled with yang energy which is good for a young couple but could be excessive to older folks.

You can design very chic looking bedrooms and still follow feng shui principles at the same time. As long as you position the bed auspiciously according to your **lucky KUA directions** while observing the basic guidelines on bedroom feng shui, you will not go far wrong.

Here are additional tips you will find beneficial to follow:

- Keep the bedroom **regular in shape**. No matter how chic an irregular shape may look to you, resist the temptation of agreeing to an L shaped, U shaped or triangular shaped bedroom. Regular size and shape brings better luck.
- Keep plants and any kind of **landscaping out of the bedroom**. I know Balinese bedrooms look very good, but plants in the bedroom cause ill health and sap your energy.
- Make sure your **bed is not too small** or excessively large. Beds that are too small will cramp your growth and development while beds that are too large cause the entrée of too many relationship problems.
- Stay clear of **abstract designs** – art décor designed rooms are dangerous. Keep the lines of the bedroom soft and curving. Never sharp or pointing.
- In terms of colours, use **soft pastels** rather than loud primary colours. A bedroom dominated by red is suitable for young people, but red is a very yang colour which is not very conducive to rest.
- Keep **wealth and other deities** as well as the celestial creatures out of the bedroom. It is not advisable to energize the bedroom with feng shui symbols of good fortune and definitely the dragon should be kept out of the bedroom.

110 Living room ambience

This living area is simply too cold and sterile. The ambience lacks warmth and yellow lighting plus more leafy plants, flowers, colored cushion covers and a rug or carpet would improve the living feng shui greatly.

The living room should be **warm, inviting and friendly** and this is the best paint of the home to activate with lucky symbols and auspicious images. The arrangement of furniture should be regular while colors should reflect the presence of all five elements. It is also a good idea to keep living rooms **energised with sounds**, activity and bright lighting. Some conduit of energy from the outdoors would ensure the continuous inflow of cosmic chi to benefit the household.

Basic Guidelines

1. The living room should be regular in shape.
2. The living room should be neither too small nor too big. It must have enough room to allow the energy move around.
3. It should be located in the outer half of the house.
4. Hang a large family portrait to enhance the importance of the family members.
5. The living room must not be higher than the dining room.
6. Do not have a mirror reflecting the main door.
7. Avoid poison arrows or protruding corners in the living room.
8. Keep the living room well-lit, best achieved with a crystal chandelier.
9. Do not place furniture under exposed beams.
10. Do not display pictures of fierce or aggressive animals in the living room.
11. Enhance the elements of the each corner using element energizers.
12. Avoid exposed shelves in the living room, as this can send out killing energy.

111 Dining room furniture

The earth tones here make this an excellent dining area for the Northeast, Southwest and center location of any home.

Dining tables can be square, round, rectangular or eight sided in shape. These are regular shapes and will not give too many problems. However, if you have a **rectangular shaped dining table** like the one shown here, make sure that no one sits at the corners. Never eat with the corner pointed directly at your stomach as this is very inauspicious. The mirror reflecting the dining table below is excellent.

High backed chairs are to be preferred over low backed chairs, and chairs with arm rests are more auspicious than the chairs shown in the two pictures above. Both dining rooms are well lit and have good colour schemes suitable for the dining area. The feng shui touch can be provided with the presence of Fuk Luk Sau or the Laughing Buddha.

This picture shows a very warm dining area that is both well balanced and inviting. This dining area is excellent in any part of the home.

112 Kitchen cabinets & layouts

Almost all modern kitchens look good and do not present any major feng shui problems. The important thing in the kitchen is the placement of the **stove/oven**, which should be positioned to take advantage of your auspicious directions based on your KUA number.

White colour schemes are suitable for West located kitchens.

Red is not so suitable for the kitchen, as this would signify excessive fire energy.

QUICK TIPS TO KITCHEN FENG SHUI

- The **sink** should not confront the stove since this pits water against fire, which represents a clash of elements.
- The **refrigerator** and dishwasher should be placed away from the stove/oven.
- The actual cooking area should not be in the Northwest part of the kitchen, as this represents Fire at Heavens Gate.
- All **shelves** should be closed with doors, which can be glass, wood or plastic.
- Colour schemes of the kitchen should harmonize with the element of its location direction.
- **White kitchens** are excellent if they are located in the West and Northwest of the house. Kitchens in this part of the house should not have a red colour scheme.
- **Yellow kitchens** should be in the earth corners Northeast or Southwest. Here avoid using a colour scheme dominated by green or blue.
- **North located kitchens** can be blue, black and white, but not in yellow, beige or cream.
- Kitchens placed in the East and Southeast benefit from a green dominated colour scheme, but should not be in red or white.
- **Kitchens in the South** should not be in red even though this is a fire element location. Use pink or beige, but not red. Red in the kitchen is a danger colour as this would signify excessive fire energy.
- Always use tiles for the **floor of the kitchen** as this gives it excellent grounding energy. Do not use wood, carpets or linoleum for the kitchen floor. Kitchens that have windows are better than kitchens that do not. Never allow odours to get too strong and most important, do not allow your kitchens to get cluttered up with left over food.

113 Explaining personal elements

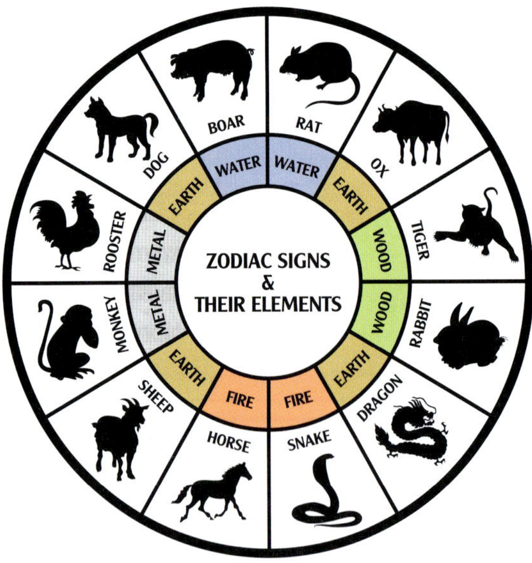

Many people get confused when it comes to identifying their personal element and this is understandable, because every person is influenced by more than one of the five elements. We are influenced by a **whole basket of elements**. Based on your birth details, it is possible to generate the following elements that impact on your luck cycle and influences:

- The **year of birth** gives the YEAR heavenly stem and the earth branch elements
- The **day of birth** gives the DAY heavenly stem and the earth branch elements
- The **month of birth** gives the MONTH heavenly stem and the earth branch elements
- The **hour of birth** gives the HOUR heavenly stem and the earth branch elements

The above creates the basket of elements generated from what astrologers refer to as your **PAHT CHEE CHART** or Eight Characters chart. It is from the basket of elements that fortunetellers are able to read your destiny luck cycles in conjunction with **Purple Star Astrology**. Of this basket of elements, the element of your zodiac sign is the YEAR earthly branch element and the objects in your living space should always strengthen this element.

To get the best luck chi from the furniture around you, and especially from your bed and the sleeping area, you should use the element defined by your **zodiac sign**. The illustration here enables you to check your element according to your zodiac. To enhance the personal chi of your space, you can use the **productive cycle** of the five elements to help you decide on the colours, shapes and materials of your surrounding furniture.

However, do remember that personalizing element enhancement should only be **limited to one's bedroom**, since there are other residents in the home. When applying element enhancements in the rest of the house, feng shui masters usually use the various feng shui compass formulas to do so. Thus using the Eight Aspirations Pa Kua method that identifies the elements for different parts of the home and different corners of a room is one method. KUA number Eight Mansions feng shui is another method.

ELEMENT ACCORDING TO KUA NUMBER

You can use your personal element as defined by the KUA formula to apply to bedroom furniture, clothes, jewellery, and other personalized accessories. Using your personal KUA element is especially potent when applied to personal adornments like colour of clothes, jewellery and make-up colours and styles. (KUA numbers are covered in Chapter 3). Almost all of feng shui sciences are based on the elements. Knowing which element to use is what makes up much of the skill of feng shui expertise.

114 Shapes and dimensions

The shape of tables, book cases, cupboards, sofas and their dimensions can either add to or detract from the energy of any room, thereby affecting the subtle movements of chi around them. When shapes are in balance and are harmonious to the intrinsic chi of that part of the room and house they occupy, the effect is positive. When they are out of sync, the effect is negative. And when **dimensions are auspicious**, they add to the luck. I never used to believe much in feng shui dimensions until I used it to design a new office desk for myself years ago in 1982. That year I was promoted so many times it became embarrassing! I have believed in feng shui dimensions ever since.

SUPERIMPOSING THE PA KUA

Lets take a look at shapes and see how they can be utilized to improve the flow of chi in your rooms. It all depends on which compass sector the room occupies.

EXAMPLE: From the illustration below, note the Pa Kua of directions can be superimposed over the whole house and also in each individual room. This enables us to know the dominant element of each room as a whole, as well as the individual corners of each room. Since the house faces **SOUTH**, we know that the master bedroom for instance is located in the **Southwest** making the dominant element here the earth element. This bedroom thus benefits from *fire* energy, which enhances earth. So triangular shaped objects, lights and red carpets and curtains would enhance the luck of this room. However, because it is a bedroom, too much red would be excessive yang. So it is better to enhance only the Southwest corner of the room. **A triangular cabinet** in that corner is thus auspicious.

SUPERIMPOSE THE PA KUA ONTO THE HOUSE FLOORPLAN ACCORDING TO ACCURATE COMPASS READINGS

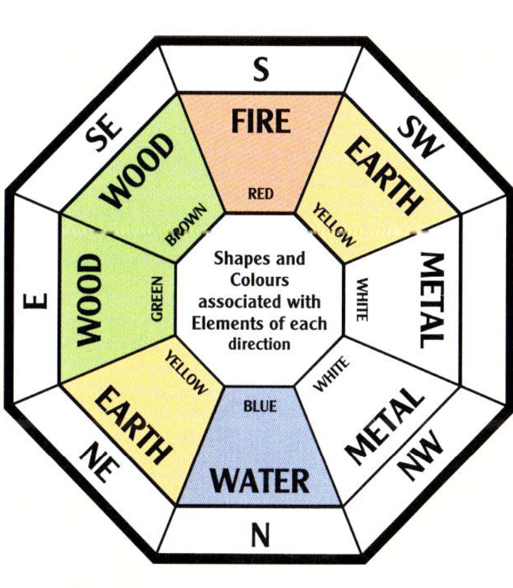

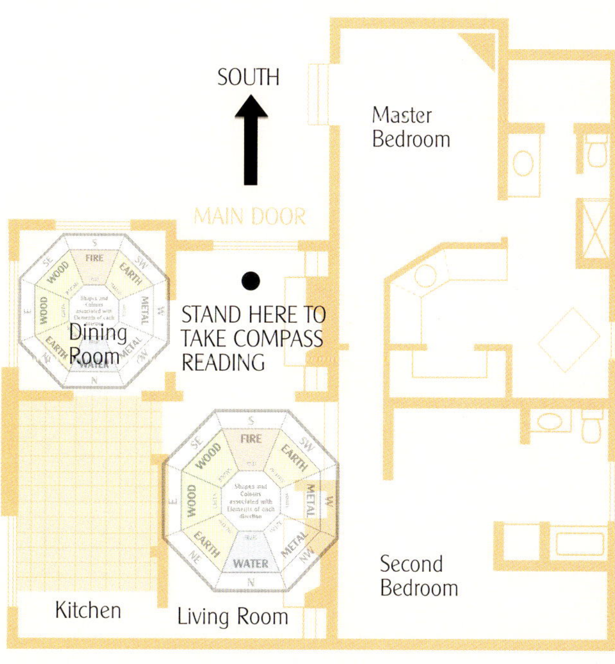

115 Colours and colour combinations

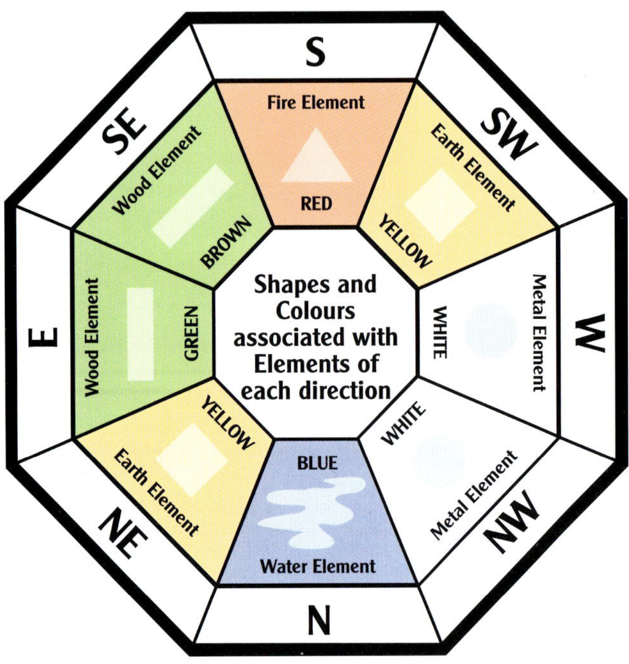

The Pa Kua here shows the correlation between directions and colours. This same Pa Kua can be used to help us select auspicious ***shapes*** for the different sectors of the house and the different corners of individual rooms. Now we can also focus in on the **choice of *colours***. Thus we see that the South parts of the home and rooms are of the fire element. So in South corners, red is the complementing colour, and green is the enhancing colour, because wood feeds and enhances fire.

What would hurt would be blue (water), which puts out the fire or earth, which exhausts the fire. So for each sector, there are auspicious and inauspicious colours. There are also auspicious colour combinations which in the South would be green with red, and also blue with green since water strengthens the wood which feeds the fire. Blue on its own would not be good, but blue with green would be auspicious.

Use these **guidelines on colours** according to the Pa Kua to select dominant colours for curtains, carpets, cushions, paintings and other interior decoration items. They will add tremendously to the harmony of your home interiors.

In the **North**, the element is Water, which is enhanced by Metal. So white is excellent. Colour combinations that are auspicious are white with blues, or metallic with blues. Green would be bad because it exhausts the water and earth destroys it. So yellow is also not a good colour for the North.

In the **West** and **Northwest**, the element is Metal, which is enhanced by Earth, so yellow is great and yellow with white would be very good. The combination of gold with white or with yellow is also good. Red would be disastrous and blue would exhaust the sector.

In the **East** and **Southeast**, the element is Wood, so greens would be auspicious. Blue is also very nourishing and combinations of blue and green would be excellent. Avoid reds and whites or combinations of these colours.

In the **Southwest** and **Northeast**, the element is yellow, it being of the Earth element. So red is excellent because Fire feeds Earth. All the bright vibrant shades of red and orange would work well in these corners. The colours to avoid would be green, which hurts the corner, or white and gold, which exhaust it.

116 Lighting for yang chi

The lighting in this corner is bright yet restful. This is good. What is missing are wall decorations - a painting or family portraits - and some plants and a coffee table.

Lighting is one of the most powerful of feng shui tools. As an energizer of powerful yang chi, it has few that can match its potency. If in doubt about wanting a remedy for whatever affliction, try using bright lights. They work for practically all sorts of feng shui ills, **except** in overcoming the Flying Star annual affliction of 5 Yellow. Indeed lights would enhance the 5 Yellow, but for most other feng shui problems caused by cramped spaces, stagnant energy, dark corridors or places which have become excessively yin, nothing works better than bright lights.

But lights **should never be harsh or direct**. Spotlights transform benevolent yang energy into hostile yang chi. Light wall washes work exceptionally well and in the corners of the room that benefit from fire energy, it is a good idea to keep the lights turned on all through the day and night. The corners that benefit most from lights are South, Northeast and Southwest. Rooms in these corners of the home will really benefit enormously from being kept well lit.

Bright lights in the SOUTH bring fame and recognition. These should be warm lights.

Bright lights in the SOUTHWEST bring love, romance and family joyous occasions. Yellow light is best.

Bright lights in the NORTHEAST bring the luck of scholarships and also excellent for scholastic success.

117 Interior poison arrows

The beauty of this bedroom is spoilt by the presence of secret poison arrow from above (exposed cutting edges of ceilings) and from sharp edges of the black display shelves.

Hostile chi inside home interiors usually emanate from protruding corners and exposed overhead beams. **Structural beams** create the most hostile chi and the effect can be very harmful. Feng shui practitioners with many years of experience have frequently made known their observations about the harmful effects of these interior features. It is for this reason that I am always wary about having ceiling designs that seem to cause silent killing chi to come from the ceiling.

Do watch out for these potential killers in your home and try **never to sit under a beam** or in the line of fire, so to speak, of hostile chi coming out from a protruding corner. Also, try arranging your furniture such that their edges do not face sitting or sleeping areas. The negative effect usually shows up in serious disease or illness.

DISARM BEAMS WITH BAMBOO FLUTES
Older and frail people are particularly vulnerable. Their beds should never be under these features. If you cannot move from under beams try hanging two bamboo flutes with the mouth side down in an A configuration to reduce their ill effect.

118 More poison arrows

The architectural concept of this living area is dominated by the three overhanging wooden slabs which can be the source of hostile energy.

It is extremely beneficial to look out for "hidden" poison arrows inside the home. These come in the form of **heavy looking beams** and overhead exposed ceiling designs which tend to have the effect of "pressing down" on the luck of residents.

So exposed **structural beams** can be very dangerous to the health and well being of residents.

The **corners of furnitures** especially of big cabinets and heavy tables can also be dangerous as they create plenty of "killing energy" inside the home.

Likewise **open shelves** that look like sharp blades cutting into your back or when you sleep. These and other hostile looking strucktures and objects inside the home are what causes hidden obstacles and aggravations to arise.

For those sensitive to feng shui vibrations, these "poison arrows" are immediately obvious. They should be either blocked from view or removed altogether if possible.

119 Modern homes can incorporate feng shui

This is the living room of Jennifer's home - note all the feng shui friendly features.

There is room for plenty of creativity in feng shui. I have seen some remarkably beautiful and well-designed modern homes that cleverly incorporate auspicious feng shui principles in the subtlest ways. There is no need to use anything old, antique or Chinese if you do not like this style in your home. You can be as modern as you wish. My son-in-law, Chris who is an architect, for instance, designed his living room to look modern, but he added a **water feature** at precisely the correct spot to tap the auspicious water star under the Flying Star method, and he designed the sitting arrangements in the living room to tap both his and Jennifer's ***sheng chi*** directions. And to obtain recognition luck, they invested in a very good copy of a Tang dynasty horse for their South corner. You can see how modern the look is. Notice there are no exposed overhead beams and the living area is not hit by any poison arrows whatsoever. The water feature is a family size swimming pool, which lies beyond the sliding doors.

Notice that all homes will have sharp corners that are potentially dangerous in that these edges send out *shar chi* or killing energy. So it is important to **arrange seating arrangements** in a way that no one sits in the direct "line of fire".

At the same time, all homes will have structural pillars. Once again, the important thing is to arrange the layout of furniture such that the edges of pillars do not hit at anyone sitting on the sofa set. Where such pillars hurt you, you can always camouflage with foliage plants or wrap mirrors around the pillar. This effectively causes the pillars to visually disappear, thereby not causing feng shui problems.

120 Feng shui art

Art is something that is extremely personal. Art reflects the mood, tastes and attitudes of different people, so it is impossible to say what is good or bad art. Irrespective of personal tastes however, it is vital to take a feng shui perspective towards the hanging of art in the home. This is because the chi emanated by **hostile images can sometimes be very harmful**. Art images can cause misfortunes to occur – and you would not even know why.

The bad luck and misfortune caused by art hanging on the walls of homes and offices work quietly and quickly indeed. I am especially mindful of art that is old, art which has been hanging in unhappy homes, **art which feature grief**, art which feature images of ferocious animals, art with dour looking faces and of grim looking portraits. The list of potentially harmful art is impossible to quantify. So many aspects come into play – colours, tones, and history of the piece, its provenance and so forth. Even **images of auspicious objects** can be harmful when drawn in an inauspicious way.

Many people have asked me about feng shui and art, and I have to say that nothing gives me greater pleasure than visiting art museums in Paris, New York, Saint Petersburg and London. I am a great fan of the Impressionists and love the way they capture sunlight, water and flowers – full of colour and yang energy. They are excellent examples of **happy art** that create positive vibrations wherever they are hung.

Below: Happy Family

Right: Weeping Woman

Look at these strikingly different art images by Picasso. Both paintings are worth millions and they were painted at different periods of the artists' life. The painting on the bottom is entitled WEEPING WOMAN – implies sadness and depression. Would you have a print of this so called masterpiece in your house? On the other hand, look at this stunning painting on the top. Also from **Picasso**, it comes from his happy blue period. Having a print like this hanging in the house is definitely auspicious, as it indicates a happy family. So the feng shui perspective applies equally well to western or eastern art. Look at the colours and symbols – then decide.

121 Art can create bad luck

I would suggest you think about the following feng shui aspects of hanging art:

- Avoid art that has **dark foreboding colours** – the chi created is very yin.
- Avoid **war scenes** and fighting – this will cause residents to be confrontational.
- Avoid portraits of **wrinkled old men** and women. This creates illness chi.
- Avoid paintings of **fierce animals** inside the home. Tigers, leopards can turn ferocious.
- Avoid art that has sharp angular lines suggesting **knives and weapons**. Chi is killing.
- Avoid art that depict **silent ghost** like scenery e.g. of marshlands and forests.
- Avoid art that show houses that look **haunted**, poor or dirty.
- And finally avoid **art of old portraits**. The Chinese believe that eerie spirits like to make a home hiding behind paintings with faces and especially those with piercingly intense eyes. We cannot be too careful about this.

SIGNS FROM THE UNIVERSE

I took a sudden liking to two old-looking "Shanghai posters" of with two sweet looking girls. **They were also very inexpensive** and I could see they were genuine because the paper looked dry and faded. I felt irresistibly drawn to them, so I threw caution to the winds and bought them. I arranged to have them framed and here's the mystery.

During framing, one of the posters suffered a tear that ran across the head of the girl. Immediately I sensed something wrong and realized I was breaking my own rules about art. There was no way I would hang the poster in any part of my house now. I never keep anything chipped, torn or broken in my house, so I threw the posters away. **I read the tear as a sign that I should not "invite" the posters into my house**. That day, I had such bad luck, fell twice and almost broke my leg, received some bad news and fell ill with a sore throat. Uncanny coincidence but I am always very sensitive to signs from the Universe.

MY HORSE PAINTING

Ten years ago I had a similar experience. We had a horse we loved terribly. He helped Jennifer win many riding competitions and so we decided to have him painted by a famous modern Chinese artist. We gave the artist a picture of Jennifer leaning on the horse, both looking smiling and happy. Unknown to us, this excellent artist had a famous trademark – he always included a **little cloud in all his paintings** and so he put a cloud just above the horse's head. Shortly after the painting arrived, we hung it in pride of place in our living room.

Our horse **JUSTY BOY became lame** soon after that and did not recover for several years. One day, I sat in the living room and suddenly noticed the cloud in the painting. I thought maybe I should take the painting down. Believe it or not, that month, after several years of treatment and a lot of vet bills later, Justy Boy recovered. Since then, I have been ever alert to little details like that.

When I related this experience to an old Taoist master from Hong Kong, he nodded his head wisely, telling me **never to have anything in the home appear as if it is under a cloud**. It is not that clouds are inauspicious, only when it seems to be just above you, **blocking out the sun**. The old master also taught me how to read clouds, telling me how he could detect oil under the ground just by looking at the clouds directly above. Very powerful, but I have never put this particular skill to the test!!

122 Art can also bring good luck

Here is a painting by the celebrated Impressionist artist **Claude Monet**. Look at the vibrancy of the sunlight shining on these **lush growing plant**s. The trees look like they are alive and well, so the energy that emanates is sure to be auspicious, bringing growth energy to wood and fire corners. This kind of art would be great for the East, Southeast and South, but unsuitable for the North. This is because these plants would soak up the water energy of the North, leaving the corner depleted of this vital element.

Here is another auspicious painting by **Monet.** The sailing ships are already auspicious for these bring **good fortune from the wind** and waters. But here we see also beautiful water, blue skies and bright sunshine – all of which are sources of yang energy. Hanging a print like this on the North, East and Southeast walls would be excellent.

This stunningly colourful painting is by **Renoir,** another French Impressionist. This is an excellent print to hang in your living room as it brings in the energy of a **happy scene**. They are having a good time socializing on a lazy afternoon. The ambience and energy created from this image are positive and joyous. During my university days, I hung this print in my room simply because I liked it so much. The feng shui man said it also brought me a great social life.

123 Mountain images give support

One of my very favourite photograph of a Golden Mountain.

Probably the single most powerful art subject to have in your surroundings either at work or at home would be that of mountains. There really is nothing as supportive as having a beautiful painting of a mountain range behind you – something that can simulate the celestial **protective Turtle** or the powerful yang creature, the Dragon.

Mountain paintings should be selected with great care. They should look majestic, unshakeable and friendly, and emit a balance of elements that is in sync with the wall where you plan to hang it. Mount Everest is an excellent example of a powerful earth element mountain, suitable for walls on the Southwest, Northeast, West or Northwest.

Mountains that are **lush with vegetation** are excellent on walls on the East, South and Southeast of your living room. Mountains white with snow are excellent for the East, Southeast and North of your home or room. Mountains that look barren or are excessively sharp with lots of triangular sharp peaks are hostile and not recommended. Mountains that are yellow, brown and which look stony, suggesting rocks and granite, would be excellent for the Southwest, Northeast, Northwest, and West walls.

Mountain paintings should always show the **mountain dominating the valley**. If there is a valley in the foreground with the mountains far away, the painting is useless, as it offers no support at all. This suggests you will fall over backwards and also that the mountain is subservient to the valley. In feng shui, this is quite fatal if the painting is hanging behind you. But if such a painting were hung in front of you, it could be auspicious. The idea is to be clear what energy we are tapping.

Mountain paintings should also **not have water flows** and water falls, unless these are so tiny as to be dwarfed by the sheer size of the mountain image itself. This is because when we use mountain energy, it must be stronger than water energy.

124 Traditional lucky symbols

Chinese homes are replete with good fortune symbols painted on art in all kinds of media. Thus our porcelain ware, Chinese paintings, sculptures, dining plates, utensils, furniture, screens, room dividers and just about anything made for the home are decorated with beautiful paintings, carvings and embroidery of all the traditional symbols of good fortune.

I have seen the power of these symbols work so often that I am no longer surprised each time I visit any one of the cities of China and see the enormous influence of auspicious symbols. In the Eighties when I first visited China, it was the images of the Forbidden City that amazed me - gigantic cranes, tortoises, dragons and every kind of good fortune flowers. With China opening its doors to the world now, anyone can visit any of the cities of China and see for themselves the powerful role played by auspicious symbols in the life of the Chinese. Indoors and out, homes and gardens are decorated with traditional auspicious good fortune symbols.

It is an excellent idea to offer auspicious symbols as gifts to our loved ones. The gift of traditional auspicious symbols is the best – the Laughing Buddha image, for instance, is an excellent offering of happiness vibrations. And it is always a great idea to present peaches, or the God of Longevity to your parents or grandparents for their birthdays. The gift of longevity is like an amulet, which protects against unnatural death. Always find images that are well made and decorative enough to add lustre to your home interiors. Never get cheap plastic imitations – the more valuable the medium, the better. Thus symbols fashioned as fine jewellery or made from precious stone carvings are the best.

Shown here are two stunning gifts I treasure simply because they have such auspicious meanings and were given to me with such good sentiments. My partner in the Dragon Seed deal presented the prized porcelain bowl decorated with five dragons to me many years ago. She said it was a gift of five dragons, and the bowl has brought me a great deal of happiness. Next to it is this exquisite porcelain peach presented to me as a birthday gift to wish me a long life. My daughter gave this to me.

Five Dragon Porcelain bowl and Golden Peach to bring happiness and longevity.

125 Four seasons of good fortune

Chinese art is always drawn with auspicious decorative symbols. Five red bats around a longevity symbol is popular simply because it attracts such good luck. Likewise, the God of Longevity is a deity that has a place in many homes because it symbolizes good health and long life. The deer, the peach and bamboo are also auspicious. Here is a list of potentially lucky images for you to consider.

Certain animals in art are especially auspicious e.g. horses are an excellent subject since horses bring recognition, strength, courage and a sense of adventure. Horses should never be running in fear. Frolicking horses with courageous postures are very auspicious. Tribute horses are excellent subjects. Workhorses and injured horses are not auspicious. Other lucky animals featured in feng shui art are deer, elephants, camels, as well as the celestial creatures – the dragon and tortoise.

Birds of every plumage bring good fortune and almost every kind of bird brings good luck of some kind. Bird feathers in the car protects against accidents. And a bird picture placed strategically near the door of a house ensures it gets sold as soon as you put it on the market. The Phoenix, peacock and rooster are three birds associated with feng shui – their images connote a variety of good fortune meanings. A pair of birds, mandarin ducks especially, suggest romance.

Flowers – the chrysanthemum, plum blossom, magnolia, peony and orchid – all have different auspicious meanings. It is suggested that homes with young girls always benefit from flower images, especially those painted with butterflies, since this always suggests the presence of many honourable suitors. The peony is the king of flowers but the presence of the lotus and water lilies also ensure that young ladies find happy matches. Flowers must never be drawn with thorns – nor should there be any flowers that are faded or wilted.

NOTHING MORE AUSPICIOUS THAN THE NINE DRAGONS

Of all the images, there is nothing more auspicious than the Dragon, so if you ever come across a painting of a single Dragon, do get it. Even more auspicious than a single Dragon is to have Nine Dragons. The power of 9 some believe is even more potent than the power of 8, as it is the "ultimate number".

126 Traditional Chinese art

Above: The Eight Immortals captured in art bring auspicious feng shui

There are simply so many auspicious images depicted in traditional Chinese Art that it is really no problem at all finding a suitable art that brings good fortune to decorate the home. The key to whether a painting is suitable for displaying in the home lies in the **legend or the story behind the art.** Hence before you hang up a piece of painting do some research on what it means – especially if that art piece is large, and will dominate an entire wall at your entrance area, living room, or dining room.

Finding traditional Chinese art that can blend into modern homes can pose a challenge to the modern interior decorator. My advice is to go your own instincts. There are many auspicious images to choose from so unless you like a piece of art you should not hang it in your house.

Here is a magnificent painting of the **Eight Immortals** all of whom possess a special power that can bring health, wealth and success. All prominent Chinese families have at least some version of this painting in their homes as it is believed to bring excellent good fortune not only to one's own life, but for all one's future generations as well.

Here is a painting of Liu Hai, the immortal who is shown holding a string of coins which he used as a fishing tool to bait the Chan Chu. Where there is gold coins, is where you'll find the three legged toad!

127 The Three Legged Toad

Another favourite painting with the Chinese depicts the legend of **Liu Hai** and **Chan Chu.** This is a universal favourite amongst business people familiar with the wealth attracting symbolism of this humble three legged toad. Here coins symbolize gold and it is used to flush out the toad that is said to be the wife of one of the 8 Immortals who was punished or stealing the peach of Immortality.

The legend of the three legged toad has made this a popular symbol amongst many wealth symbols. The Chinese believe that simply placing this creature in the home will attract money-making opportunities into your home. Place this painting in the living room and the toads under sofas and on low shelves looking at the door but not directly in front of the main door.

The 3-Legged Toad brings money luck with you when worn as a pendant.

128 Powerful Heroes

Traditional Chinese art is rich with symbols and deified warriors who attract power and protect your home from the bad intentions of others. The most popular **God of War and Wealth** is the immortalised **General Kuan Kung.** He is famous for his integrity, excellent military prowess and victory through fearlessness. The police and the triads look to this powerful deity for protection and businessmen engaged in corporate takeover deals always have his image nearby to assure themselves of victory in the highly competitive field of business.

Another highly revered figure in Chinese legend, famous for his unbending loyalty and unsurpassed ability in martial arts is **General Yue Fei**, a War General during the Song Dynasty. In the history books, Yue Fei is often credited for playing a strong role in preserving the Song Dynasty due to his seemingly divine abilities to win battle after battle! Legends, poetry and biographies speak of Yue Fei's extraordinary skills in archery, kung fu and Praying Mantis boxing. Senior managers in large organisations believe that merely having this image in the office, especially placed behind them, would make them leaders in their chosen field and rise victorious over their competitors.

Yue Fei is highly regarded as one of the most loyal and skilled military war generals in Chinese history.

129 Art in children's bedrooms

The best kind of art to hang in children's bedrooms are paintings that relate to their studies, the acquisition of living skills and images that attract recognition for their work. Children's rooms should have images and enhancers that help them gain good exam results and major scholastic honours. Thus images of the **carp jumping over the dragon gate to become dragons**, three carp holding a crystal globe, or a fisherman teaching a young boy how to make a living are all suitable images for a child's bedroom.

Here is a wonderful painting for attracting mentors into children's lives. This painting depicts a student with his old and wise master. Portraits of experts or geniuses in their chosen field is also very suitable. For example, a portrait of **Albert Einstein** or **Sir Isaac Newton** placed in the **Northeast** of the child's bedroom invites the luck of wisdom into their lives.

Above: This auspicious art-piece portrays the mentor-student relationship between and a wizened master and a young pupil.

Left: An Einstein potrait hung above your child's bed brings fabulous mathematical abilities.

130 Art to attract romance luck

If you want to attract love and romance into your life, hang romantic art inside your home. You can go with the traditional images of **mandarin ducks**, double happiness, the dragon and phoenix, or you can opt for something less esoteric and less Chinese, and go Western.

There are many stunningly romantic art pieces painted by legends such as Austrian artist Gustav Klimpt. His painting **THE KISS** is probably the most universally acknowledged painting of love. There are also other very beautiful European sculptures and paintings that send out some very powerful love vibrations.

Always hang the symbol of love in the corner that benefits romance, which is the Southwest corner of the bedroom or the living room. You can also use two other alternatives:

1. Your nien yen direction according to the Eight Mansions KUA formula because this is your personal romance direction OR

2. The direction that indicates your status in the family. This means Southeast if you are the eldest or only daughter, West if you are the youngest daughter and South if you are the middle daughter. For boys, it means East if you are the eldest son, Northeast if you are the youngest son and North if you are the middle son.

You may, if you wish, activate all the walls and rooms of your home that directly benefit your love life. Do this if you are very desperate to find someone. But if you are this desperate, then I do strongly suggest you get the double happiness

Above: This beautiful photograph of a loving couple makes an excellent contemporary love energizer in the Southwest.

image, a pair of mandarin ducks image or the dragon/phoenix image either as a piece of jewellery to wear or as a cloisonné decorative piece to hang on your romance wall, or placed beside your bed.

Remove all animal or people images, which show alone-ness. Keep things in pairs to attract the chi energy of a couple. If you are a woman, look for some male images, and if you are a man display some female images. It is really important to balance out the yin and yang energy in the home if you want to attract a spouse.

Mandarin Ducks are famed for their eternal dedication to each other.

7

REVITALIZING ENERGY

When we focus our attention on the chi that pervades all living space, we create an awareness that gives us a feel for the cosmic dimension of our homes. The chi inside homes brings good luck when it is positive and healthy. It brings bad luck and disasters when it becomes negative, stagnant or stale. Negative chi creates obstacles that impede the harmonious flow of chi.

Negative chi is less harmful than killing chi or dead chi, but it brings problems, loss, depression and unhappiness. It causes illness and accidents. It blocks success. So it is just as much to be avoided as killing or dead chi.

Negative chi can be caused by any number of factors. Homes that are dirty and cluttered contain negative chi. Home which have seen illness, loss, unhappiness, violence, anger and suicides suffer from the lingering energy left behind. Negative chi must be cleared, cleansed and purified. And it is always important to keep homes clean and well groomed. This unlocks good fortune continually.

A clean home that is well groomed and tidy has greater potential for prosperity than a place that is cluttered and untidy.

Can you feel the clarity of energy in this dining room space? Energy coming in from the side door here is both benevolent and bright. The mirror on the right wall draws in this energy. The direction here is Northwest, where the flying stars are excellent so opening a doorway here also helps bring in the good energy.

131 Tuning in to the room energy

Compass formula feng shui allows us to investigate the distribution of intangible energy in internal spaces as revealed in the trigram charts and natal charts. At the same time it is also beneficial to learn to focus on the energy that is present in the home and in the different rooms. Everyone has the **ability to "feel"** the energy of spaces. Some have a more heightened awareness of energy than others, but everyone has the potential to sense the quality of energy around them. It is only by tuning in to energy that we can improve it.

When you walk into anyone's home you can usually sense if the home is a happy or a sad home. Homes with strong invigorating yang energy usually belong to strong successful people. Similarly, home that exude a defeated or tired energy usually belong to rather more **exhausted people**. Homes can be friendly and warm or cold, angry and hostile.

There are kind homes and aggressive homes, lucky homes and unlucky homes. The more intense the energy is, the easier it is to become aware of it. Usually, the energy of homes mirror that of its residents. Sometimes the energy of spaces is stronger than the combined energy of its residents and other times the personality of the homeowner dominates. It is different for different people. But almost always, the home (and office) will mirror and reflect the attitudes, directions, moods and well-being of its residents. Develop awareness to the energy of your home, as this will help you to improve its feng shui by leaps and bounds.

132 Developing awareness

Feng shui is about energy – both the tangible energy created by physical structures, shapes and objects that affect its flow and its accumulation, and also the more subtle intangible energy caused by other influences such as the inner spirit of the home, its hidden history, the lingering energy left over from other earlier residents, or simply the inherent earth energy of the space on which the home was built. Sometimes, homes are afflicted with the energy brought by spiritual entities transcended from other realms.

Tuning in to the pattern and flow of chi inside any living space requires nothing more than the focusing of one's concentration. Stand at the entrance of your home for a few minutes. Face out and feel the energy that is coming at you. Try to get a feel for whether it is benevolent or agitated. You will find that if the entrance is being hit by some hostile physical structure, the energy will not be smooth. When the house faces an open field the energy is much more restful.

In feng shui, energy is chi, generally referred to as *sheng chi*, the dragon's cosmic breath, if it is benevolent. It is referred to as *shar chi* or killing energy if it is harmful.

There are also other kinds of good chi and bad chi. Thus good chi can also be **wang chi** which is **ripening chi**, and bad chi can also be **negative or dead chi**. These are subtleties in the practice of advanced feng shui. At first, you can develop eye sensitivity to gross energies that are good or bad, but as you progress, you will start to feel the differentiations of good and bad energy. The idea of developing awareness of energy is to be able to design different kinds of good energy for the interiors of your home.

Take the entrance for instance. Here the focus is on protection feng shui. So when you place protector images such as a pair of Fu Dogs, or Chi Lin or lions, you can develop the concentration to feel their relative strengths. When symbols of protection are positioned correctly, they emanate powerful energy. Inside the foyer of the home you might want to consider having a table on which to place a Kuan Kung image that you like. A powerful **Kuan Kung** is excellent for those in business. Those in politics might want to look for the even more powerful Nine Dragons Kuan Kung. But if your work does not require such powerful energy, then there is no necessity for something so strong.

Similarly, you would want to have a **Wealth God** inside your home because everyone wants to be richer than they are and inviting the Wealth God into the home does attract wealth chi. But if you are in business, and especially if it is a competitive business, then the **Military version of the Wealth God** might suit you better. Attention to detail adds much to the development of eye sensitivity.

When you *survey the inside of the home always use your eyes*. Develop awareness of shapes, colours, lines, dimensions and the placement of objects and furniture inside the home. Be sensitive to art that hang on the walls, to porcelain vases and figurines on tabletops, to the general cleanliness of the home and the amount of clutter lying around.

Note if rooms are welcoming or whether the energy is putting you off. You will be surprised at how many things you used to miss out on. Feng shui can rightly be called the **"art of seeing things in your environment"**. It is by developing this ability to see that will elevate the effectiveness of all the feng shui measures you put into place.

133 Be conscious of the flow

One of the most important factors affecting the feng shui of any home or office is the flow of traffic within the space. The flow of the traffic establishes the flow of chi inside the home. Generally, the more people there are in any sector of the home, the more yang will be the energy deposited there. Thus high traffic areas tend to see a higher accumulation of yang energy than low traffic areas.

The flow of traffic is affected by the way you place the furniture. Rooms that are too cluttered leave little space for the chi to flow, and the result is that it tends to get blocked. When chi gets blocked, your path in life also gets blocked. And success literally also gets blocked. This has nothing to do with taste, or style. Feng shui is about the flow of energy and what may look good to someone could well offend the aesthetics of someone else. So it is not so much what you put into your rooms ***but how you place them*** *that affect the flow of chi.*

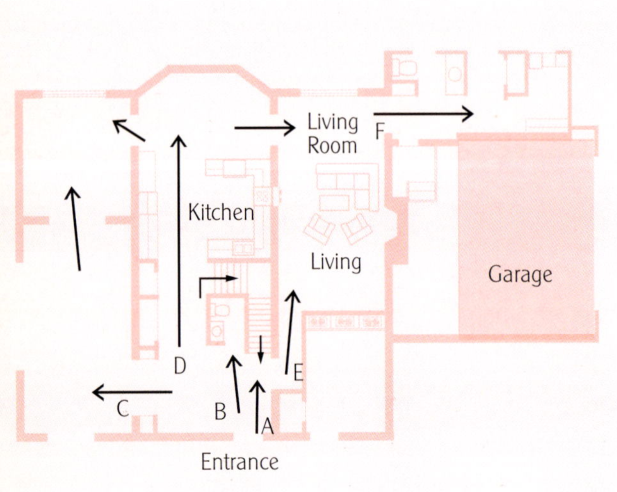

Try to map out a route, that reflects how people move within the home. By doing this, you can identify feng shui afflictions. At the entrance the flow of traffic should lead to a bright hall and never to staircases and toilets. Look out for rooms that do not get used as frequently. Also take note of corners that are ignored and rooms that are hard to get to. The idea is to balance the flow of chi in the home.

1. Identify corners that tend to get ignored and install a bright light in that corner. Remember that all corners represent some kind of luck and when they stay too quiet, it affects that aspect of your luck. This is because that corner will succumb to **Yin Spirit formation**. So shining a bright light there will counter it with yang energy.
2. Identify rooms that are not used. If you have such rooms in your home – e.g. bedrooms of children studying overseas – do go in regularly to **open the windows**, turn on the fan, turn on the lights for a while. This will balance the chi and prevent the energy from getting excessively yin.
3. Identify parts of the garden or house compound which may be ignored and do the same thing. Always make sure the chi in every corner of the home is kept moving in a healthy manner, since this affects the well being of residents in a very direct way.

EXAMPLE:
Many things can be improved in the layout here where the flow of traffic is quite inauspicious. The arrows indicate the flow of traffic in this house. At the entrance, attention is focused on the door leading to the toilet **(B)** and the staircase taking you upstairs **(A)**. Both create feng shui afflictions to the flow of traffic which must be countered by having a bright light. A third line of flow is too long and straight as indicated by **D**. Meanwhile the door into the living room is through a narrow passageway. **(E)** . Note that the kitchen of the house is in the center, which is not an ideal placement.

134 Clearing Clutter

One of the things that almost all feng shui practitioners agree on is that clutter in the home does not attract good feng shui. In fact, **clutter in the home causes luck to become severely blocked** so that success luck will be hard to come by. Homes do not need to be as clinical as a hospital, but when living rooms and bedrooms are allowed to get piled up high with old newspapers, dirty clothes, piles of old magazines, unwashed clothes and so forth, the flow of energy in the home is certain to get blocked.

The result is a sickness of the home. Just as the flow of chi inside the human body must not get blocked, as otherwise the person gets sick, so also the flow of chi inside the home should flow smoothly, unimpeded. It should not become blocked. When the energy of the home gets sick, it affects the residents' luck as well.

The clearing of clutter in the home can actually be very **therapeutic**. Try it sometime when you are feeling lethargic. Clear your desk, moving from one drawer to the next and culminating in the clearing of your desk top. File all your letters and notes and throw away all the junk that inadvertently accumulates over time and as you clear your desk feel your energy getting lighter and brighter. This is one of the best ways to get out of a state of lethargy and also revitalize stale energy.

It is the same with the clearing of junk inside the bedroom where clothes tend to choke up wardrobe space and stuff swept under the bed can cause all sorts of bad feng shui manifesting for the sleeping couple. Spend time cleaning the bed and the bedroom space of clutter built up over time. **Throw out old clothes and out of date clothes**. Unless you make room for new clothes, your energy will remain static.

A home free of clutter attracts good chi to settle!

Taoist feng shui masters always advocate making space for new things to come into one's life. It is for this reason that they **never like rice urns to be full to the brim**. There should always be some room for new opportunities and new goodies to enter into one's life. Clearing clutter implies making way for new energy to flow through.

In the kitchen, space must really be kept absolutely clean and clear of clutter. Never leave food lying on tabletops and do keep garbage disposal closed so that there is never any stench. Do not attract the creepy crawlies as this brings negative energy into the kitchen.

Nothing hurts feng shui like stale food and dirty unwashed plates and dishes. The kitchen shown here is not only uncluttered- it is also clean and happy looking. There is absolutely no clutter here so food is cooked within a clean and auspicious environment.

Those who live a bachelor existence usually find it hard to prevent clutter and junk from building up. Unless they make an effort to have their homes regularly cleaned and cleared of clutter, they are certain to suffer from bad feng shui brought on by invading clutter. Stale energy also builds up and transforms into yin energy. There is lethargy and bad luck as a result.

135 Moving the chi

The energy of the home must never be allowed to stagnate. Chi must be kept vibrant and alive, moving all the time. When chi is quiet it simply **stagnates** and attracts what is known as yin spirit formation – a situation of chi energy that is interpreted by feng shui masters as being too still, quiet and dull, and hence has little power to attract good fortune.

If you understand the tai chi or yin and yang symbol, you will understand that primordial yang energy is constantly moving and primordial yin is always still. For good fortune of the material kind to get created, there must be an abundant supply of yang energy. **Yang chi is constantly moving** - never coming to a standstill; only then can there be the vitality that contributes to continuous good fortune. It is important to keep the chi moving.

This is one reason why it is always such a good idea to move furniture – sofas, beds, and small sideboards – in order to get at the dirt that accumulates beneath. This slight movement of furniture is such good feng shui medicine for the house. In addition to cleaning the home thereby ridding the surrounding space of the dead corpses of insects, spiders and so forth, the movement of furniture on a regular basis moves the chi. Chi never gets a chance to stagnate. The energy of the home is therefore vital and alive and never becomes lethargic.

The **revitalizing of interior space results** in a very magical change of energy. You will find that successful businessmen who are in the property business – hotels, apartments and shopping complexes for example – are very smart at keeping the energy of their multi million-dollar properties alive with moving chi. Properties that are allowed to "die" and are never given fresh new energy almost always get progressively weaker and more lethargic until eventually they literally die. Until someone comes along to revitalize the space that has gone to sleep.

When I first set forth on Hong Kong soil I was there in my corporate role as a banker and I was amazed at the huge numbers of "redevelopment " projects where literally whole apartment blocks, office buildings and hotels were frequently pulled down and rebuilt. Naïve to the world of property development and feng shui practised at the highest levels of commitment I was at first surprised, but when the feng shui masters of Hong Kong explained to me that this was one of the best ways of **rejuvenating valuable plots of land** in the heart of the city, it opened my eyes to the huge benefits of moving the chi.

I have since then applied this same principle to my own home and to the homes of many of my friends with great success. Keeping the chi moving keeps good fortune rolling.

For exactly the same reason it is a good idea to:

- Clean under the **carpets** regularly since this moves the chi.
- Move **cupboards** to get at the dirt that accumulates behind.
- Give the **undersides of beds** a good vacuuming to clear the space we sleep on.
- At least once a year to undertake spring **cleaning**.
- Have a program of **repainting the home** once every two or three years.
- Have a program to revitalize the home through **minor renovations**.
- Occasionally change the furniture of the home.

136 Creating fresh new energy

Negative energy of any kind can be overcome by bringing new energy into the space. New energy is young, fresh and has greater vitality – it replenishes the home and keeps the chi inside robust and growing. Chinese Taoist Masters stress that yin and yang must be assessed according to their strength. **Yang energy is either young yang or old yang. Yang energy that is exhausted tends to dissipate and transform into yin** unless given a new lease of life. For homes to enjoy robust good fortune the yang energy within should be young yang, strong, vital and vibrant. The secret of keeping yang energy this way is to replenish it constantly and keep it moving.

This is why I urge house owners to move their furniture around at least once a year – to keep the chi moving. Energy is never allowed to stagnate under sofas, in corners and behind furniture. These are places where dust tends to collect because here is where they find accommodating parts of the room which is beyond the reach of cleaning brooms and mops. Thus moving furniture aside to enable these places to be cleaned instantly refreshes the energy of the corner. Create a new arrangement for the furniture to give it a new lease of life.

The best time to do this is just before the end of the old year. It is amazing how much strength you will feel when you undertake a major house re energizing exercise. Include the cleansing rituals (using bells, singing bowls and incense) that appeal to you – they generate positive shifts of the intangible forces that will enhance the energy of your home. I do these cleansing rituals in the fortnight before the lunar New Year but you can choose anytime you wish.

Another thing I recommend to keep the chi of the home robust is to give it a **make over once every three to four years**. Sometimes this is just a cleaning and repainting of walls. Other times more serious renovations in accordance with changing flying stars may be undertaken. This is not something that everyone can do, but if you can, I recommend it strongly. There are few things that bring faster results than using one's feng shui knowledge to revitalize the home. Look on feng shui enhancement as an ongoing process.

Each time you make these changes you must be conscious that you are changing the energy by moving the chi. Houses always feel so good after a well planned feng shui renovation. It causes a rush of new chi into the home, which has the most revitalizing yang effect.

USE INCENSE TO CLEANSE YOUR SPACE "SPIRITUALLY"

Giving the home a regular "incense" ritual cleansing once a week is excellent for appeasing the spiritual energy of the home. Use fragrant aromatic incense like sandalwood burnt in an open charcoal fire to get the best results. An incense burner adorned with auspicious symbols such as the 8 auspicious objects further infuses the incense with auspicious chi.

137 Releasing trapped energy

Left: The big open windows here let in a good flow of fresh energy on a daily basis. This room also benefits from its daily sunshine bath. Such a home will always be well energized.

Many homes and offices have trapped energy that becomes negative because it has been stifled and locked inside tiny rooms. It is important to release this energy allowing fresh new air to blow through. Otherwise it is like keeping an ever-expanding harmful presence within the home.

These are also **homes whose windows and doors are seldom opened to let the air in**. In the tropics where outside temperatures get so hot people live in air conditioned homes, travel in air conditioned cars and work in air conditioned offices some people never get to breath fresh air. Over time those who have no regular regime of exercise will find they get sick from breathing stagnant air day after day. People like that are so badly in need of new chi. Homes that never get fresh air are also so desperately in need of new energy.

In temperate countries it is the intense cold of the winter months that cause homes to stay locked up tight. But the result is the same. The chi **within homes is recycled chi that cry out for release**. This is a problem that seems to afflict city homes, as a result of which an entire range of new ills and diseases have been discovered in the last fifty years. All caused by living in excessively yin spaces.

Breathing yang chi becomes a luxury for these city dwellers. Tune in to the chi of your living or work space. See if there has been too much recycling of stale air. Try opening the doors and windows and feel the energy shift instantly. The simple act of opening doors and windows in the home to suck in air and winds from the great outdoors have a fabulous revitalizing effect.

Make the effort to regenerate like this at **least once a month**, if not more often. You will find that you need to open at least two openings (doors or windows) to create the flow of chi. Simply keeping one door open will not bring in the chi from the outdoors. You will need to create the flow. And then you will feel the gentle energy of wind and breezes breathing new life into your space. Do this during the morning hours before the environment becomes polluted.

138 Negative chi from neighbours

If you live in a link house in a residential neighbourhood, the triangular shaped roof design shown here might also feature in houses from across the road. These sharp edges are like poison arrows and if the neighbour opposite is also hostile, then the negative vibes sent your way would be worse.

Unfortunately for some people, negative chi can come from across the hallway or from the house next door. When neighbours are friendly the energy from them is reinforcing. When vibes are hostile, however the energy can be harmful. When neighbours send intimidating chi on a regular basis you are sure to succumb UNLESS you tune in to it, recognize it for what it is and do something to dissolve it. **Hostile chi** coming from neighbours can be the harmless chi of frivolous gossip and small time envy, which can be easily dissolved by using your own stronger energy to ignore it, and then it dissipates. Sometimes the chi is simply annoying, like when your neighbour has a house full of screaming children who disturb your rest, break your things or simply irritate you. Overcoming this is easy. Just place a large urn of water with a wide mouth and a narrow bottom. This will effectively soak in all annoying loud noises and create an invisible absorbing vehicle.

It is when the energy being sent your way is full of venom, poisonous jealousy, bitter hatred, spiteful gossip or represents something more sinister that you might want to seriously consider countering with stronger measures. There are ways to **protect from being harmed by this kind of *hatred motivated* killing energy**. Use a round mirror to reflect everything being sent to you from across the road (i.e. coming from the opposite direction.) Send everything back with a reflective surface. The Chinese use the round mirror surrounded by the trigrams placed in the arrangement of the Yin Pa Kua symbol – and this is really powerful but it is also harmful. We call it the Pa Kua and it has the power to bounce back the bad energy and even to magnify it a thousand fold as well.

It is unnecessary to use such a strong counter measure. A round mirror of about twelve inches diameter should be adequate. I find that **hanging bells** is one effective way of dispersing incoming negative energy. The only problem with using bells is that if you inadvertently magnify any quarrelsome chi that may be present there or if there are quarrelsome flying stars they may be very strong, and things could get worse. I prefer to use the mirror cure supplemented **with an urn of still water**. I call this the YIN water cure and it is excellent for absorbing hostile vibrations.

139 Energy from previous residents

Before signing the lease to buy or rent any residential property do ask about the background and history of previous occupants. Negative chi caused by traumatic events such as a murder, a serious burglary, or a suicide tends to linger unless cleansed and dissipated. Sickness of the terminal or mental kind also tends to generate very sticky chi. The walls and floors and ceiling contain left over unhappiness and pain, which simply must be cleared.

Negative chi of the **angry aggressive** kind can also have been left over from occupants whose lives were consumed by anger, bitterness and violence – these are strong emotions that inadvertently get stuck on to the walls and ceilings of the home. Sometimes they are so stuck on that no amount of scraping and repainting can get them off. This is the case when the home has been closed most of the time with heavy drapes and dark coloured walls – yin chi captures and stores the spirit of anger and unhappiness very well. The negative chi of the place has seeped into the spirit of the home and simply must be released.

Fortunately, clearing any space of left over negative chi is not so difficult to do.

Ringing a space clearing bell instantly clears away stale energy.

There are powerful spatial purification techniques and cures, which anyone can use to sweep away old negatives – these include the use of metal objects such as bells, cymbals and singing bowls. Get those, which are specially made from seven types of metals to represent the seven chakras of the human body and the seven important planets that affect the energy of our world. These special space-purifying implements are very effective in dispersing negative energy.

Look for feng shui space-clearing tools and learn to use the striking of bells, cymbals and bowls to create sounds that absorb the negatives in the environment. Note that it is the harmonics of metal on metal that can be so powerful.

Using the **space-clearing bell** is probably the easiest way of lifting the energy of any space. These seven metal bells can be obtained from China, Tibet and Kathmandu. They are usually hand made and come with a wooden mallet. Or they can also come with a ringer inside the bells. The latter creates the effect of metal on metal and can be more powerful under certain circumstances.

Ring the bell in a rhythmic way so that the clarity of harmonics is heard and walk round your rooms three times in a clockwise direction. You will discover that as you ring, the sound becomes clearer and purer as the energy gets lighter and cleaner. As negative energy dissipates the sound of the bells begin to resonate with greater purity.

You can also use the **singing bowl**, which is even more effective because here the negative energy is drawn into the bowl, and then transformed into positive chi. The singing bowl has wonderful harmonics and once you get the knack of making it "sing", you will discover that clearing your space with it on a regular basis does wonders to make residents generate feelings of well being.

140 Using singing bowls to clear space

The use of the singing bowl is exactly the same as for the bell. Place it on a soft cushion in the palm of your hand – this will cause better harmonics to flow from the bowl and then strike the bowl three times to "awaken" it. Then walk round the room three times in a clockwise direction. Keep striking the bowl allowing the sound to linger as long as possible. You will find that as you grow in confidence, and as the energy of the space becomes clearer the sounds too will become purer.

You can always accompany your space clearing work with the burning of incense. In Malaysia we can easily find the "ingot incense" – this is sandalwood incense fashioned into the shape of a gold ingot, and burning this incense while clearing the space with the singing bowl creates wonderful chi for the home.

Now that you know how to "purify " the energy of your space, you do not have to be put off an otherwise beautiful home going for a good price just because there was a death, or some unpleasant incident, happened there.

Over the millions of years since Earth began all space must have experienced negatives of some kind. **Energy swirls and moves**, gets cleaned and gets muddied. The ancients knew of simple methods to clear the space – and much of this knowledge is now seeing the light of day brought about by a revival of interest in the energy that permeates time and space. Many old masters from different traditions are now sharing their secrets with the world – the use of metal cures, bells and bowls and incense – come from old Chinese and Tibetan traditions.

Singing bowls are much easier to get these days, but because they cannot be mass-produced, and are handmade, there is no guarantee of consistent quality. The sound emitted from each bowl will be different. So you must develop a sense for the singing bowl and tune into its harmonics to see if it has affinity with you. Sometimes it is so easy to just "know" the bowl that will work for you and other times you may try out a dozen and none seems suitable. When you do find a singing bowl you like and can tune into, do look after it. **Never allow the singing bowl** to fall onto a hard surface as this destroys its clearing powers instantly. Then you will have to get a new bowl. On the other hand, a bowl that you have used over the years becomes increasingly efficient at clearing your space. Soon it becomes a trusted and powerful ally of the home. There is no need to get singing bowls with designs or symbols and in fact I prefer the plain bowls. Always remember to place a cushion below to preserve the harmonics of your singing bowl.

A Singing Bowl uses the sound of metal to purify energy in a space.

Do note that you can also use singing bowls to temporarily overcome bad feng shui. When feng shui changes cannot be undertaken immediately, you can use the singing bowl daily to cleanse the atmosphere of inadvertent negative energy caused by any of the feng shui afflictions, both tangible as well as intangible.

141 When there has been an illness

An unoccupied guest room attracts illness. Clear the space before letting your guests use it.

When serious illness strikes it is often due to "sickness stars". This can affect young children or older people of the household. They are more vulnerable to changes in energy. When the family falls ill, the best cure are the **metal cures**, and especially the **sound of metal**. This is when the wonderful singing bowls are so precious. When used correctly, the bowls create a powerful metallic resonance that is incredibly efficient in absorbing and dissipating sickness chi.

The use of singing bowls is something you need to practice and get used to doing and the best way is to invest in a **really good singing bowl**. You can get a small one as the harmonics of the smaller bowls tend to be sharper and of a higher octave. Some people, however, do prefer the lower sounds of the larger bowls – it is up to you really as both are equally efficient at dissolving sickness chi.

Walk round the room three times in a clockwise direction, striking at the singing bowl or rubbing its edges with a wooden mallet. This will make the bowl sing and in singing it creates vibrational force that cleanses the air of sickness chi. Keep on creating the sound of metal – within minutes you will feel the room get lighter and brighter. Illness stars will be considerably weakened.

To take care of sickness causing flying stars, you can also hang **six rod metal windchimes**. In the flying star system of feng shui there are several number combinations that indicate the presence of illness causing energy, and for these the metallic windchime is an effective cure. Whenever illness strikes, I would recommend hanging metal wind chimes and using the singing bowl to clear the space of the intangible forces that is causing the illness. As a short term measure, this is an excellent cure even if you do not know flying star feng shui.

It is advisable however to investigate further and see if you can effect a long term cure as well. For this, an understanding of the illness stars of flying star feng shui is essential. It is by knowing that illness stars are actually Earth element stars, that we know how to use metallic energy to weaken them. Here we are using the exhaustive cycle of the elements.

Another way to control illness stars is to paint the walls pure white. Few people realize the immense power of white. This is the colour of metal but it is also the colour that contains all the **seven colours of the rainbow**, making it intensely powerful. So when someone is ill, placing him or her in a room with white walls is excellent. White flowers are also the best flowers to send as a "get well soon" offering. And since we are on this subject of flowers, do refrain from sending red flowers to someone who is ill. **Never send red with white**, as this is really a very unfortunate combination indeed. In fact, to the Tibetans red flowers sent to someone ill is a sign of death. So stick to white.

142 Sunshine water clears death vibes

Where there has been a death in the family it is very re energizing to complete the clearing of homes ritual with sunshine water. After the ritual cleansing with bells and incense follow through after the seventh day with thorough cleaning using sunshine water.

It is believed that by the seventh day the soul of the person who has passed on will have left the premises and gone on to what is known as the state of bardo – the in between state between death and rebirth. By the 49th day the soul will have taken rebirth or gone on to pure land. These are traditional beliefs that are part of the spiritual tradition of China and many other Asian countries. Rituals and practices associated with the three major events of life – births, marriages and deaths - are based on these beliefs. After death there is always symbolic cleansing done to aid the departed soul along its way. The space left behind should also be infused with living yang energy to benefit the living.

Sunshine water is water that has been left out in morning sunshine for at least three hours. The Chinese like to keep urns filled with water in the outdoors that are able to absorb the energy of the sun, the moon, the wind and air as well as the rain. In modern times when we get our water from the tap, leaving water out for a while is also a good way for harmful chemicals like chlorine to evaporate. This softens the water considerably and makes it really excellent for a variety of purposes, one of which is to give the house a thorough cleansing.

When you clean the home with sunshine water, you have to make sure that the floor is covered with water. This applies only to the ground floor of homes. Sunshine empowered water seeps into the base of the home, revitalizing it and cleansing it of any **lingering death energy**. If you live in an apartment, you cannot do this ritual, as it will be ineffective. In this case use a damp cloth soaked and rinsed with sunshine water to mop the floor and wipe tabletops. This will symbolically regenerate the energy.

Washing bedsheets amd pillow covers in sun water removes stale and negative vibrations.

143 Purifying with fragrant smoke

The use of aromas to revitalize spatial energy has been universally accepted by the cultures of many traditions and in recent times, this has become popular again. When you work with energy, you will understand that aromas permeate the consciousness of space. This helps to lighten it, thereby dissolving negative and hostile energy. There are many types of aromas commercially available today and it is a matter of personal preference what scents you use. However, some scents are more powerful than others.

Sandalwood for example, has been acknowledged as particularly uplifting. It is also a very spiritual scent with its wood revered in China and India. When sandalwood incense burns, you will experience its healing essence very quickly. Sandalwood absorbs negative energy that stick on surfaces, clothes, walls, floors and even the air itself. It is wonderful to finish spring-cleaning with whiffs of burning sandalwood incense. If you are ill, have a clogged nose or are down with the flu, light a stick of sandalwood incense to feel instantly embraced in an aura of healing energy. Sandalwood is more popular with Asians – Chinese and Indians. Westerners prefer other aromas and one whose popularity is similar to sandalwood is lavender.

Lavender is also very conducive to reducing heaviness in the air. It is said to bring out the creative spirit of our consciousness and is especially wonderful for transcending into other dimensions of consciousness through meditation therapy.

Aromatherapy today blends easily with many feng shui rituals. The release of natural aromas into space through the burning of incense invokes subtle energy fields and it is these that determine the quality of chi in any space. I do believe that fragrance and aromatic oils have tremendous healing power, and anyone can incorporate these into a powerful space purifying ritual with great success.

Lavender fragrance when sprayed into any space has a lovely calming influence. You can also use aroma diffusers to calm the energy of a room.

USING INCENSE

When you use incense to create fragrant sacred smoke, begin by generating a quiet mind and a good motivation. Open doors and windows to bring in new winds, then follow through with the sacred smoke ritual, using fragrant incense or aroma sticks. Many circumstances get improved by using fragrant smoke cleansing. The actual ritual itself is not different from smudging; a practice very popular with Native American Indians who use bunches of dried fragrant leaves to clear their homes of bad energy. Closer to home, I learnt my method from my mother and grandmother who used the "kemenyen" to burn fragrant incense over burning charcoal – allowing the smoke to dissipate through the rooms of the home.

Use incense burning saucers and bowls made of metal and decorated with auspicious symbols. I always use incense burners with auspicious images – the Nine-Dragons, the Pi Yao, the wu lou or the lotus shaped incense burners. I use the Nine Dragons to create the chi of courage and strength and the lotus when I want to generate a more refined ambience. I use the wu lou to spread health chi and the Pi Yao for all-round protection.

You should **develop your personal preferences** and choose from a wide variety of incense burners – today they come in many sizes and shapes – and they are usually very well made. The Chinese really are going upmarket in terms of the quality of their products, unlike the old days.

In recent years, I have discovered there are many variations to using sacred smoke rituals to cleanse home space. These can be either very simple or rather elaborate. It is up to you. All the sacred incense ingredients needed are easily available.

More important than ingredients is to generate focused concentration directing the mind to the cleansing process and creating the motivation, which is to keep the energy of the space light, thereby keeping illness and misfortunes at bay. **Always undertake space clearing, with a good motivation**. My advice is that you should undertake something like incense rituals within your own home. Incense has the power to transcend into other realms and it is best to stay on familiar ground. In your own home, your own energy and identity are very powerful – even if you may not be aware of it. When you unwittingly try to do someone a favour by performing some feng shui ritual, and especially rituals that involve incense, you may not be aware of things about the other person's space. And then instead of helping, you may be creating more problems. So do resist the temptation of trying to undertake space cleansing for other people.

This is one of the most auspicious ways to burn incense, with a Nine Dragon incense burner.

144 Creating yang chi with sounds and lion dancing

These lions created loads of auspicious yang energy for the **World of Feng Shui flagship store** at the Mid Valley shopping mall in Kuala Lumpur. The lions rolled gold ingots into the shop to create big success and good fortune for all the shoppers coming in to get their feng shui energizers.

The energy of homes come alive instantly when you use **sound therapy** – the sound of music, of people, of children, of chimes, of pets, of bells and bowls, and of drums and cymbals. Every tradition uses the throbbing and rhythmic sounds of various instruments to breath *yang* life to a special day, a celebration, or a happy occasion. The Chinese tradition always uses sounds – the sudden burst of firecrackers exploding during the New Year, the beat of drums to bring in the lions at festivals where colourful lions bring in yang energy. Bells and cymbals are also extensively used to awaken the chi of spaces. Thus when wealthy people move into their homes they go through the ritual that always includes drumbeats, bells and cymbals clashing. Better yet when there are lions dancing and prancing around.

In your home, the use of **sound therapy can be done on a less grand scale**. Home energy need not be so powerful. Thus *windchimes* are such an excellent way of capturing natural sounds from the winds. These chimes can be made of metal but they can also be made of bamboo. The sounds emitted are very different – you can use both types – metal for the west and northwest corners and bamboo chimes for the wood corners east and southeast, Notice these are **directly facing corner directions of the compass**. This is because the two elements being enhanced here – wood, which brings prosperity, and metal, which brings gold and success – are those most commonly associated with material success.

Hang these sound enhancers in the corners of your home, but also bring in the sounds of laughter as often as possible. The yang that comes from happy people is very powerful so keep inviting your friends over to collectively have a good time. It is far more powerful than you realize. And when you have a shop opening for business, or a wedding, or you are moving into a new home, or simply to celebrate the start of a new year, **bring on the lions** ... the combined use of cymbals clashing, drums beating and a few red and gold lions prancing around in happiness creates a store of yang chi that is incredibly powerful.

145 When there are a series of accidents

Negative energy in the home often causes a series of unrelated yet discernible pattern of accidents occurring. Someone banging your car in the morning, reversing into a drain; hitting your head against a beam, falling down on a misstep – when you notice a series of little things like this happening to you, one of three things can be out of sync in your home:

1. It could be that the **annual and monthly flying stars** have brought some bad luck to your front door or to the bedroom you occupy. Check this out if you can, before something more serious happens. Usually the entree of the star numbers 5 and 2 either singly or together coming in to the part of the house where the front door is located can cause a whole month's worth of bad luck, unless it is remedied with 6 rod windchimes. So even if you do not know flying star feng shui, hang a small all-metal windchime near the front door and see if the accidents or illness stop. If so, leave it there for about 30 days and then remove it.

2. The entrance of the house has become afflicted with excessive amounts of the **element that destroys the element of the main doorway**. This affliction can also have occurred in your bedroom. You need to be familiar with your home. Know which part of the house is North and which is South and so forth, then know the elements of each part also and you will then know if there is a conflict of elements. If there is, remove the offending element. An example: If you suddenly decide to place a tree in the Southwest of the house and your front door is located here, the chi of the front door gets sapped. Remove the tree! More examples: If you unknowingly place a water feature in the South, you will be putting out the fire. Remove the water immediately. Or you could start parking your new car in the East or Southeast – here metal hurts the wood energy, so you get sick if these are the directions of your front door. Everything that happens to your environment affects the chi.

3. The **entrance is severely blocked** by boxes, newly arrived furniture, etc which has not been moved for various reasons. This can cause a series of misfortunes unless rectified. Never allow unopened boxes to become clutter. No matter how busy you are, putting off clearing of newly arrived packages for the house can sometimes lead to bad consequences.

If you cannot find anything that could be causing the series of accidents, you can always use the space clearing rituals referred to earlier and see if it helps. **Combine the use of the singing bowl with incense rituals**. Sometimes a member of the family may have inadvertently picked up some "dirty energy" and brought it home, thereby causing the energy of the home to go out of sync. If this is the case, then using space-clearing methods will ease the situation.

Leave the incense burning each day inside a Pi Yao incense burner. The incense activates this protective creature. The Pi Yao is an excellent symbol used in the appeasement of the Grand Duke Jupiter.

146 When relationships go wrong

If things start going wrong for you in your interaction with people at work and socially, you can suspect that something in the energy of your space is having a negative effect on your relationship luck. This is usually caused by **afflicted earth energy** in the home, which in turn can be caused by the simple passage of time. Or it can be due to the **placement of plants in the wrong part of the home**. Plants signify Wood energy and when these are inadvertently placed in Earth corners (Southwest and Northeast) they cause problems in your social interactions with people.

Sometimes in cleaning your home, you could unwittingly place all sorts of junk inside spare rooms and bedrooms, or perhaps such junk is just left in corner. If your luck is bad, this can trigger off negative effects simply because the newly created junk has been dumped into corners that cause feng shui afflictions to manifest. The most vulnerable is when main doorways and bedrooms are affected. So when things suddenly start going wrong, do check that nothing is blocking the flow of chi and that plants have not been placed in Earth element corners.

If all seems well there, it could be your flying stars; in which case, to be on the safe side, hang a small metal windchime near the door and watch if things get better. If they do, you are on the right track, and hanging another windchime will strengthen the remedy. If things get worse, then it is a good idea to arrange for a *flying star natal chart* reading of the house – this will immediately show you what has gone wrong.

Quarrels are another way that afflicted feng shui can manifest. When husband and wife start quarrelling for no apparent reason, the cause is usually an **afflicted bedroom**. In flying star feng shui, there is a quarrelsome star number which "flies" into bedrooms either as annual or monthly stars, and this causes quarrels to happen. The Chinese use the Almanac to calculate these afflictions and there are remedies that can be used to overcome these quarrelsome stars. Usually, the most effective remedy is *to place something in red and gold in the bedroom.*

I have discovered that when my family is going through a period when everyone is being argumentative and confrontational, it is almost always due to the quarrelsome star having flown into the dining room. I have thus taken to having something **red and gold hanging** in the dining room permanently.

If you discern a sudden rise in family tensions, look for something in **red and gold**. Even a painting of goldfish will help. At the same time, reduce noise levels in those rooms where the family gathers. Noise will trigger the hostility star.

Plants in the Southeast erode relationship luck. If you have plants here, better to move them away.

147 Dissolving tension and anger

Another excellent way of dissolving tension within the home is by placing at least **six round crystal balls** in the family areas of the home, especially in the Southwest or Northwest corners. Having round crystal balls suggest smoothness in relationships. The number 6 signifies heaven and the crystal balls indicate a union of the heaven trigram with the earth trigram – Chien with Kun. Crystals are the most potent symbols of Earth energy. I have found them to be such wonderful enhancers and also so auspicious.

Make sure they are crystals. Do guard against having plastics that pass off as crystals. **Natural crystals** are superior to manmade crystals and if you can afford them, it is excellent having a large single-pointed natural crystal displayed in or near the center of your home with a light shining at it and lighting it up. This activates the crystal's Earth energy, and since the center of the home is always enhanced by the Earth element, everyone living in the home will benefit from the enhanced energy triggered by the light shining at the crystal. All tensions within the home will dissolve. Any tendency towards anger, violence and hostility will be considerably reduced.

Left: Clustering six crystal balls together are most effective in absorbing quarrelsome chi.

If the problem in the home is continuous anger that leads to violence and quarrelling, invest in a vase to apply the YIN water cure. The Chinese word for **vase is "ping"** which stands for peace, and many Chinese homes display many beautiful vases to create an atmosphere of peace and harmony in the home. Vases however work their potent magic only when displayed in homes that are clear of clutter, and when they are filled with still water. This is YIN water, which has the power to absorb and dilute anger in the home.

CLEANSING WITH SALT

Here is a preliminary cleansing ritual to perform when you bring crystals into your home. Always cleanse them of other people's energy by placing them in a salt solution. Use either sea salt or rock salt. Or use salt to rub all over the surface of the crystal. Think that the salt is drawing out all the negative energy and then wipe it with a damp cloth. If the crystal is very large, you might want to soak it in the salt solution for seven days and seven nights. Once crystals are cleansed, the continuous shining of a light onto the crystal will keep its chi fresh and vibrant.

148 Burglary, lawsuits & gossip

BURGLARY – use salt and saffron

Houses which have just suffered the nasty after-shock of being robbed, burgled and broken in need to be instantly cleansed of the negative energy. Usually, the same few houses in a neighbourhood tend to be the targets of burglars. The Chinese believe that such houses suffer from the robbery affliction star and unless this is corrected, there is always the **danger of being burgled again and again**.

When your house has just been burgled, use a mixture of **salt and saffron water** to cleanse the doorways and windows of the home. All the openings of the home should get a wipe with this solution. Move three times round the openings in a clockwise direction. Next place a salt and saffron water solution at the entrance of the doorway, leaving it there for three days. Also keep the lights turned on for at least three days.

Another cure is to use the **singing bowl**. Usually when a home has been burgled, residents live in fear during the following weeks and it is necessary to lift this cloud of apprehension. Otherwise, negative energy gets created that can act as the catalyst for some other type of misfortune to occur. Using the comforting harmonics of a singing bowl to absorb the negative energy is very helpful. The internal chi of residents will get stabilized in a shorter time and the air becomes lighter.

An effective antidote to being burgled is **having an inverted broom placed by the wall** next to the door. This is said to ward off the chi of robbery. The Chinese also believe that placing a pair of Chi Lin or lions flanking the doorway acts as a powerful deterrent.

LEGAL ENTANGLEMENTS – use birds or yin water

Yin water is said to be powerful in absorbing the quarrelsome vibes that lead to legal entanglements. Remove all windchimes, clocks and other moving objects from near the vicinity of the door. Place an image of a bird in flight near the door flying outwards – this is believed to reduce the negative impact of legal battles and could even solve the problem altogether. Birds are excellent **symbols of appeasement** and also for warding off accidents. The Chinese and Hindus, believe that the placement of birds feathers in the home will ward off legal battles and accidents. Keeping bird feathers or the image of a bird in the car is also said to have the same effect. If you are presently involved in a lawsuit, wear birds fashioned into jewellery, preferably appearing to fly.

GOSSIP - display the Rooster or wear the Mystic Knot

If you suffer from negative gossip the best way to reduce its occurrence and its effect on you is by using sounds to scare away the *devil of chatter* – and the best is by using metal cymbals. Hanging a pair of cymbals just inside the home will symbolically override the negative effect of gossip as well as go a long way towards reducing its occurrence.

Another effective way to reduce gossip is by displaying a Rooster image with sharp claws. This will calm the chatter that focuses on your love life. Wear this symbol in green (made of a non gem quality jade) to put a stop to idle gossip that pertains to your business, in gold to reduce all frivolous gossip and with diamonds to counter gossip that harms your career. You can also wear coloured crystals to overcome gossip.

149 Amulets to ward off jealousy & politics?

The Taoist feng shui cure for jealousy at work that leads to really harmful gossiping is the Rooster image. The **Rooster** is believed to be the most effective counter measure for those who become victims of malicious politicking at work. Place a white (or gold and red) Rooster on your desk at the office – and let it peck away all your problems one by one. The Rooster cure is especially suitable for those whose desks are placed in tight corners or who may be sitting in what I like to refer to as the *centipede arrangement* – one desk behind another in two rows. Such an arrangement gives rise to the sting of gossip and malicious backbiting. The rooster on your desk will clear away all negative energy created by the situation.

To ensure you are adequately protected, also carry an **amulet brass mirror** in your purse. The *brass mirror cure* was a popular method used by the mandarins of the Emperor's court to overcome political intrigues. In those days, the danger of death caused by the politicking maneuvering of ministers and court advisers was very real. Any fall from grace would result in imprisonment or death not only of the patriarch but also of the entire family. Belief in symbolic feng shui was something everyone took for granted – and especially the advisers in the Emperor's court. Today's corporate and office intrigues are not dissimilar from the Court intrigues of the old days, so the use of feng shui cures used in those times might give some relief.

If you are the target of jealous rage and envy, you could become the unwitting recipient of negative vibes sent your way. These can come from jealous colleagues, spurned lovers, envious friends or business enemies. In today's highly competitive environment, everyone needs protection against negative vibrations sent out by unscrupulous people.

Many Asians believe in wearing amulets, which are said to have the power of warding off negative energy. The Chinese are great believers of amulets and many believe that simply wearing **a dragon pin** has the power to ward off negative vibrations. Other popular amulets are the tortoise, the Chi Lin and the mystical symbols.

If you feel that you could be attracting jealousy wear a Dragon pin. The Dragon is a powerful celestial creature, which can protect and also attract luck. This is the most simple amulet image, which has been used for many centuries. Women should wear the dragon on their left, while men should wear the dragon pin on their right. The pin is necessary because it must resemble a needle capable of piercing through negative chi. In the old days, Taoist masters would sew needles into the clothing of children to ward off jealousy.

In the home, the presence of **9-ring swords** are a powerful deterrent. These swords are made from old Chinese coins tied together with red thread, and are said to slice through invisible negative energy with great accuracy and effectiveness. Place them behind you at work to curb the negative impact of jealous thoughts sent your way by envious colleagues.

Curved knives made of metal are also effective in clearing negative intangibles that may affect your well being.

8

SPIRITUAL FENG SHUI

Taoist feng shui engages the inner chi of man, using secret techniques that unite heaven, earth and man to create awareness of shifts in the subtle chi. These movements affect man's well being, facilitating direct communication with nature, and with winds and waters. It enables us to read signals from the environment and from the realms of animals, from weather changes, from cloud formations, from signs sent from the cosmos - seen within the context of time and space.

Inner feng shui engages **meditation, breathing and visualizations** to empower the clothes and jewellery we wear with powerful chi, helping us to transform ordinary symbols of nature, from the animal realms and from mysterious past traditions into powerful amulets and talismans. Like the exquisite gold and diamond longevity symbol shown above and the stunning tribute horse jewellery shown below, complete with gold ingots on its back. Here the natural treasures of the earth – gold and diamonds- can be fashioned by man and empowered by special mantras powerful talismans and amulets.

Every home will be made more prosperous and safer when powerful spiritually empowered amulets and plaques containing secret mantras are placed in the home. Such sacred objects can be modern and contemporary in design but as long as they contain special mantras they become extremely powerful.

150 Spirituality and feng shui

One of the most exciting dimensions of spiritual feng shui is its focus on the mysterious connections between mankind and the cosmic chi of the Universe. Spiritual feng shui is inner feng shui, a set of principles and practices that produce shifts in self-awareness that improve the way we interact with the environment. The common thread that connects man and his environment is chi, the life force we describe as energy.

Spiritual feng shui embraces the whole mysterious world of "magic" that deals with the empowerment is the opening of one's body and mind to shifts in the chi. This involves developing expertise in breathing and visualizations. At a higher level, meditations become part of the training. With years of practice, the reading of and awareness to energy becomes second nature. The mind manifests energy in ten thousand different ways. Spiritual Feng shui tunes into chi to understand the workings of the Universe and their manifestations.

It is this awareness that gives rise to an understanding of the environment, of nature and of its effect on the fate and fortunes of man. This understanding can be so accurate, so stunning in its veracity, that sometimes we think of it as magic. And this goes back to the shamanic heritage of ancient China. Our cultural traditions and legends are filled with stories of celestial masters who seemed to have such amazingly yogic powers – they could fly through the sky, be in several places at one time, appear and disappear at will. **And communicate with Deities from different celestial and hell realms**. Speak to any Chinese brought up on the weekly TV shows of Hong Kong and Taiwan that are based on Cosmic heroes and heroines, and they will describe physical feats

Above: Green Tara is the Mother of the all Buddhas.

beyond your imagination.

Feng shui really only scratches the surface of Chinese mystical and magical traditions. Here we watch in awe as celestial masters demonstrate a kind of yogis power that is truly magic, do things with their bodies that defy gravity and stun the senses.

Every physical feat that goes beyond ordinary human endurance is attributed to empowered chi. **Every piece of good fortune and every occurrence of misfortune is related to negative energy chi**. A falling leaf is chi. A child crying is chi. Meeting the man of your dreams is chi. Getting a great job offer is chi. Striking the lottery is chi. Winning is chi. Losing is chi. The Eight Immortals personify all the highest manifestations of chi and having their images in the home symbolize the ultimate of all good chi. Better than 8 Immortals are holy images of the Buddhas and the Goddesses. They will bring new and amazing insights into spiritual feng shui to enhance any home!

151 Creating seven types of awareness

When there is no chi we are dead. When it is available in abundance life is a ball.

Spiritual feng shui focuses exclusively on the chi. Tuning in to the chi, Masters are able to read signals from nature, understand the signs that reveal things to us about forthcoming events, people and situations. These signs also reveal when the chi needs replenishing and when chi has turned bad.

Spiritual feng shui enables the Master to **read faces, palms, bodies**, so he can tell us the level of the life force, is able to predict when death will occur and when recovery will take place. The Master sees a painting hanging in the hallway and is able to forecast how it will affect the family, watches the demure maid bring in the tea and can say unhesitatingly that she is with child.

Such Masters can look into the eyes of your son and predict the next twenty years of his life, share a meal at your dinner table and can tell you the outcome of that job interview you had this morning, witnesses the flight of swallows and tell you a stranger is coming with a happy message.

Spiritual feng shui takes us into another realm of space enhancement – one that engages the **mind at inner levels**, and with training enables us to use our body centers as sensors. These engage the seven types of awareness that reflect the seven energy centers of the body.

The development of awareness at these levels is not the same as the seven energy centers of the chakra system. According to the Chinese, energy source is at the center of the body – **the central tan thien** just below the navel. Energy flows through the body via the vertical axis known as the central channel and the meridians, and a field of energy is created inside our bodies. We can activate both solar and lunar chi to empower our life force.

The seven types of awareness are:

- **Visual** awareness – engaging the sense of seeing
- **Hearing** awareness – engaging the sense of listening
- **Tasting** awareness – engaging the sense of eating
- **Feeling** awareness – engaging the sense of touching
- **Sensing** awareness – engaging the sense of tuning in
- **Inhaling** awareness – engaging the sense of breathing
- **Transcending** awareness – engaging the mind in meditation

Solar chi kung uses sun energy to activate the nine orifices of the body to an awareness of energy and doing this successfully is said to be excellent for improving health and mental clarity. It also detoxifies the body and contributes to the build up of a strong immune system. **Lunar chi empowerment** uses moon energy to balance the two vertical axis of the body. This method regulates the internal flow of fluids and opens up the five psychic channels of the body.

To learn the correct physical exercises, breathing and ultimately meditations and visualizations that help you develop a heightened sense of awareness, you will need to find a **perfectly qualified Spiritual master.** It is quite beyond the scope of this book to offer you the methods. But knowing the basic concepts of Spiritual feng shui will empower your practice and lift its effectiveness to an amazing new level.

152 Concept of "Like with like"

One of the primary doctrines of Taoist feng shui is the concept of matching **"like with like"** which uses an intuitive approach. Basically this refers to the matching of your personal chi with the chi of your immediate space and environment. How you interpret this tenet is up to you. It is a matter of judgment. You can take a totally simplistic approach OR you can make the matching as complex as you wish. As long as you follow your own developed intuition (based on meditative practice engaging your inner chi) applying this concept will bring you good feng shui. Basically, the concept of "like with like" refers to the mind's symbolic associations. Using inner chi, you can ask yourself the following questions:

Do your directions match? The answer is "matching your date of birth, your KUA number with the season of your birth. Use this simple approach to check the season of your birth and determine the direction that brings you good luck. Taoists associate the East with Spring, North with winter, South with summer and West with Autumn. So if you move from your place of birth towards your seasonal birth direction, you will have good fortune. *So if you were born in the winter in Texas and you move to Nebraska you will be moving towards your birth direction which is North so the move will bring you good fortune.*

Do your days match? For instance if you were born on the 1st of any month, then the number 1 is good for you. And if you were born on a Thursday, then every Thursday is lucky for you. This is a simple approach. It is an approach to numerology that focuses on the number we remember the most easily, and uses the inner feng shui consciousness to tap subconscious lucky numbers. Say you were born on the 11th day of any month, the number 11 is lucky for you. A house address with the number 11 means that house will be lucky for you. If you were born on the 25th day of any month, it means a house address with the number 25 or 125 or 225 etc is good for you.

Do your numbers match? Your numbers are based on your date of birth. According to Taoist feng shui, there is no need to change this to the lunar date since your inner chi identifies with your western birth date. Hence, if you were born on the 18th March 1976, then your numbers would be 18 3 1976 – Any of these numbers appearing on your address, telephone number, car number would be in affinity with you. So a car number 1831 is good for you. A telephone number with at least half of these numbers will be good for you. An address without any of your numbers is said to do nothing for you. If you add up all the numbers of your birth date, you will obtain a single digit number that is lucky for you. In this case 183 1976 adds up to 8, so 8 is the number that brings you *like with like.*

Do your colours match? This is based on your birth season. If you were born in the Spring, your colour is green; in the summer it is red, in the winter it is black, in the autumn it is white and in the in between seasons it is yellow. Wearing your colours will bring you *like with like* good fortune. Taoist feng shui further indicates that red or pinks will bring you a lover or spouse, wearing yellow will enhance your wealth luck, wearing green will reduce stress and aggravation and wearing white will help you recover from an illness. This simplistic approach to feng shui is said to be as effective as using the concept of the five elements.

153 Concept of double goodness

The feng shui concept of double goodness is one of the secrets of magnifying good fortune. Here the reasoning is that when you have determined a number, a colour, a direction or an element that brings luck for you, then having it doubled will bring you double the luck, double the goodness, double the happiness. They get magnified!

Thus you can apply the concept of **"double goodness"** much like the double happiness concept, the symbol of which is shown here. The double happiness is a very powerful symbol of conjugal bliss and happiness in marriage and family life. It connotes double blessings from heaven. When you apply the concept of double goodness, think of all the good things in your life doubling in magnitude i.e. your wealth doubled, your success, and your generosity doubled as well.

SELECTING DOUBLE GOODNESS DIRECTIONS

Applying the double goodness principle to the use of directions is something that is also advocated in the practice of EIGHT MANSIONS FENG SHUI – under which it is stated that if a certain direction is said to be auspicious for you, then having it as your facing as well as sitting direction will bring you a double dose of good fortune. So if NORTH is your romance direction, then if your houses faces **NORTH** and your bedroom is located in the NORTH section of your house, you will enjoy double romance luck.

And if **EAST** is your prosperity sheng chi direction, then if your houses faces EAST and you sleep with head pointed EAST you will enjoy double goodness luck.

And if **WEST** is your health direction, then sleeping with your head pointed to the WEST and your bedroom is placed in the WEST room of your house will bring double goodness health luck.

Or if **SOUTHWEST** brings you romance luck, then sleeping with your head pointed SOUTHWEST and if your room is also located in the SOUTHWEST corner of the house will bring you double the romance luck you seek.

You can also apply the double goodness concept to your directions based on your birth season. Thus, if you were born in the spring, your lucky direction would be EAST. Then if your house faced EAST and you were occupying the EAST room of your house, you would be enjoying double goodness luck.

SELECTING DOUBLE GOODNESS DAYS

So if 1 is good for you then the 1st day of the first month is double goodness for you. If 2 is good for you then the 2nd day of the second month is your double goodness day. And if 8 is good for you then the 8th day of the 8th month is good for you. And so forth. You can regard such a day as being doubly excellent for you to move into a new house, to start renovation, to get married or to undertake any of the happiness events in your life. Applying the double goodness concept to the selection of lucky days is one of the easiest ways of finding a day whose chi is said to be in affinity with your chi. This method does not necessarily over ride the use of the Almanac. Instead, if this selection of day is good for you, and the Almanac also says it is a good day, then by all means consider this day as having a heavy dose of double goodness. I like Taoist feng shui because its concepts are simple and uncomplicated.

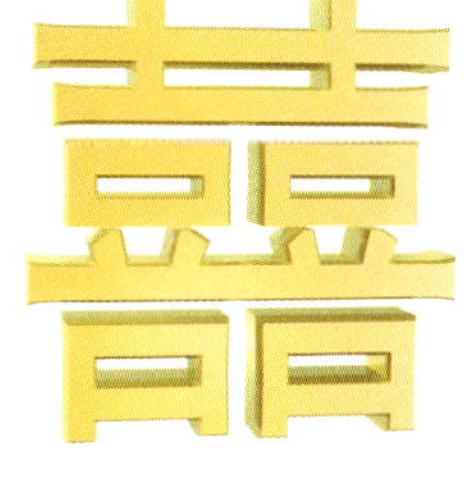

154 Going with the flow

The flow of chi within the home should flow naturally. The idea is not to cause physical flows to be stopped abruptly or for there to be obstacles in its path. Energy moves according to the physical patterns of the home. So watch the patterns on your floors, on your curtains and in the lines and traffic patterns of the home.

Spiritual feng shui teachings always stress the benefits of **moving along with nature**. Going with the flow means not fighting against the direction of the wind, not swimming against the currents, not attempting to turn back the clock and refraining from creating imbalances to the energy around you. Going with the flow also suggests symmetry, so that a natural balance of energy is achieved at all times. It is for this reason that feng shui recommends regular rather than irregular shapes, rounded curves rather than angles and sharp edges, a meandering rather than a straight line. There is rhythm to the flow of life, to the changing of seasons, and to the transformation of yin into yang and back into yin again.

The simplest example of going with the flow can be experienced in how we react to the change of seasons. In winter, when it is cold we wear heavy clothing for warmth. In summer we cool ourselves with lighter clothing. In the materials we use to build our homes, we must ensure the wood we use has the grain running in the same direction, that the **marble on the floor** flow in generally the same direction and the slate tiles we use also move in generally the same direction – all going with the flow.

155 Spiritually Testing the wind

Feng shui captures the essence of wind and water. You need to test the wind – see if it is excessively dry or wet, if it's gushing too fast or murmuring gently. Dry winds contain no moisture and do not bring goodness. Fast winds drive all goodness away. The winds also bring signs – messages from the cosmos. Here is how to read the wind for signs:

- **Choose the correct hour** to undertake the testing. This should coincide with the hours of your animal sign. RAT - [11pm to 1am]; OX – [1 to 3am]; TIGER- [3 to 5am]; RABBIT - [5 to 7am]; DRAGON – [7 to 9am]; SNAKE [9 to 11am]; HORSE – [11 to 1pm]; SHEEP - [1 to 3pm]; MONKEY - [3 to 5pm]: ROOSTER – [5 to 7pm]; DOG – [7 to 9pm] and PIG- [9 to 11pm]. If the time falls in the middle of the night, use the time frame that is directly opposite. For example, instead of 2am, use 2pm.

- **Test the wind from outside the main front door**. Take three big steps outside, and then use a compass to determine your orientations, turn to face south. Next, relax all your body sensors. Focus in on the seven types of awareness and open yourself to the wind that is blowing at that precise moment. Remember to stay relaxed at all times. If there is a **gentle breeze**, the signs are excellent. If the wind is gushing and strong, good luck is swept away. The more windy it is, the more protection the house needs. If there is no wind at all, the energy is stuck and the house requires to have its energy woken up. You can use sounds, music, or throw a party to bring in an infusion of yang energy.

- If you are testing the winds for **ROMANCE luck**, look for signs related to the earth element. Look for things in pairs, such as birds, bees and butterflies. Look out for things passing by that are **red or yellow** in colour. Look for the moon, women, smiling faces, flowers blooming. Anything in Nature can be read as answers to the questions in your mind at that moment in time you decide to test the wind. If you are doing this investigation for a friend, use their animal hour instead.

- If you are testing the wind for **WEALTH luck**, look for signs related to both wind and water either combined or singly. The most potent signal for wealth and prosperity is rain. Light rain is excellent. Beware of hurricanes and storms. Thunder and lightning are claps of approval. Also check clouds. The presence of light white clouds is always a good sign. **Look at the cars and vans that drive past.** When something that suggests money, or a harvest or a fully loaded lorry drives by these are instantly good signs. A busload of children, a neighbour's cat jumping by, even a garden **iguana** are all good signs. Once I came out to test the wind and saw an iguana while on my morning walk. Imagine seeing something like that in a city residential area! That evening, I received a fat check in the mail. Another time a vicious Rottweiler who had escaped from his home came straight at my two cocker spaniels and attacked me. I recall screaming and a car pulling up. The car stopped the dog in its track. He slunk away when his owner came, but it left me shaken. Two weeks later, I collapsed while on a lecture tour of India. Coincidence? Not at all. I should listen to all the signals sent to me by the cosmos. So should everyone who is interested in understanding energy.

156 Mystical mudras to detect chi

Kuan Yin, the Goddess of Mercy.

You can use mystical hand signals (called mudras) to check the energy chi of your house. The time to use these mudras is when you feel there might be something wrong with your feng shui, but you are unable to see what it can be.

Sometimes the chi works in such mysterious ways that the cause of a family problem could be hidden from being known. For instance if your children, first one and then another start having speech problems, or a member of the family develops a mysterious illness, or things go wrong with frightening suddenness or frequency and you have called in the feng shui man and still are unable to find anything wrong - you can then try using these mystical mudras.

Always start with the **protection mudra** shown above here. Hold both your hands out in front of you in the protection mudra.

First close your fingers into a fist and then straighten the index and the little finger. Hold your hands with palms facing upwards in this position and slowly walk round the rooms of the house. At first you will feel nothing but after a while you will start to get a small tingling sensation in your hands. This is the protection mudra in that it **ensures you do not 'collide" with negative energy** as you walk around the room. Remember to keep your spine straight and erect as this will ensure chi flows through your body unimpeded thereby facilitating your investigation.

FEELING FOR DIFFICULT ENERGY

To investigate and uncover negative energy that may be causing you harm but which is not easily obvious, use the investigation mudra shown below here.

To do this bring the two hands together and join the fingers of both hands, index finger to index finger, little finger to little finger, and the right thumb to the left thumb. Use the illustrations on this page to practice the mudras.

With the two hands joined together at the fingers you can walk around the rooms of the home a second time. Your hands will help you to **resolve and detect difficult chi energy**. When the energy is negative you will feel a tingling in your hands. This should cause you to stop and investigate the vicinity of that area. The mudras assist you to penetrate the chi of that part of the house. Often closer inspection will reveal the cause of any illness or problem area.

The Protection Mudra

157 Playing feng shui detective

To use the mystical mudras effectively you must learn to synchronize the use of your eyes with that of your hand mudra of investigation. You must have some idea of what you should be looking for, but do keep an open mind. Energy works in strange ways and bad energy can be caused by any number of things. Let me share some personal experiences with you to give you an idea of what to look for. Using this same method to play detective in my own home, here are some examples of the things I discovered.

A nest of red ants near the base of my rambutan tree. When I appeased the ant nest with incense offering, they left after a week and so did the mysterious red rash that had sprung up across the front body of my maid. The tree was just outside her window.

A line across the face of a mature lady that was part of a beautiful Chinese screen I used to hang along one wall of my living room. It was a hairline crack and it struck me as most inauspicious. I had developed a very severe pain across my face and was reluctant to see the doctor because there seemed to be no particular reason for the pain and I had used the investigation mudra to get a feel for the energy, which could be causing me this problem. I dismantled the screen as soon as I spied the hairline crack across the face. I folded the screen and kept it in my storeroom. My pain left me almost immediately.

A huge crack in our rice urn. That time I had just returned from Hong Kong to stay in Malaysia and was going through a really hard time. Try as much as I could, I simply was unable to shake off the feeling of dread and fear. It was totally illogical and unreasonable so I suspected something could be wrong with the energy of the home. I used the mudra to go round my house and stopped in front of the rice urn.

There was a huge crack that ran the length of the urn from the mouth to the bottom. The maid had turned the crack to the back so it was not immediately noticeable. Once I changed the rice urn my feelings of dread disappeared completely. I became more confident of myself and succeeded in shaking off some very real and debilitating feelings of self-pity and fears for the future. So sometimes when you feel afraid and uncertain of yourself, you might want to use the *investigation mudra* to see if you can find anything wrong in the objects around your home that could be causing you to feel the way you do.

The joints in the underside of my bed had come loose. I had been sleeping very badly and could find no reason for it. The mattress was dry and had been put in the sun to energize it with yang energy. I had also undertaken space clearing to improve the quality of chi in my bedroom. It would work for a couple of nights and then I was back to being unable to sleep. I tossed and turned at night. The lack of sleep was affecting my work so badly I decided to make a thorough investigation and it was then that I noticed that the underside of my bed was loose. Somehow, the tongue and groove that held my bed together had come loose. I was lucky the bed did not just collapse. As soon as I had the bed fixed, I went back to sleeping like a log.

So now you try playing feng shui detective in your home!

158 Sensing the chi

Each time you suddenly become aware of the sun shining through trees, or coming out from behind clouds it is always a sign of recovery.

Chi is really the wind, just as money is water. Chi brings all the attributes of happiness as well as facilitates the water, which brings wealth. So while water is vital and important, chi is even more so. When you test the wind you are in reality sensing the chi around you. *Here are important signs to look out for.*

When testing the wind for **HEALTH** luck, look for signs of movement that reveal the presence of yang chi such as a **gentle breeze**, or the colour white which always means healing and a renewal; the sun suddenly appearing from behind clouds. This latter sign is such a powerful symbol of yang energy that recovery is certain. Once, many years ago while I was nursing my sick horse who was suffering from colic, an illness that can be a potential killer, I prayed fervently for a sign even as I comforted him. He was lying on the ground inert. I thought he was dying. And then suddenly, the sun shone through the heavy foliage of trees. I knew then he would recover and he did. That was over ten years ago and I have since sold him to someone else as I have given up riding, and he is still going strong!

When sensing the chi for clues to **BUSINESS** luck, look for signs related to the **wood element**. If you see a lorry carrying a load of logs, or transporting furniture these are excellent signs. Flowers, plants, a view of water, or suddenly turning on the a TV and there is a picture of forest of trees, or a field of flowers blooming – these are excellent signs that your business is going to succeed. If precisely at your birth hour a visitor arrives bringing his young son (below the age of 9) this is an excellent sign, especially if the little boy seems to like your home and starts playing. If he starts to cry and frets and wants to leave, you better think twice ... recently I was in Singapore looking at the house feng shui of a friend. She is starting a new business venture and wanted to ensure her feng shui was auspicious. **At the precise moment I started looking for signs I looked up to the clouds above her house** and spied truly auspicious cloud formations that took the shape of dragons. I was very excited by these signs and then her phone rang. When she had taken the call she ran out of the house grinning. "This is the first time someone has phoned me asking me to collect money due to me." she said. That was indeed a good sign. According to Taoist feng shui this indicates that her luck is good and her business will succeed. She will certainly not have any collection problems.

To sense the chi for **SUDDEN MONEY LUCK**, look for signs of prosperity e.g. the appearance of coins, or suddenly seeing an image of a river – on television as you turn it on, or in a magazine on the page you open to, or rain suddenly falling, or a bird

Painting of cranes symbolize longevity for the residents.

flying towards you. **Birds** are generally speaking, the **BEST indicators of sudden wealth**. When you hang pictures of birds or paintings of many birds, it suggests great good fortune coming towards you. I know of at least three very successful tycoons in Hong Kong who have huge paintings of birds in their homes. They tell me these paintings brought them quantum leaps in their financial fortunes.

Paintings of cranes (which are symbols of longevity) are also said to bring sudden money luck when they are painted as a flock and flying in the skies. *When a plant that rarely flowers suddenly blooms it is also a very good sign.* On the day my lotus bloomed they did so in pairs – one white and one pink, as shown in the picture here we received confirmation that my lama was coming to stay. For me this was fantastic good news indeed. I associate the lotus to the manifestation of spiritual happiness rather than business luck, but my lotuses also brought a wonderful financial windfall.

As with birds, flowers also indicate extreme good fortune when you are looking for signs for that indicate how a business venture will turn out. Flowers blossoming suggest a project coming to a successful fruition. Yellow flowers indicate money success while white flowers can suggest a bad situation getting better. White blooms also suggest someone sick getting well.

Pink flowers suggest good fortune associated with romantic luck. When you want your steady date to pop the question, pink flowers are much better indications than red flowers. Indeed, sending red roses to someone you love is usually frowned upon by those who practice feng shui, since red roses can cause relationships to end. This is especially true of roses that have thorns. Better to send pink or peach roses with the thorns removed. The indications of auspicious colours for flowers should be observed when displaying flowers for the home. Displaying fresh flowers that are yellow in colour are said to be the most auspicious in terms of attracting wealth luck; pink to attract romantic luck and white to attract health luck. When you get up in the mornings, let these auspicious flowers be the first thing you see. This is one of the best reasons for placing auspicious symbols in the home. Then they become the first thing you see in the morning when you wake up and the last thing you see at night before you sleep. This creates powerful auspicious vibes within your mind. This is the stuff of Taoist feng shui.

159 Signs from children

Happy children bring yang energy into your.

Young male children under 9 years old are said to reflect the good and bad side of energy that dominates any home. When they are young, and especially when they are young boys they personify ***"pure yang"* chi**. Their behavior and the way they dress can be translated into special signs that tell you about the quality of energy in any space. Young boys are also used by Nature to communicate with us. So be alert to their behavior if they should suddenly appear at the exact hour you are testing the wind and sensing the chi.

The appearance of children on the scene of any feng shui investigation is itself a potent sign. If they smile and seem happy to watch you work, it means your feng shui consultation should go well. If they start to fret, or whine or seem uncomfortable or unhappy for whatever reason, I would suggest that you stop working. It is either a sign that it is not a good time to do the feng shui of the place, or that the house feng shui is so negative it requires some space cleansing before any feng shui alteration can be made. **Be sensitive to the behaviour** and responses of young children as they can reveal much about the energy of any space.

READING SIGNS FROM CHILDREN.

Observe what they do.
If they are playing, watch the games they play. Are the games stable or unstable? Are they happily reading? Are they building something? Does it suggest anything related to what you are doing? For instance, if you were in business, then anything they do that is related to building, growing or eating would be good signs. If they offer you anything – some sweets, coins, or paper – these too are excellent signs.

Watch their moods.
Are they crying, happy or unhappy? Are they smiling and laughing? Are they drinking water, slurping an ice cream or watering the plants, wanting to go to the bathroom, restless? Are they feeding your fish? Remember that a happy child always suggests good feng shui, while an unhappy fretful display of anger or tears always suggests that there might be pockets of negative energy, which may be cause for concern. When the child screams that he or she wants to go home, it is almost certain that there is something negative in the energy.

Look at the clothes they are wearing.
What are the colours? Are they in harmony with your home? Are their clothes too tight or too loose? Do they look comfortable? For instance, we always associate children wearing yang colours, seldom black. Thus when you see children coming into your home wearing a black outfit, it signifies yang confined in yin. It is a very bad sign indeed. If your friend brings her son to visit and you see the child wearing a black outfit, try to make an excuse quickly and divert the child to someplace in the garden. Children who wear white, green, yellow, red or bright blue bring the yang vibrations of the four directions.

Remember that the reaction of young children to the energy of your space is usually a reliable indication of the quality of its energy. Young boys under the age of nine are especially reliable indicators of energy.

Also look at photos or paintings of children in the home.
When you hang pictures of children on the wall, do **make sure they are not of tragic children**. There are few things as auspicious as young children grinning broadly and looking happy. Pictures like that exude pure yang energy that is favourable, while pictures that suggest children are in discomfort, in pain or in grief are to be avoided. I once knew an artist who was so moved by the suffering children of Africa she did collages that depicted their sufferings. In her home, she hung many of these art pieces, which sent sad vibes all through her home. I was not surprised years later to hear that both she and her children suffered severe illnesses and accidents.

Photo of children crying is very inauspicious.

160 Signs from birds

If you ever see a flock of birds (flying ducks or geese) like this it is an incredibly auspicious sign – it precedes a wonderful advancement in your career. Paintings of thousands of birds are especially auspicious and if you can find such paintings, hang them in your home to attract prosperity into your home.

In feng shui, birds are powerful symbols of new opportunity and so the Crimson Phoenix – the celestial queen of all feathered creatures is the ultimate symbol of new opportunities during times of adversity. The Phoenix is the ultimate bird symbol and having the Phoenix image in the home is said to attract prosperity and abundance. Having a hundred phoenixes would be a hundred times auspicious.

Other birds, even bird feathers are also regarded with favour. This is because all birds are regarded as lucky symbols of good fortune.

Birds signify protection for those who take financial and business risks. When placed in the South, birds ward off bad business luck. Roosters deflect gossip and politicking. Birds of prey bring wealth and bird feathers protect from accidents during travel. Hanging even a toy bird with real bird feathers at the back of a car is powerful protection from accidents. In Taoist feng shui, birds are regarded as cosmic messengers. So one can really tell a great deal just by tuning in to the timely appearance of birds.

Birds flying towards you are the best signals. Birds flying away from you suggest a missed opportunity. A bird flying upwards is a good sign. Birds singing in the morning bring good news. When birds build nests in your garden, it is a very good sign heralding prosperity or increased income.

WHAT BIRDS DO YOU SEE?

Do you see a single bird, a pair or a family of birds?

A pair of birds means love is coming your way. A single black bird indicates an important message. A family of birds, such as the family of ducklings shown below suggests the possibility of a new addition to the family or a family reunion, which brings happiness.

Do you see healthy or injured birds?

An injured bird is a warning. Be careful for the rest of the day. Drive slowly. A healthy lively bird suggests a happy occasion. Several birds chirping merrily means increased social partying. When birds are singing, it is a happy sign suggesting a busier social life.

What colour birds do you see?

A white bird means healing. If someone close is desperately ill, this is a sign of recovery. A bird with red markings means an honour of some kind is coming to you. A yellow bird means sudden wealth or a happiness occasion (e.g. a pregnancy.) A blue bird means promotion at work.

What kind of birds do you see?

Magpies mean new friends coming into your life. Birds of prey always mean wealth; The **Eagle** for instance suggests good fortune. **Small birds** such as sparrows indicate good news – these are happy messengers. **Lovebirds** suggest romance or meeting a soul mate. **Crows** mean some divine message can be expected perhaps having a prophetic dream. **Owls** indicate a teacher of great significance coming into your life.

From the top: A single black bird indicates an important message. A Sparrow indicates good news. An owl indicates a teacher of significance coming into your life.

161 Strengthening the earth chi

An easy Taoist feng shui way to enhance the quality of energy of your home is to strengthen its **earth chi**. Earth chi is so important that in the old days this was almost synonymous with good feng shui. Taoist feng shui accepts that heaven and earth combined establishes the natural phenomena upon which man builds. This is the trinity of **tien, ti, ren** or heaven, earth and mankind. In the trinity of heaven, earth and mankind, it is earth chi, which has the most significant influence on your fortunes.

Here are six ways to strengthen the earth chi in and around your home.

1. Always use earth materials as your ground floor. **Use marble, granite or tiles**. Solid slabs of tiles or marble are better than broken marble or broken terrazzo. Anything broken or a haphazard design suggests an unstable foundation. Also avoid having wood or carpets on your ground floor. Always use *earth* materials.

2. Surrounding your home with rocks brings good vibrations. This does not mean having rocks all along the boundaries of your home, but placing a few large rocks at the four corners suggests earth chi is strong and stable. These rocks need not be large. A large rock signifies mountains and these should really be placed in accordance with flying star indications. You can also use a pile of stones to build a mountain of gold and this creates a direct connection with the earth/heaven axis. A pile of rocks with some gold leaf stuck to the rocks can thus symbolize a *mountain* of gold in a residential house. It is very auspicious indeed.

3. Create a support wall behind the home to signify the mountain giving you support. This need not be a massive wall – anything four feet and above is sufficient to signify support. A support wall is always better than having trees to give you much needed support.

4, Create a square patch filled with sand or pebbles to strengthen the earth chi of the front of the house. This strengthens the symbolism of earth element energy.

5. Manifest the earth numbers of 258 – these are the three *earth numbers*. When you place 2 round crystals, five yellow rocks and eight medium sized pebbles it is one way of manifesting these powerful earth numbers. You can stress whichever number you wish or have the crystals, pebbles and rocks in any quantity you wish. Since the period of 8 is coming, emphasizing 8 will bring good fortune. These three special numbers 258 are also described as *parent string numbers* in the flying star system of feng shui. When they occur together, they manifest great good fortune. This is one of the secrets in the combined practice of flying star feng shui and numerology.

6. You can hang a painting of a mountain in the home to simulate mountains. A painting of mountains has many feng shui uses. Ideally mountain images should look solid and strong to simulate support for all your endeavors. The key is to hang the mountain image in the correct spot in the home, and to hang the right kind of mountains. If you know flying star feng shui, then hanging a mountain image in the corner of the house or living room which has the mountain star 8 brings enormous good fortune in health and relationships. The mountain painting is also incredibly lucky when hung behind you at work or wherever you are sitting. This symbolism of powerful earth chi is required for upward career mobility as well as the preservation of one's wealth.

162 Using mystical symbols

Taoist feng shui has many versions of mystic symbols which can be empowered to become talismans and amulets. In the past the patriarchs and ladies of the upper classes wore these mystic symbols. The mandarins and official at court also wore them as part of their official attire. These symbols were treated like amulets and talismans and were often worn as jewellery pieces either as rings or as pins. Some were worn as hairpieces and yet others were worn hidden inside robes and secret belts.

Protective amulets were often drawn with sacred prayers written in fancy calligraphy and then consecrated by monks or other holy men. Special auspicious and sacred gemstones such as blue **lapis lazuli**, red **coral, turquoise**, yellow **amber**, green **jade** and pearl coloured **moonstones** were also incorporated as finely embedded decorative energy enhancers. The selection of stones was usually based on astrological calculations. Whenever coloured stones were used these would be fairly large pieces as they often doubled as symbols of authority and also represented the five elements.

Popular talismanic jewellery worn by the senior court members and army generals included symbols such as the ***Ru Yi, the longevity symbol* as well as the *mystical* knot.** These three symbols had significant meanings and when empowered were believed to bring better health, strength and vigour as well as protecting the wearer from unnatural death such as by accident or by execution. I have searched out some of these old talismans, extending my search to surrounding countries around China as well since many of these countries had close ties and links with China and over the past twenty years have amassed quite a personal collection of auspicious stones and treasures.

I have found some truly really mystical and stunning *treasures* from unlikely places such as Kathmandu, Tibet, Mongolia and India as well as China. Indeed, these old pieces are the inspiration behind my line of feng shui jewellery. My reasoning is that the wearing of jewellery has huge significance in every culture and it makes a lot of sense to wear **jewellery and gemstones** that have auspicious meaning. Mystical symbols and powerful gemstones transcend the passage and time and are as potent in today's modern world as they used to be in past eras. I have repeatedly discovered this to be true.

One of my particular favourites is the **mystic knot**, which is of course the infinity symbol, extended three times. This is such a powerful sign that merely drawing the symbol in the air with your hands will transform bad energy into good energy. I have made the mystic knot into a ring and a pendant as part of my own collection of auspicious jewellery and ever since I started wearing the mystical knot pendant (it is done in white gold and embedded with tiny diamonds) I have felt incredibly re-energized. It seems like my creativity is magnified a thousand-fold.

There are many other symbols that can be fashioned into powerful amulets I have repeatedly found that many of the symbols of other cultures are similar to the symbols used by the Chinese.

Thus the symbol of the **Sigil** which is the Lo shu movement of numbers, the symbol of the **cicada**, the symbol of the **sun and moon**, to name just a few are also special symbols and they feature as strongly in Egyptian as well as Chinese cultural history.

163 Protecting from excessive yin chi

YIN forces can be harmful to the energy of *yang spaces* and this manifests in different ways, often as illness, but also as relationship problems that reflect a discord in the energy of the home or office. At home, **sickness and insubordination** problems with maids as well as quarrels between spouses and siblings can be the result of strong yin forces. At work in the office, yin chi cause severe stress, politicking, and lots of backstabbing. The result is the pernicious presence of hidden enemies. Friends can become adversaries under such conditions. This kind of work environment is very stressful indeed.

Yin forces should be kept at a minimum and never be allowed to dominate any space. In feng shui, this affliction is referred to as *yin spirit formation*, which, at its least harmful causes inconvenient illnesses, small accidents, backbiting and harmful gossip but at its worst can cause severe illness sometimes requiring long hospitalization. YIN forces also cause backache, arthritis and sciatica pains and older people are much more susceptible to yin chi attacks. Thus yin spirit formation should always be chased away, or transformed into yang energy. If your home has many older people residing within, it is very important to give your **home a yang energy bath frequently**. Opening the doors and windows of home and work places to receive new flows of energy should be a regular monthly thing. The playing of music, the holding of dinner parties and the presence of young people all imbue the home with precious yang energy. So whenever friends and relatives drop by make them welcome because they are bringing you yang energy.

Strong natural stone formations that resemble dragons such as this one are highly revered. I found this nine dragons rock formation in the courtyard of a rich man's house in Suzhou city near Shanghai

OVERCOMING OFFICE POLITICKING

When yin forces get too strong and seem to be hitting the more vulnerable of the residents in a home you might need specific cures. In this context, yin forces caused by problems of office politics is probably the most common problem. Many people suffer from this problem at work, and it is something far more widespread than many people realize.

So many people are unhappy at work simply because there is someone at the office gossiping and putting them down. I am very familiar with this problem as I witnessed a lot of this when I used to work in the corporate world so I can sympathize with people who are victims of office politicks. It is easy for those who have never been the victims of such nonsense to advise others to ignore it but the truth of the matter is that office politicking is a yin force that just will not go away. It has to be acknowledged and to be coped with.

Taoist feng shui the **rooster** image is the most popular cure. The rooster symbolically gobbles up all negative gossip and politicking. A porcelain *rooster painted in gold is powerful. So are rooster images painted in white or in red and gold* because fire and metal energy will overcome any quarrelsome and sickness energy, which might be nearby.

Red and gold Buddha of Happiness images are equally excellent cures for *flying star* afflictions caused by the quarrelsome star 3. Those of you who know how to practice flying star feng shui might want to remember this. When you meet the stars 3/2 or 2/3 use a Laughing Buddha image painted in gold and red. Let the Buddha sit facing the direction of anyone you suspect is causing you trouble. This transforms potential grief into actual happiness.

Coin swords can very effectively supplement roosters. This should be placed on the wall that is on your left side of your facing direction at your desk. Hang such a coin sword with its hilt up and its blade side pointing down. This is of course not a real sword as it is made of coins – the meanings are symbolic but the symbolism is a powerful remedy when used with respect and diligence.

Support symbols behind the office desk, such as **Kuan Kung**, the **Dragon Tortoise** and of course **mountain paintings** are excellent. When I was running a bank in Hong Kong in the Eighties I had the opportunity to visit the offices of many banking CEOs there. I was amazed that almost every Chinese CEO had stunning paintings of mountains hung behind them. In the Chinese banks originally founded by prominent families, their mountain paintings have often been in the family for many generations.

I noticed that these paintings rarely had water flows in them. Instead the **mountains usually looked solid and imposing** sometimes resembling the dragon and at other times resembling the tortoise.

These mountain paintings provided the symbolic presence of mountains, which in turn provided valuable support for them and their financial business. It was while I worked in Hong Kong that I became truly convinced of the potency of lucky symbols placed for protection as well as to attract good fortune.

Even today in the newly emerging modern China, anyone visiting the fast growth cities of Shanghai, Beijing or Canton surely cannot ignore the presence of symbolic images all round the city – tortoises and dragons in parks, protective **Fu Dogs** and **Pi Yao** images in front of department stores and museums and just about every kind of auspicious image painted on artworks, ceramics, embroideries and other decorative items.

Every symbolic image is a legend with a specific meaning of good fortune. The presence of these images indicates that Taoist feng shui that incorporate the use of symbols is once again alive and well in modern China.

The use of the celestial creatures of good fortune all round the cities of China indicates the powerful presence of yang energy. Yin forces now have less chance of taking hold as China races into the new millennium with a maximum of yang chi. If you had visited China even in the early Eighties you would surely have been struck by the huge prevalence of people dressed in the yin colours of blue, gray and black. This was what I remember the most of my visits to China during the 1982 and 1983 years. Today all the colours prevail and the yang colours of reds and whites and yellows have become very popular.

Above: Dragons become incredibly powerful when they are awakened.

164 Dotting the eye of the dragon

Taoist feng shui considers that there is vital energy in every celestial creature and when these creatures have their spirit awakened by dotting their eyes, they become even more powerful. Herein lies the rationale behind "dotting the eye of the dragon".

This is a ritual which involves the **symbolic awakening of the creature**. It can be undertaken in a simple dotting the eye ceremony with respect to dragon paintings and dragon images placed inside homes and offices. When the dragon images in your home are energized this way, they bring prosperity, protection and happiness occasions such as births and marriages.

To dot the eye of the dragon all you need is a **black brush and black Chinese ink**. The ritual can be as elaborate or as simple as you wish, so you can do it yourself dotting the eyes with black ink or you can engage a skilled professional to do this part of the ritual. No matter how you do it, however, it must be accompanied by an infusion of yang energy.

The loud clashing of cymbals and drums can represent this, OR having bright lights shining at the dragon can also represent yang energy. It is advisable to dot the eyes of the dragon during the *dragon hour* in the early morning. This means between 7 am to 9 am.

So if you have just invited a dragon image into your home try dotting and thereby opening its eyes and watch as your dragon brings you good luck. A useful tip about dragons is that they should be placed near water, or at least, near an image of water. This is said to *activate lucky outcomes luck* for those living in its vicinity.

There are Taoist masters who insist that the tall multi level buildings of the modern age signify the eyes of the dragon. Thus, in Kuala Lumpur, the Petronas Twin towers symbolizes the eyes of the KL dragon, so bringing prosperity to the country.

165 The power of smooth crystal balls

Taoist feng shui also acknowledges the efficacy of round smooth crystal balls, especially when they are made from natural rock crystals. Displayed in clusters of six or nine in the living or family areas of the home, crystal balls create energy which foster loving relationships and ensures a smooth ride through life for residents. Quarrels are kept to a minimum and in fact soon become a thing of the past. Projects will succeed and victory is often within reach.

I always recommend crystal balls as a **cure in quarrelsome households**. At the same time crystals signify the nurturing energy of mother earth, so they also benefit the household matriarch. Placed in the Southwest corners of the home they bring wonderful family and romance luck. This can mean the Southwest of the living or bedrooms, or of the family or study rooms. To activate the power of the crystal even more, try hanging a bright light shining at it. Remember that in the Southwest location, crystals bring love and a steady relationship. This relationship will be very smooth and pleasurable if you place six crystal balls here. They can be any size but those that are about 3 inches diameter are the best.

Crystal balls carved with the map of the world into crystal globes are excellent for study and examination luck especially when placed in the Northeast of any room. In this case one crystal globe is usually sufficient unless your child is a hyperactive child requiring constant stimulation. A Crystal globe in the Northeast will add great strides and improvements to your child's school grades and attention span.

Shown here are my crystal balls placed in the living room to activate some very auspicious flying star numbers in this part of the house. And because this is also the Northwest corner, the crystal balls really benefit the father. The earth energy of the crystals also benefits the mother.

SOME POWERFUL RITUALS WITH CRYSTALS

Here are three Taoist feng shui rituals using crystals, which will enhance the energy of your home.

1. **MOUNTAIN PEAK CRYSTAL FORMATION** overcomes all negative chi. Bury three crystals in a triangular pattern in the ground in front of your home. You can use the driveway if you wish, or cover it with tiles but do make sure the peak of the triangle is pointing outwards. You can use crystal balls or single pointed crystal. This is a very powerful secret way of preventing bad energy from entering into your home.

2. **SEVEN CRYSTAL FORMATION UNDER THE BED** overcomes evil and attracts wealth. Place seven pieces of single pointed crystals under the bed in an arrow formation with the peak pointing towards the head of the bed. On either side have three crystals thus making a total of six. With the central crystal making an arrow, the formation makes up seven crystals.

3. **SIX ROUND CRYSTALS ON YOUR WORK DESK** attracts recognition for your work. Place six crystals on the top right hand corner of your desk to improve your concentration and creativity. If you write powerful mantras onto your crystals, they really bring extreme good fortune in all aspects of your work.

166 The power of amethyst geodes

The purple stone or amethyst is regarded with great favour in Taoist feng shui practice. It is especially useful for fortifying the bonds of marriage and when placed under the bed directly under the feet of the sleeping couple it symbolically "ties them to each other". When husbands tend to stay out too late, wives would tie the amethysts geode to the bedpost on her side of the bed. This was believed to attract the husband home.

Amethysts geodes with deep "pockets" are also said to be extremely powerful in attracting wealth energy. A very successful department store owner I know has the most amazingly deep-pocketed amethysts geode, which he places at the entrance into his office. It brings him enormous good fortune. If you want to activate the power of crystals in your home or office, you can use either the amethyst or the **quartz crystal**. In either case always look for thick formations of crystal. Geodes that have thin crystal formations indicate poverty vibrations and are simply of no use. You must look for those that have thick crystal formations.

Inside, the crystals formed should be deep **purple in colour, since this indicates wealth**. Amethyst geodes made into display tables are very auspicious in the living room since this creates strong harmonious energy. They also have the power to transform negative energy into positive energy. Yin vibrations are also transformed into yang vibrations.

Displayed near the front of the house Amethyst Geodes attract great friendship and meaningful relationship.

167 Useful tips on displaying symbols

DRAGONS

... bring prosperity and success but do note that they are most potent when placed near water. So if you have a water feature or an aquarium, or a swimming pool in your home, do invest in a dragon to be placed near it. For such purposes a dragon image carrying a pearl would be the best. **Place one, two, five, six or nine dragons**. These are numbers that activate the dragon image. Never place dragons near fire, in the kitchen, inside the bedroom, or on the floor. Also make sure you do not keep your dragon image imprisoned in glass cases. They should be free to fly upwards. Wear the dragon image as a brooch pin to ward off bad energy and protect you from being cheated or conned. Wear it as a locket to activate your heart chakra, which gives power to your powers of persuasion. The best dragon images are those made of real gold and decorated with precious gemstones or diamonds.

HORSES

... bring recognition and fame. Tribute horses in white and led in by the God of Wealth bring prosperity. **A single black horse** such is the victory horse. The symbol should be proud and magnificent. The red background accentuates the fire energy of the horse. It is very auspicious. **Running horses** that appear like they are in a panic bring extreme fear and misfortunes. **Workhorses** also suggest work without recognition. They should never be displayed in the home. Horses are best displayed singly or in **groups of eight**. They should never be displayed as five horses, and four horses suggest a terrible accident or death. In old China a horrible form of execution was death through being tied to four horses. Thus having four horses in a painting is a most unlucky symbol.

LIONS

... can be quite dangerous for your neighbours, so it is better to use Chi Lins or Fu Dogs – those that are shown with the child and the ball. Lions when used for protection should be placed on the ground and never high up on gateposts. Remember they are very fierce.

TORTOISES

... bring loads of good energy. You can keep any number of tortoises, but a single tortoise is usually the best form of protection. They are best placed at the back of the home or in the NORTH part of the garden. **Golden tortoises** with dragon heads are even more potent as protector images in the home and office.

168 The significance of trees

The presence of trees around one's living abode as an essential component of good feng shui although there are simple guidelines to be followed. Basically broad leaved trees are to be preferred to thin spiky leaved trees. Bamboo and pines are exceptions as these are regarded as powerful symbols of longevity. But bamboo should always be planted in the front of the house for it to bring good fortune. When planted at the back bamboo can cause misfortune.

A single tree planted in the center of any home means "difficulty" and although readers may think this is an unlikely situation I have seen several wealthy homes with central open courtyards planted with a single large tree. I was not surprised that despite their wealth these families were always short of cash. Their businesses always seemed to be having cash flow problems.

Five trees behind the house simulate the mountain support. If they are fruit trees the symbolism is that the support is also nurturing. These trees should look healthy and strong, not dead or tired looking. **A dead tree** behind the house is bad luck but a dead tree in front is even worse. So do chop off dried trees that have died. If there are old people staying in the home they will be especially susceptible to dead tree energy

Decaying old trees can sometimes cause harm to the health of the house although I have to confess that my "old" mango tree, shown here is nearly 27 years old, and still going strong. It continues to bear fruit. In such cases the old tree can be the source of nurturing and protective energy. Taoist masters who are skilled in the art of extracting powerful tree energy often consider old trees as sources of powerful wisdom energy. However certain types of trees are more auspicious than others

- **Red date trees** as well as pomegranate plants are said to bring pregnancy and recovery luck.
- **Apple trees** bring peace and harmony to the home.
- **Orange trees** bring wealth and prosperity.
- **Willow trees** bring tears and hard work.
- **Lime trees** gets rid of bad energy.
- Trees and plants on the **left side of the home** (i.e. the dragon side) will control the husband's anger and benefit him while plants on the **right side** will control the wife's anger and benefit her. It is therefore a good idea to plant trees and plants on *both* sides of the home.